# YOU
## Were
# BORN
## for
# THIS

# BRUCE WILKINSON

Author of the **New York Times** #1 Bestseller
**The Prayer of Jabez**
with DAVID KOPP

# YOU
Were
# BORN
for
# THIS

7 Keys to a Life of Predictable Miracles

RANDOM HOUSE
LARGE PRINT

Every story in this book is an account of an actual event. No composite anecdotes or other fiction techniques have been used. However, details in some stories have been modified slightly to improve readability or to protect privacy.

All rights reserved. Published in the United States of America by Random House Large Print in association with WaterBrook Multnomah, an imprint of Crown Publishing Group, *R. H.   10/13/09*  New York.   *23.*
Distributed by Random House, Inc., New York.

Jacket Design by Kristopher K. Orr

ISBN 978-0-7393-7732-1

Library of Congress has established a Cataloging-in-Publication Data record for this title.

www.randomhouse.com/largeprint

FIRST LARGE PRINT EDITION

PRINTED IN THE UNITED STATES OF AMERICA

10 9 8 7 6 5 4 3 2 1

This Large Print edition published in accord with the standards of the N.A.V.H.

# DEDICATION

To Him who is able to do exceedingly abundantly
above all that we ask or think,
according to the power that works in us, to Him
be glory.

**from Ephesians 3:20–21**

# Contents

# Part 1

---

# WELCOME TO EVERYDAY MIRACLE TERRITORY

# 1

# A New Way to See the World

**You were born to expect a miracle today**

**W**hat if I told you I'm certain you missed a miracle yesterday? And not just any miracle but one that Heaven wanted to do through you to significantly change someone's life for the better—maybe your own?

I would understand if you were doubtful.

But right alongside that doubt, most of us can identify a nearly universal experience. Almost everyone in the world—whatever their religious belief—can point to an event in their lives that seemed directly orchestrated by Heaven, that seemed impossible to explain without using words like "I can't believe what just happened! That was a miracle!" We call these experiences divine coincidences, miracle moments, supernatural provisions. Whatever we call them, we tend to value such events so highly that we recount them over and over, often for years. "I'll never forget the time . . . ," we say, or "Sooner or later my daughter is going to tell you about . . ."

Why do we remember such events so clearly? I think it's because we feel that we have been touched by Heaven. It's as if God Himself stepped through the curtain that separates the seen from the unseen to make something wonderful happen for us, something only He could do.

But here's the best part. In the experience we hear a personal and unforgettable message from God. Something like, **I'm here. I care about you. I can do for you what you cannot do for yourself.**

Beginning with this near-universal experience, this book asks a few simple but intriguing questions:

- Why are these experiences of the miraculous so rare for most people?
- What if Heaven actually wanted you to experience them on a regular basis?
- What if ordinary people like you and me are invited to partner with God to deliver miracles to others?

If these questions put a picture in your mind of people everywhere walking around expecting to be a part of miracle moments on a regular basis, you're not far wrong.

## A mysterious encounter

Let me tell you about a mysterious encounter I had in a restaurant outside Denver with a waiter named Jack. I call it mysterious because on the surface everything looked so ordinary. Five friends at a table for six, waiters coming and going, voices, clatter—just what you'd expect in a busy restaurant. But by the time dinner was over, we all knew beyond a doubt that we'd been present for a divine appointment.

It was as if God Himself had walked up and said, "Thank you for saving Me a place. I've been wanting to do something for Jack."

Here's what happened.

During the course of the meal, Jack had served us well. But apart from the usual exchanges about the menu and our orders, we hadn't spoken much. Around the table, meanwhile, the conversation revolved around some of Jesus' more extreme teachings—ones like "Ask, and you will receive" and "It is more blessed to give than to receive." During the conversation I felt unexpectedly nudged by Heaven to try something I'd never done before. At the same time I sensed it was meant to involve Jack.

My experiment involved putting three hundred dollars "at risk." Now, don't let the amount throw you. The money wasn't mine, and believe it or not, the person who was letting me carry it around was expecting me to give it away. (But more about that in a later chapter.)

When Jack came by to refill the water glasses, I

posed a question. "Have you ever heard the saying 'It is more blessed to give than to receive'?"

"Yes, I have," he said.

"Do you believe that?"

"Sure, I guess I do," he said, looking puzzled.

"Good!" I said. "I have an interesting opportunity for you." I placed a hundred-dollar bill on the table. "You have an unusual choice, Jack. You can either receive this hundred dollars as a gift, not a tip . . ."

I paused. I definitely had Jack's attention, and the two couples with me didn't appear to be breathing.

I looked at Jack. "Or you can say no to the money and instead give each of us a dessert. But this would be **you** buying the desserts, not the restaurant. You can't do both things, and there's no right or wrong. So what would you like to do—give or receive?"

Jack just stood there holding the water pitcher. He asked twice if I was serious. Then finally he said, "I'll take the hundred dollars."

True to my word, I handed him the bill.

"Thank you!" he said. Then he walked back to the kitchen.

After he left and my friends started breathing again, we all tried to figure out what had just happened. Was my unusual test about giving and receiving even fair? What was Jack thinking now? And what in the world was he saying to the crew in the kitchen?

All the while I was feeling increasingly uncomfortable. You see, earlier I had slipped another two hundred dollars under my plate. If the waiter had chosen to buy us desserts and not take the hundred—believing that it is more blessed to give than to receive—I was going to give him the hidden two hundred dollars. I had really hoped he would make the self-sacrificial choice because I'd strongly sensed that God wanted to encourage him with the larger sum.

The next time he came around, I said, "I'm curious, Jack. Do you feel like you made the right choice?"

"Absolutely!" he said excitedly. "In fact, it was a miracle. You see, I'm a single dad." He pulled out his wallet and proudly showed us a photo of his three-year-old son. "Isn't he something!" he said with a big smile. Then he explained his reaction. "I have to work three jobs during four days of the week just so I can take care of my son the other three days when my ex-wife works. But I'm having a tough time making ends meet. Just this morning I had to mail my alimony check of a hundred dollars even though my account was down to zero. Driving to work this afternoon, I actually prayed, 'God, please! I need an extra hundred dollars, and I need it tonight!'"

Well, I was speechless, and so were my friends. How could we have known of our waiter's crisis or of his prayer for a hundred dollars?

Then it was my turn to explain. I told him that even if he had decided to give instead of receive, I'd planned to give him the hundred dollars. "But now that I know your story, I agree. You made the right choice."

Suddenly I knew what needed to happen next. "You have to know that none of this money was mine," I told him. "The owner wanted me to pass it on as a kind of message to the right person. And I'm sure that person was you."

**God had used one person to deliver something that met a big need for another person—and in a way that was clearly miraculous.**

I reached under the plate for the other two hundred. "Obviously God wanted you to have the hundred dollars, and He wants you to have this too."

## What God thinks is normal

What just happened here? Let's break it down:

• Jack drove to work that evening to wait tables, but he brought with him a secret, pressing need.

• I had come to Colorado from Atlanta on business and ended up having dinner with friends in Jack's restaurant.

• Unbeknown to Jack or my friends, I was prepared to meet someone's financial need with money that wasn't mine.

• By the end of the evening, God had used one person to deliver something that met a big need for another person—and in a way that was clearly miraculous to everyone involved.

You might react differently to what happened around that table. You might think, for example, **Well, I don't have a hundred-dollar bill lying around. And if I did, why would I give it to a stranger?**

**For that matter, how would I figure out whom to give it to?**

We'll look closely at these reactions and more like them in the pages ahead. You'll see, I promise, that God is just as likely to have plans for five dollars or twenty dollars as He is for a hundred dollars and that He never asks you or me to serve Him in a way that doesn't fit us personally and perfectly.

For now, though, put yourself in the story of our dinner with Jack. Imagine how you would have felt leaving that table and knowing you had played an active role in delivering God's pro-vision for a young man's desperate need. Better yet, imagine a lifestyle of such encounters, where God works through you in unexplainable ways to do a miracle—and on a reg-ular basis.

> **God did not place you on this earth to notice Him at work only once or twice in your whole life.**

This kind of life is not only possible but is what God thinks of as normal when He thinks of you.

You see, He did not place you on this earth to notice Him at work only once or twice in your whole life. He did not create you to consistently miss out on the won-der of His presence and power.

The truth is, you were born to live a supernatural life doing God's work by God's power. You were born to walk out your door each morning believing that God will use you to deliver a necessary miracle today.

This book will show you how.

## The Everyday Miracle Territory

When it comes to miracles, most people I know see the world as divided in two.

On the far left is a region we could call the Land of Signs and Wonders. In this land amazing miracles seem to happen a lot, although only for a select few. Mostly this world reveals itself on television, in a few unusual churches, and in faraway places. Still, Signs and Wonders is a remarkable place. In this land the blind regain their sight and invalids throw away their canes to run around like school kids.

On the far right is the Land of Good Deeds. Nobody is putting on a show here. Fortunately, though, the place is full of good people watching out for each other, doing good works. And certainly God is pleased with that.

Interestingly, in Good Deeds land a lot of people believe in miracles and spend time studying them. They just don't expect to actually see any miracles, much less be a part of them on a regular basis. When they praise God for miracles, they're grateful for things that occurred long ago. Good Deeds land doesn't dazzle like Signs and Wonders, but things are more manageable there. More predictable.

What's the one big disadvantage in Good Deeds land? God rarely shows up in a supernatural way. Why would He? No one is expecting the miraculous, and besides, everything is running just fine. Or so it seems.

Which land would you say you live in most of the time?

A large majority of people live in the Land of Good Deeds. Even though some would say they have experienced meaningful personal miracles in the past—at a point of spiritual awakening or in a time of crisis—they believe those experiences are rare. More important, they believe we don't have a role in whether one happens again or not, so there's no point in leaving the house today on the lookout for one.

What I want you to realize is that if you live in either land I've described, you've overlooked the most promising region of all. You see, between the dazzle of Signs and Wonders and the duty of Good Deeds lies a broad and promising middle ground.

In this book we call this in-between land the Everyday Miracle Territory. Here people believe that God wants to intervene—and does—in supernatural ways in human affairs on a regular basis. Here unmet needs are seen by ordinary people as golden opportunities for God to show up, and to do so through them, at almost any moment. They're not waiting for special powers for themselves or for God to part the skies on their behalf. They have experienced miracles and know beyond doubt that miracles are for them and others like them, right here and right now.

Those who live in the Everyday Miracle Territory have already made two startling observations.

One is full of hope. Everywhere they look, in every situation, they see potential for an unforgettable "God-incidence"—not a coincidence but a moment when God steps in to meet a real need through them in a way that only He can. Some days it actually feels as though God has a pile of miracles ready to be delivered!

Their other observation is full of dismay.

They are nearly alone.

Would you agree that few people today are living in Everyday Miracle Territory? I wrote this book to help you see that the land of personal, everyday miracles is your rightful home turf. Instead of focusing on the nature-defying acts that God **is able to** do, this book invites you to encounter the miracles that God **does** do on a regular basis—and to embrace your exciting part in partnering with Him to make them happen.

You'll discover that what God chooses to depend on for these divine encounters is simply a willing servant. No previous experience required. No record of perfection. No special religious gift or qualification. In this book we call these refreshingly ordinary folks "delivery agents" for God. They are men and women who say to Him, "Please send me to do Your work by Your power today!"

That's exactly what Jimmy said.

## Jimmy the "delivery guy"

Jimmy is one of the most down-to-earth men I've ever met. He can fix anything, find anything, make do with anything. You're stranded with a handful of folks on a desert island? You want Jimmy in the handful. You want to program your iPhone to walk your dog? Jimmy's your man. Just don't ask him to spend time over tea talking about relationships or contemplating the meaning of the universe.

The first time Jimmy heard that he could cooperate with God in supernatural events on a regular basis, he thought, **Not likely.**

He worked in construction, after all, not ministry. He struggled to come up with even one time in the past ten years when he could say with certainty that the supernatural had clearly showed up. The idea of a lifestyle of miracles felt about as real to Jimmy as taking a road trip through an asteroid belt.

But over the course of a You Were Born for This conference, Jimmy realized that he really did want to learn how to partner with Heaven to do God's work on earth. Taking a big step into the unknown, he committed himself to being God's delivery agent when and where he was called upon.

The next morning, while Jimmy was dropping off windows at a job site, he struck up a conversation with a carpenter named Nick. Nick let it be known that his marriage was on the rocks and that he didn't hold out much hope. He just seemed to want to vent.

Normally Jimmy would have expressed sympathy for a man in that kind of misery, then quickly steered as far away as possible from such a sensitive topic. This time, though, Jimmy hung in there. He listened, identified with Nick's struggle, asked a few questions. Then, sensing that the man's heart was open, he asked a simple but miracle-inviting question he had learned at the conference: "Nick, I really want to help you. What can I do for you?"

Without hesitation the carpenter said, "You could tell me what to do next. I'm tied up in knots, but I really want this marriage to work."

Jimmy panicked. Tell another guy how to fix a relationship? **Not likely!** But he took a deep breath and then took an outrageous step of faith. "Why don't you get something to write with," he told the carpenter, "and when you come back, I'll tell you how to save your marriage."

The truth was, Jimmy was stalling. He didn't have a clue what he was going to tell Nick. But as he explained to me later, he was holding on to a couple of things I had said at the conference: "Relax, the miracle is God's to do, not yours" and "Give God a minute." Something or Someone seemed to be leading the way in this conversation with Nick, and Jimmy was determined to follow.

When the carpenter returned, Jimmy heard himself saying, "You need to go home and make your bed."

Jimmy had no idea where that had come from or what good it was. "That's all I have to say," he told Nick apologetically. "I guess you don't even need to write it down."

But the carpenter was staring at Jimmy with his mouth open.

"How did you know?" he gasped. "That is a giant source of conflict for us! I'm the last one up, and I **never** make the bed. My wife says it's a sign of everything that's wrong with the marriage. I don't get it. But you know what? I'm going to drive back at lunch and make the bed before my wife gets home."

To me, this story demonstrates God's willingness to do a personal miracle if we are willing to deliver one. Nick wasn't expecting help from a stranger. And Jimmy didn't think he had help to give. What he had, though, was a readiness to pass along what God prompted him to say.

But the best thing the story shows is God's heart. He cares about the personal struggles of a carpenter named Nick—and He wanted Nick to see that. He cared enough to show Nick a practical step he could take that might say more to his wife than a love letter and just might turn things around for the couple.

All He needed was Jimmy, delivery agent.

## Doing what God wants done

You might be like Jimmy, completely unprepared and unqualified but ready to try something different. You may have grown up in the church and have a long list of religious accomplishments to point to. You may be like Nick, uncertain that God exists or that He cares for you. But Heaven works in ways that seem to apply no matter what our spiritual mind-set happens to be.

Perhaps you've heard about my book **The Prayer of Jabez.** It shows how a little-known prayer from three thousand years ago can still result in great blessing and influence for God in our time. Millions bought the book, prayed the prayer . . . and were astonished at what God began to do in their lives. One reason the message of that book resonated with so many, I believe, is that it made ministry (which simply means doing what God wants done in the world) accessible as a way of life.

Jabez lived in ancient Israel. The Bible says that he was "more honorable than his brothers," but as far as I can tell, it wasn't because of his superior spiritual status. Perhaps he was "more honorable" because he asked with all his heart for God to do for him and through him exactly what God already wanted to do.

And the Bible says, "God granted him what he requested."[1]

Through the prayer of Jabez, millions learned to ask God to expand their territory of influence for Him and then to put His hand of power on them. Not surprisingly, as soon as they took these brave steps, people started seeing miracle opportunities all over the place. And thousands wrote excitedly to me to report what was happening.

Here's what I want you to see: **The Prayer of Jabez** showed ordinary people how to ask God to greatly expand their opportunities to serve Him. **You Were Born for This** shows ordinary people how to be intentional about and skilled at inviting the miraculous into the midst of that larger life.

Think of **You Were Born for This** as **Jabez** to the miracle power.

For all the Jimmys and Jabezes in the world, this

book reveals in practical terms how God works supernaturally through His willing partners to make a difference in people's lives. It's the most rewarding and
significant life imaginable!

Wouldn't you know it, in answer to my own prayers
during those years, God expanded my territory beyond
anything I could have imagined.

He sent our family to Africa.

## When good deeds aren't enough

In 2002 my wife, Darlene, and I experienced a clear
call to move to Africa to tackle some of the most daunting challenges of our time. "Will you go?" God said to
us. "Will you care?"

This was happening during the busiest months of
my speaking and writing about Jabez. Why would God
ask us to leave behind an exploding ministry based
on a book He was so clearly blessing? We didn't understand it.

You might think that someone who has studied the
character of God in graduate school and dedicated his
life to serving Him wouldn't be surprised when God
radically redirects his life. I will confess that until then
I had enjoyed a lot of clarity about what God had called
me to do. I saw myself as a Bible teacher, leader, and
disciple maker. My publisher saw me as an author. And
that was that.

But almost overnight we experienced a spiritual
awakening to the needs of a continent. Poverty. Preju-

dice. Hunger. AIDS. Orphans. God seemed to be say-ing to our family, "My heart breaks over these things. I want your hearts to break over them too."

Without knowing what it might mean, we said yes. Then, believing we had been called to a three- to five-year personal mission, we said good-bye to friends and family and moved to Johannesburg, South Africa.

**Good deeds alone will never be enough to meet the desperate needs of our time.**

What does this have to do with **You Were Born for This**? From the start we knew that trying to meet any one of those needs would be far too big a task for us. God would have to show up in extraor-dinary ways or nothing of signifi-cance would get done.

And He did. We started not by asking, "What can we do?" but by asking, "What does God want done?" We set some high-risk goals in the areas of greatest need. Our min-istry plan expected—even depended on—God to intervene. Finally we set about working with others, including charitable groups, African organizations, government agencies, churches, and thousands of First World volunteers, to meet faith-stretching goals. Of course not everything we tried succeeded. But we kept asking for miracles and taking risks of faith, and God **did** show up, as I'll share in the pages ahead.

By the time we returned to the States, our thinking had changed in two important ways.

First, we'd become convinced that good deeds alone

will never be enough to meet the desperate needs of our time. This is true whether the needs are personal or global in scope. We simply need more of God. We desperately need miracles!

Second, we had learned that it's often longtime Christians who resist miracles the most. Many have stopped expecting miracles, asking for them, or even knowing how to partner with God to invite them. In other words, they have abandoned the Everyday Miracle Territory and often measure success by how **little** they need God.

> **You Were Born for This is a bold initiative to reclaim the miraculous as a normal way of life.**

As you'd expect, the consequences of limiting what God does on earth to what we can do for Him are disastrous. Just look around. The most pressing personal and global needs go unmet while a generation asks, "Where is God? Doesn't He care? Does He even exist?"

But it doesn't have to be that way.

## Miracles are for everyone

**You Were Born for This** is a bold initiative to reclaim the miraculous as a normal way of life. Through biblical insights, true stories, and practical how-tos, I'll show you what that new normal could look like for you.

In part 1 you'll see why everyone you encounter has an unmet need that God strongly desires to meet, very possibly through you. You'll discover that the Everyday

Miracle Territory is real—and you're standing in the middle of it.

We define a miracle as "an extraordinary event manifesting divine intervention in human affairs."[2] It's true that most of us will never be empowered by God to heal someone or walk on water. The Bible is clear that not everyone has been gifted to carry out such miracles. Yet the Bible is also clear that we are all invited to do God's work by God's power. That's why in this book we only focus on the personal miracles that are within the reach of all of us.

I'm audacious enough to call these miracles predictable. By that I mean that when we do God's work in God's way, He reveals Himself to be a miracle-working God. I mean that miracles will take place so regularly that their occurrence will seem predictable to you—not because of how or when they occur but because they **will** occur.

In part 2 you'll be introduced to four keys to a life of miracles. They will enable you as a delivery agent for God to

- make a very specific, urgent request;
- understand and accept His miracle agenda for you;
- know how to partner with an unseen power;
- take a promising but life-changing risk.

In part 3 you'll discover practical advice on how to deliver a miracle to someone in need. First you'll learn five universally identifiable signals that will guide you in your partnership with Heaven. Then you'll learn five steps for delivering a miracle. When you learn and apply these truths regularly, you can invite God to do a miracle through you for anyone at any time.

That's a startling statement, isn't it? But as you'll see, God is so intent on meeting people's deepest needs that He is always looking for volunteers who will become living links between Heaven and earth.

In part 4 you'll be introduced to three more keys that unlock what I call special delivery miracles. These miracles meet needs that matter to everyone: finances, life dreams, and forgiveness. Each chapter is based on surprising insights from the Bible and is illustrated with stories you'll find both instructive and highly motivating.

**You Were Born for This** will change how you see the world and what you expect God can and will do through you to meet real needs. You will master a few simple but powerful tools and will come to say with confidence, "I want to partner with Heaven to deliver a miracle to someone in need today—and now I know how!"

If that's what you want, I invite you to turn the page.

# 2

---

# The Tiny, Enormous Difference

## You were born to do God's work by God's power

**I**n the first chapter I described an exciting new life of miracles. And I promised that experiencing the supernatural on a regular basis is the "this" you were born for.

But if waking up to our miracle potential is so wonderful, and if this is what God wants for us, what keeps so many from actually living this way? Why do we continually fall into a rut of trying to help others on our own, of trying to avoid any situation where we would be forced to depend upon God for success?

The truth is, we can be in relationship with God and active in helping others for years without really understanding His ways or allowing Him to work through us in supernatural ways. At the heart of the problem, I believe, is a small distinction with big implications. I'm talking about the difference between knowing about God's power and actually partnering with Him in delivering miracles.

An event in my life illustrates that tiny but enormous difference.

Some years ago I was invited to speak to eighty men at a retreat center. The evening of the event, I asked the person in charge, "What would you like me to do if God shows up tonight?"

He seemed startled. "What do you mean?"

I repeated my question. "If the Lord moves and does something unusual, what do you want me to do?"

He gave it some thought. "Well, it would be important for you to bring things to a close in thirty minutes," he said. "Like we agreed."

"All right," I said. "But if something else occurs that might be unexpected, I'm going to look at you. If you want me to end things, just grab your right ear, and I will close in prayer."

He didn't seem pleased with my backup plan. "I don't need to grab my ear, Dr. Wilkinson. You just close in thirty minutes."

I confess, at this point I imagined God shaking His head in disappointment. You see, I wasn't there only because I'd been invited. Before I'd agreed to come, I'd had a strong sense that I'd already been "sent." (More about that in chapter 4.) Then, as I had prayed about what to say, I'd sensed that Heaven might have something unusual in store.

When the time came, the roomful of men welcomed me warmly, and I launched into my message. No more than five minutes in, I received a divine nudge (more about that later too). In a way that was both unusual and impossible to ignore, my attention was directed toward a man sitting four rows back on the left side of the center aisle.

I decided to trust the nudge—in fact, to risk looking like a fool because of it. I stopped talking, walked down the aisle, and introduced myself. The man's name was Owen. "I sense there is something unusual going on in your life," I told him. "Is there anything I can do for you?"

Alarm was written all over Owen's face. "No!" he exclaimed. "No, not at all. Really, I'm fine."

Now what to do? Nothing but apologize to Owen and get back up front. On the way to the podium, I thought, **Well, Lord, that was unusual.**

You should know, audiences I speak to aren't accustomed to speakers who stop in midsentence and march into the crowd with a point-blank, personal question. (I'm not accustomed to it either, for that matter.) Some men in the room were eying me now as if I might be dangerous.

Once I'd collected my thoughts, I began again. But almost immediately I felt another nudge from God.

Same nudge, same man. This time I debated with Heaven, and my case was airtight. **I just did that, Lord, and nothing happened!**

But the nudge was clear. **Go again.**

Have you ever come to a point in your life where you've had to make a choice between everything visible, everything expected and sensible . . . and something invisible, something inaudible, something known only to you that you can't possibly defend **but that you know in your heart is true**? When God nudged me again, I had one of those moments. My sentences stumbled, then stopped. And I decided to take another risk of faith.

So I picked up a chair from the front, carried it down the aisle, and sat right next to Owen. "Sir, please don't be offended," I said calmly, "but you're not telling the truth."

You could have heard a pin drop.

Owen wore the same look of alarm, but when he finally found his voice, he said, "How on earth did you know?"

"I don't know, really," I said. "But God does, and He has something in mind for you tonight. I sense that something is deeply troubling you."

"The truth is, I'm quitting the ministry tonight," Owen said soberly. "I called my wife this afternoon and told her my decision. Right after your session tonight, I'm done."

We certainly had everyone's attention.

## A roomful of witnesses

"Would you mind sharing why you're quitting?" I asked Owen.

Haltingly, Owen told his story. He'd been a successful businessman. But when he felt called by God to work with men, he'd given up his business and put heart and soul into his new ministry. Financially, nothing had gone as expected. "My wife and I have gone broke trying to keep this thing afloat," he said. "We love what we do, but we have lost our savings and our retirement. I've remortgaged our house. My credit cards are maxed out. On top of all that, I'm sixteen thousand dollars in debt . . ."

Owen was struggling to talk now. "I've had enough," he said quietly. "After tonight, I quit."

Every man in the room could identify with Owen's painful dilemma. If God wanted him to stay in the ministry, why were the circumstances so impossible for him and his family? I said as much to Owen, and I told him that my wife and I had experienced similar testing numerous times.

Then I said, "I have only one question. When you changed course and launched your ministry, was that a career move on your part, or would you say it was in response to a divine call?"

"God called us," he said. "I have no doubt."

"Okay. Would you say that God is now calling you out of the ministry? Is He asking you to leave?"

"No."

"Are you sure you want to leave?"

Owen became agitated. "Well, I'm up to my ears in debt. I **have** to quit! How am I supposed to do this?"

"I understand. But has God asked you to leave?"

A long pause.

"No."

As this little drama played out, the other men listened raptly. And I'd forgotten about the guy in charge who didn't want to have to pull on his ear to get my attention.

"What are you going to do?" I asked Owen.

And then God's Spirit moved into the room—a noticeable awareness that His presence was among us in peace and power. Many in the audience were struggling with their own emotions.

Owen's eyes filled with tears. Then with great effort he said, "I shouldn't quit unless He asks me to leave. I won't quit."

I wanted to test his resolve. "But what about the sixteen-thousand-dollar debt?"

"No, I won't quit." He had decided.

We shook hands on his decision, and when I asked some in the audience to gather around and pray for him, scores of men surrounded him. They poured out their hearts in prayer for Owen. Then we all listened while he prayed an emotional, humble prayer, recommitting himself to his calling.

Men were beginning to filter back to their seats when someone spoke up. "It's not right!" It was the man in charge. "This man is sixteen thousand dollars in debt. My wife and I are going to give him a thousand dollars. What are you going to do?" He looked around the room. He looked at me. "What are **you** going to do? You're the speaker."

I didn't say anything while we all contemplated his challenge. And then, without a word, men started to open their wallets. One by one they walked over to Owen with their gifts. I did too. In no time at all, Owen had sixteen thousand dollars.

Owen was speechless, awestruck by what God had done, and the rest of us were grateful just to have been a part of it. What an unforgettable experience!

Standing beside him in the aisle, I said, "Do you recognize the order of things that just happened? What did you have to decide before God gave you the money?"

"Unless God calls me to, I'm not leaving."

"When you made a decision of loyalty to God," I said, "the powerful arm of God was outstretched from Heaven. Do you recognize who was behind this test?"

"God was. He was testing my loyalty," said Owen.

"How did you do on the test?"

"I almost failed it."

"Yes, but you didn't," I said. "Isn't it interesting that God sent me here on the very night you were going to quit and gave me a supernatural nudge—twice—because He didn't want you to fail the test? And He prompted all these men to meet your need!"

I never got back to my message that night. God clearly had something better in mind. The miracle for

Owen was followed by one-on-one miracle break-throughs for two other men who'd been brought to that room for a reason. But so had all of us. Our paths had been guided there, not for a program, not to hear some-one speak, but to be witnesses together of God at work in powerful, personal, and super-natural ways.

**The story shows how a small shift in how we think about the Spirit's power can have enormous consequences.**

I'll admit the whole experience took longer than thirty minutes. But the man in charge never reached for his ear.

## A small shift in how we think

How many times do you suppose you have been in a situation where God urgently wanted to do something supernatural—something unexplainable and bigger than you could imagine—but it didn't happen because someone started tugging on his ear?

Maybe that someone was you.

I told the story of the men's retreat at some length because it illustrates the kinds of personal miracles God loves to do and **will** do when He has a willing and responsive delivery agent. The story also shows how a small shift in how we think about the Spirit's power can have enormous, lasting consequences. Consider how close I came to missing out on the miracle God did through me for Owen. How easy it would have been for me to explain away God's nudges and proceed with my talk according to plan. The result would have been a perfectly fine ministry event, but would God's glory and power have been so unforgettably on display? Would Owen's critical need have been met? Not likely.

So, what made the difference?

Nothing special about me, I assure you. The difference had everything to do with what I know about God's miraculous power, who has access to it, and how it helps us accomplish His work.

As I've traveled the world, I've noticed that many of Christ's followers appear to know a lot about God's Spirit but few understand how practically to partner with Him to bring a personal miracle to another person. I've seen many who long for more of the Spirit and yet resist actively partnering with His power in their lives.

In this chapter I want to help you see some things you might have missed about God's power. I hope you'll see and experience what the men in the room with Owen did that night. The evening awakened them to the hope that ordinary men and women really can actively partner with God to accomplish the miraculous. And they went home determined to be more than witnesses of God at work. They wanted to be agents who know how to deliver His miracles to others.

I wrote this book to awaken that same hope and expectation in you. We're never more fully alive and complete than when we experience God working through us and in spite of us in a way that changes someone's life right before our eyes. Nothing compares to the wonder of seeing God's goodness and glory break through—and knowing we played a part in it.

Let's begin with what Jesus said about the supernatural power of God.

## God in motion

One of the last things Jesus did with His friends before He returned to Heaven was to hand out their new job descriptions. It made for a very short read:

> **Go into all the world for Me . . . and do the impossible.**

You'll find the complete assignment in Matthew 28:18–20 and Acts 1:4–8, but have you ever wondered how the disciples reacted? I think they might have felt two opposite reactions at the same time. On the one hand, I think they wanted to say, "Please, Lord, no! We can't possibly. Look at our limitations. Look at our failures."

And on the other hand, I think they couldn't wait to get started. They'd already learned a lot from the Master, and His mission for them was glorious beyond words. Why not get right to work?

How would you have reacted?

I want you to see that both of these responses are rooted in the same misunderstanding about how this partnership with Heaven actually works.

Which explains a further instruction Jesus gave His friends:

**Wait.**[1]

But wait for what? Look at Jesus' explanation of how the impossible would become the norm in the near future:

**You shall receive power when the Holy Spirit has come upon you; and you shall be witnesses to Me . . . to the end of the earth.**[2]

The Greek word here for "power" is one that might seem familiar to you—**dynamis.** As you might guess from its English derivations (**dynamite** and **dynamic,** for example), **dynamis** means a certain kind of power. Not potential power, like still air or water, but power in motion. Power like a gale-force wind or Niagara Falls. **Dynamis** means power at work.

When Jesus told His followers to wait for Heaven's dynamis, the message was clear: What I'm sending you to do you cannot do in your own power. You can only do it as My power moves through you.

So wait for it.

The disciples got the message. They waited. And when the Spirit came in power, the world changed. If you've read the stories of the early church in Acts, you know what I mean. Now all believers had the Spirit all the time, not just dwelling in them for renewal and comfort, but working through them to accomplish Heaven's desires for people in need.

What happened next was miraculous.

Imagine the stories told around dinner tables at night.

"Philip, when you followed God's nudge into the desert and that VIP got saved—I'll never forget that!"

"Paul, when you stood up in the town square to talk about Christ and people were throwing rocks, but some people listened and many believed—I'll never forget that!"

"Rhoda, when you shouted, 'Peter is at the door!' even though we were sure he was in prison—I'll never forget that!"

God's power—the dynamis of the Spirit—was at work through them to accomplish what they could never have done on their own.

It's easy to read the accounts of the early church and assume that those were special people living in special days. Some of them had walked with Jesus, after all. Some were apostles. Perhaps that's why many today think they can't expect to partner with the supernatural in similar ways.

But is that assumption true? Listen to one apostle's frank remarks about how much difference being "special" made:

**I, brethren, when I came to you, did not come with excellence of speech or of wisdom declaring to you the testimony of God. . . . I was with you in weakness, in fear, and in much trembling. And my speech and my preaching**

**were not with persuasive words of human
wisdom, but in demonstration of the Spirit and
of power, that your faith should not be in the
wisdom of men but in the power of God.**[3]

Weakness, fear, and much trembling? Clearly Paul
realized he couldn't achieve ministry success merely by
his own effort or ability. But Paul had another stunning
insight. He saw that his weakness actually made
room—**created a miracle opportunity**—for God to
demonstrate His supernatural power.

Let me pull the threads together.

Jesus commissioned every one of His followers—
from the original disciples down to you and me—to do
for others what we cannot do alone. It is too much for
us. But Heaven has released God's dynamis to work in
us and through us. Whatever our human limitations,
when we know how to partner with Heaven, we will
see that **we were born to accomplish by supernatural
means what God wants done.**

## "Unlock that door, please!"

My first clue that my friend John was a great candidate
for miracle missions came when I heard that he was taking the message of **The Prayer of Jabez** to men in jail.
In particular, he wanted to teach inmates to be intentional about asking God to supernaturally expand their
territory for Him. Only a man who understands the
astonishing power of God would attempt such a venture behind bars.

John, a business owner with a big heart, has been visiting men at a local jail for years. "I consider it the most important thing I do all week," he wrote to me. John felt that with God's help he'd been able to do a lot of good for these men. But he wanted to do more. He wanted to do ministry with miracle impact.

What would happen, John wondered, if he taught inmates to be purposeful about inviting God to intervene through them in supernatural ways?

In **The Prayer of Jabez,** I suggest a ministry question: "How may I help you?" Many times in my life this question has led to a miracle opportunity.

"I had no idea how God would use this idea," John wrote. "But the men began to practice asking, 'How may I help you?' You can imagine the jokes flying around. 'Thank you. Would you just unlock that door, please?' "

For reasons John couldn't explain, his class grew from twelve to twenty-seven men. Even behind bars— maybe **because** they were behind bars—the men seemed motivated by the notion that God's power was available to them too. They began taking risks to invite God to work in supernatural ways. Hardened convicts accepted Christ as Savior. A man who'd had continual run-ins with inmates of another ethnicity started to slip encouraging notes under their doors at night.

One day John asked Terrence, a newcomer to the class, "How may I help you?"

Terrence barely hesitated. "I have not seen my child since she was three," he said. "And the child's mother will not communicate with me. She destroys my letters, and I'm afraid my daughter will never know me. The greatest thing for me would be to see my daughter. Can you help with that?"

As he finished, Terrence's eyes filled with tears. And John's heart sank—he didn't have a clue how to help. After talking through several ideas, they both decided that they didn't really have any options.

"We decided the only one who could help was God," recalls John. "So we prayed together. I asked God to intervene for Terrence and to bring his child for a visit."

Terrence agreed to write a letter once more asking the child's mother for a visit. Then they waited to see what God would do.

The following Sunday, when John went back, Terrence hadn't heard a thing—just like all the times before. But what they didn't know then was that his letter had been delivered and the mother and child were already making plans for a visit.

In fact, the very next Sunday, Terrence saw his daughter for the first time in years. He was able to reestablish a relationship with his family, and since that day he has been able to see his daughter regularly.

John's bold experiment in partnering with God for miracles has continued to bring transformation. "Two men received money they weren't expecting. Two other men are organizing full-time ministries for when they are released," says John. "And another guy has made plans to work at a youth camp as part of his rehabilitation."

John has changed too. "I've learned that helping other people to experience personal miracles is the most wonderful encouragement in the world."

## What is a personal miracle?

Can you see what separates John's ministry experience from many other kinds of good works for God? It is the same thing, I believe, that set my ministry at the men's retreat apart from a typical, predictably run service.

- We intentionally partnered with God's Spirit—depending on Him for success—in ways that would showcase His character and glory when He met the needs supernaturally.
- We stepped out in faith to do God's work in a context where failure was certain unless He acted.
- We took risks based on our belief that God **wanted** to show up and **would** show up in miraculous ways. And He did.

I use the term **personal miracle** to describe what happens when you help another person by intentionally relying on God's power to meet that individual's need. Why do I call these personal miracles?

First, because the kinds of miracles I'm talking about usually are completed in a person's heart. Even if the miracle itself is evidenced by something tangible— Owen receives sixteen thousand dollars from strangers, Terrence receives a visit from his long-lost daughter— God clearly does a work inside the person's heart as well.

Second, I call these personal miracles because God's purpose for doing any miracle is always the same: to meet a person's need.

And finally, the word **personal** aptly describes the aspect of God's character that is revealed by these kinds of miracles. When God takes the time to intervene in our day to meet a need in a special way that's meaningful to us in particular, we recognize how intimately God knows us and loves us.

A personal miracle is also what the Bible refers to as a good work. But not all good works are miracles. Let me explain.

Most Christians know the importance of expressing their faith through deliberate acts of service to others. Everyone's good works matter a great deal to God. As Paul reminds us, we have been "created in Christ Jesus for good works, which God prepared beforehand that we should walk in them."[4]

But what I want you to see is that good works by your own effort are good and necessary but many times are not enough. And I'm not speaking about our inability to work our way into a saving relationship with God. I mean that among the good works you and I were born to do lies a wide range of accomplishments that are extremely important to God, that we have been commissioned to do for Christ—**and that we absolutely cannot do without His supernatural power working through us.**

Think of the relationship between good works and personal miracles in your life in terms of two equations:

Your good works for God = ministry

Your ministry + God's supernatural power =
miracles

For a personal miracle, you must choose to proactively partner with God's supernatural power to do what no good work of your own could. All Christ's followers have been invited into this amazing partnership with Heaven. It's a joint but unequal venture between weak humans and an extraordinary God to pursue His agenda in His way in His time by His power and for His glory.

This amazing partnership changes what we do, how we think, and what we know is possible. We end up deciding it's perfectly natural to expect miracles behind prison bars. We stop in midsentence because God shows us there's a man four rows back on the aisle who feels forgotten by Him.

We're completely prepared to go to the ends of the earth.

## Open your eyes

I've noticed that when people start to live every day in active cooperation with the Spirit, something astonishing happens: they immediately recognize the life God intended for them. They see Jesus' promise of dynamis being fulfilled right in front of them, and the difference is so enormous that they wonder how they could have missed it for so long.

But that's the problem. You can be a Christian for years and miss it completely!

I think that explains Paul's unusual concern about this very issue. He described it as an en-lightenment problem. You need enlightenment when a fundamental and life-changing truth is just inches away but you can't see it. And if you don't see it, you can't live it. Paul under-stood that a person can be a true believer in Christ and yet not understand at all how we are to actually accomplish the business of Heaven.

> **That's the problem. You can be a Christian for years and miss it completely!**

For the believers at Ephesus, he prayed,

> **that...the eyes of your understanding being enlightened** ["enlightened"—there's the key word]; **that you may know** [have a clear mental perception of] **what is . . . the exceeding great-ness of His power** ["power"—that's **dynamis**] **toward us who believe, according to the work-ing of His mighty power** [dynamis again] **which He worked in Christ when He raised Him from the dead.**[5]

This is my prayer for you too: that the eyes of your understanding will be enlightened to your miracle potential. If you don't see the truth about God's power, you will come to a sensible but costly conclusion: "I was not born to do God's work by God's power."

Will you see and embrace the truth instead?

It's the difference between life as most people know it and your life as God wants it to be.

It's the difference between a commendable, even God-blessed human endeavor and supernaturally infused life.

It's the difference between your feeling good about what you've done to help others and others feeling astonished by what God has done for them through you.

This book is all about that tiny, enormous difference.

# 3

# Behind the Veil of Heaven

## You were born to be a living link between Heaven and earth

**I**f **I were to ask you** what you think is happening in Heaven at this very moment, what would you say?

I've asked this simple question of religious and non-religious, educated and uneducated persons the world over. And since most people believe Heaven exists, ideas tend to come quickly.

People mention angels, harps, God sitting on His throne, a lot of praise and worship. Others mention higher states of consciousness. But little involving action comes to mind.

"Any committee meetings going on up there?" I ask. "Strategy planning sessions?"

Folks laugh. They think I'm kidding.

"How about God? Does He do any work? What about God asking for opinions on important matters? Does Heaven have anything like an agenda for the day?"

People don't think so.

I love watching their faces when I ask questions like these. (They do sound a bit far-fetched, don't they?) But the responses I hear are quite revealing. The fact is, most people think God just listens to worship songs. Whenever I ask, "And what does God do when He's finished listening?" all I get is blank stares. To them, Heaven today is nice but not very exciting. It's a place on hold, a celestial waiting room for angels and great-aunts. And whatever does happen there doesn't really affect what happens on earth.

But what if you discovered that the spiritual realm of Heaven and the material realm of earth are actively linked in billions of ways? What if you discovered that God is intently at work right now on tasks that matter greatly to Him and that He's constantly looking for volunteers to help Him?

**I want to pull back the veil of Heaven to reveal what God is doing right now to connect with people in need on earth.**

We ended chapter 2 with some promises: You were born to deliver miracles for God. You can learn how to partner with Heaven to do God's supernatural work on earth. And it can happen today.

If these possibilities intrigue you, this chapter will show you something astonishing: God wants you to experience a miracle today even more than you do. To show you why that's true, I want to pull back the veil of Heaven to reveal what God is doing right now to connect with people in need on earth.

## Snorkel vision

If you've ever snorkeled in tropical waters, you know that if you get it just right, you can see one world through the bottom half of your mask, another through the top. Bottom half—a watery world of coral and colored fish. Top half—sky.

In 1 Kings 22 we get to have a similar experience. One verse shows what's happening on earth. The next verse shows what's happening at the very same time in the courts of Heaven. I think you'll see evidence of a Heaven-earth connection that will revolutionize how you view your world.

What's happening on earth, in this Bible chapter, is a turning point in the history of Israel. A ruthless and corrupt king named Ahab is trying to make a decision. Should he go into battle against Syria or not? His advisors—all of whom worship idols, not God—have told him to march north to battle because victory is guaranteed. But Ahab wavers. He wants confirmation from an outside source. On the recommendation of a friend, a prophet of God is brought in.

His name is Micaiah. Ahab soon learns that God has granted this little-known man snorkel vision: while living on earth, he can see directly into Heaven. He actually watches and listens as God responds in real time to Ahab's question.

Let's watch with him:

> **I saw the LORD sitting on His throne, and all the host of Heaven standing by, on His right hand and on His left. And the LORD said, "Who will persuade Ahab to go up, that he may fall at Ramoth Gilead?" So one spoke in this manner, and another spoke in that manner. Then a spirit came forward and stood before the LORD, and said, "I will persuade him." The LORD said to him, "In what way?"** [1]

Do you see what's happening in Heaven? It could almost be called a business meeting. God wants to rescue Israel from its evil king, but He's open to ideas on how to accomplish it.

When the spirit (or angel) proposes to mislead the king through his advisors, God not only approves but promises him success. [2]

On earth Micaiah warns Ahab that his advisors have been misled. But the king decides to listen to them anyway. He confidently marches north against Syria, only to die in battle. [3]

**But wait,** you might be thinking. **How does this historical incident help me know how to partner with Heaven to deliver a miracle?**

Let me show you. Since every miracle from God begins in the supernatural realm, we first need to find out how Heaven works. Which brings us back to Micaiah. His extraordinary glimpse behind the veil of Heaven shows a clear connection between events in Heaven and simultaneous events on earth.

And it reveals two surprising insights about what God is doing right now that could completely change how you think about your miracle potential. They did for me.

Let's start with the first one.

## God's to-do list
**Could it be that God has work to do and that He is working right now on an agenda—a kind of daily to-do list?**

The prophet sees that God is surrounded by "all the host of Heaven standing by, on His right hand and on His left." We know from elsewhere in Scripture that the hosts of Heaven are angels numbering in the millions. At least in this scene, not one of them is singing. It looks to me as though they've been summoned to a meeting with God. He wants to influence someone's day on earth, and believe it or not, He's open to ideas on how to accomplish it.

While most of us think God is still resting from the demands of Creation week, the Bible shows another picture. He has a real-time, right-now agenda on earth.

God with a to-do list? The implications are profound.

But Jesus showed that it's true. To those who criticized Him for healing a man on the Sabbath, Jesus said:

"My Father is always at His work to this very day, and I, too, am working."[4] Jesus clearly revealed that His work of healing on the Sabbath was a continuation of God's ongoing work on earth.

Then Jesus went on to describe an active partnership:

**The Son can do nothing of Himself, but what He sees the Father do; for whatever He does, the Son also does in like manner. For the Father loves the Son, and shows Him all things that He Himself does.**[5]

**It sure sounds like God is looking for a volunteer. And He's obviously open to suggestions.**

So all during Jesus' lifetime on earth, Father and Son were hard at work on Heaven's to-do list. God intervened in human affairs, and amazing miracles resulted!

Since Jesus is no longer on earth, we need to ask whom God is looking to now to complete His agenda. Micaiah's glimpse behind the veil can change how we think about that too.

Let's revisit the scene in more detail.

## Inside Mission Central

The prophet sees that God is holding a meeting. The hosts have been assembled for a strategy session. "Who will persuade Ahab to go up [to war]?" God wants to know. It sure sounds like He's looking for a volunteer. And He's obviously open to suggestions. As Micaiah watches, an angel comes forward to volunteer. He says he has a strategy in mind that will persuade Ahab.

"In what way?" God asks.

When the angel tells God his plans, God approves and sends him on his way. "You shall persuade him, and also prevail," He says. "Go out and do so."

Which brings us to the second surprise:

**Could it be that Heaven today should be thought of as Mission Central, where God is actively looking for and sending out volunteers who will carry out His agenda on earth?**

We know from Scripture that God has three options for getting something done on earth:

- **In Person,** as when He dictated the Ten Commandments to Moses
- **By an angel,** as when the angel Gabriel announced the upcoming birth of Jesus to Mary

But from Scripture and history, we must conclude that God has chosen these options only rarely. That leaves . . .

- **Through a human being**

Think about it: today, tomorrow, and the day after, our all-powerful God will choose to work through ordinary people to get done on earth what He has decided in Heaven that He wants to do.

If God is so intent on finding volunteers, it only makes sense that He would communicate His wishes to human beings everywhere. It only makes sense that Mission Central would be sending out requests—miracle missions included—to people all over the world all the time.

But that can't be true.

Or can it?

## Signals sent, signals not received

When **The Prayer of Jabez** was still at the top of the **New York Times** bestseller list, I was invited to speak in Hollywood at an unusual gathering of movie-industry insiders. The film director who called said that his colleagues—most of them agnostics or atheists—couldn't figure out why a book on prayer was outselling Stephen King and John Grisham.

"I've been working in this business for twenty-six years, and this is the first time an evangelical Christian has been invited to speak," he said when he picked me up at my hotel. "I'm guessing the crowd will be small—maybe twenty or thirty."

But God was up to something. We walked into a packed house of at least four hundred. I had just started explaining the second part of the Jabez prayer—"Lord, expand my territory!"—when a man in the back interrupted.

"I have a question!" he shouted. "Do you really believe that prayer works?"

"Yes sir, I do."

"Every time?"

"Yes."

"Get out!" He clearly wasn't buying it.

"Let me ask all of you a question," I said. "How many of you would say that at least once in your life you were clearly nudged to stop and help a person but you didn't?"

Almost everyone in the room raised a hand. Instinctively they recognized that they had been nudged to act by a supernatural force.

"That's why God always answers the prayer of a person who wants to do more for Him," I told my audience. "Because God nudges everyone, and almost everyone says no!"

Are you beginning to see why you can be a part of as many miracles for God as you want? Everywhere around us God has urgent work to be done. At all times He is looking for volunteers who will partner with Him. And He isn't just passively on the lookout; He is actively, constantly, and passionately sending out requests.

**You'll learn to be a living link between Heaven and earth, recognizing a miracle opportunity where others see nothing at all.**

Later in this book I'll show you how miracle agents can develop new sensitivities—or rediscover buried ones—that will help them stay in tune with God's intentions. For example, in chapter 8 you'll find helpful teaching on miracle-specific signals from God, from others, and even from yourself. By learning to read the signs effectively, you'll learn to be a living link between Heaven and earth, recognizing a miracle opportunity right in front of you where others see nothing at all.

By now you might be wondering why anyone would miss Heaven-sent invitations to a miracle. In my experience longtime Christians are especially susceptible to missing them because of a common misunderstanding about God's motivations.

I suffered from it for years.

## Praying (fervently) for the wrong thing

Early one morning I was asking again for God to do a miracle in the life of a friend. My part (I thought) was to persuade God to answer in a big way. Specifically, I was earnestly asking God to use me to deliver a miracle in my friend's life. What could I do or say that would change God's mind and release His favor? What kind of intensity or desperation would it take on my part to get God's attention?

Suddenly, in midprayer, I felt compelled not to say another word. I felt drawn instead to reflect silently on the assumptions hiding underneath my prayers. What did they tell me that I **really** believed about God and His desire to act? What did they reveal about how I thought God was hearing my prayers at that very moment?

It didn't take long for my actual theology of prayer

to rise to the surface. Clearly, I believed that God was reluctant to do miracles. That's why I needed to try to persuade Him—give Him reason after reason, day after day, so He would finally relent and decide to act.

In the middle of these thoughts a familiar Bible verse came to mind:

> **The eyes of the LORD run to and fro throughout the whole earth, to show Himself strong on behalf of those whose heart is loyal to Him.**[6]

Now, I'd always understood this verse to mean that God wants loyal serv-ants. And of course He does. But for the first time I read these words for what they showed me about what God is doing in Heaven right now. Do you see it?

God is not reluctant or uninterested when it comes to showing Himself strong. Rather, He is looking "to and fro throughout the whole earth" for people who are loyal to Him. Why? So He can reveal His supernatural power in their lives!

Let me summarize what we've learned so far about partnering with Heaven for a miracle:

- God is constantly at work in supernatural ways in our world, and He has much He wants to get done.
- God is actively looking for loyal partners—people who consistently care about what He cares about.

- God is regularly nudging people to respond,
  but most people miss His intentions or simply say no.

What would it look like in your life if you started
saying yes? Let me share a family story.

## A network of nudges

When our daughter Jessica was a teenager, she went with
a group on a short-term mission to Europe. Their purpose was to assist local churches in youth outreach, but
along the way Jessica found that her most important
ministry seemed to be with Leila, a girl her own age in
the group. As the two girls became friends, Leila began
to confide in Jessica. A family member was sexually
molesting her, she said. Jessica was the first person she
felt safe enough around to reveal what was going on.

Jessica listened in shock. "What's happening is not
your fault," she told Leila. She made Leila promise to
get help immediately.

Not long after Jessica returned to the States, our
family moved to Africa. But Jessica and Leila stayed in
touch by phone and e-mail. Even though Leila's circumstances didn't improve, she resisted getting help.
Then she seemed to drop off the map.

One afternoon Jessica sensed strongly that Leila's situation had reached a crisis point. She couldn't explain
the feeling—she and Leila had been out of touch for a
month. But Jessica decided to act. She called and
e-mailed a network of Christian friends, including

some friends from the mission trip. Her urgent message read: "I don't know why, but I think something terrible is happening with my friend Leila. Please pray for her right now!" Jessica still had no idea whether Leila was okay or not, but she had decided to act on the leading she felt.

The next day a friend called with news. Two hours after her friends had started to pray, Leila had made a serious attempt to take her life. Thankfully, she hadn't succeeded.

"I'm so glad I acted on what I sensed God was telling me," says Jessica. "I believe Leila is alive today because of the desperate prayers of friends. Her narrow escape convinced her to break the silence and get the help she needed."

Today Leila is full of life and happily married.

What do you think could have happened if Jessica had decided not to follow that nudge from Heaven? My second story illustrates what can happen when people ignore what God wants.

## The consequence on the corner

A few years ago our creative team was shooting a feature film in South Africa in the dead of winter. The story centered on a Zulu boy who became orphaned when his parents and relatives all died of HIV/AIDS. To survive, the boy left his village and took up a hardscrabble existence fending for himself on the streets of Johannesburg.

One bitterly cold winter morning our crew was scheduled to begin shooting at five o'clock on a particular street corner. It was so cold that production assistants had arrived early to set up tents with gas heaters where we could keep ourselves warm. We all showed up at the set wearing scarves, gloves, and heavy coats—not the attire that usually comes to mind when people think of Africa.

By the time I arrived that morning, several police cars were already there, emergency lights flashing. The film team looked as if they were in the depths of despair. I asked the director of photography what was going on.

"I can't believe this," he told me somberly. "Last night, right across the street, a homeless boy froze to death. They found him this morning."

I was stunned. Everybody was. Then, as we contemplated what had happened, the terrible irony set in.

Here we were to shoot a scene about a homeless orphan, and right across the street a homeless orphan boy died because no one gave him a blanket or a coat. No one gave him shelter.

Finally I said to the crew, "You don't think that boy's death reflects God's heart, do you?"

Based on what you've learned in this chapter, what do you think? Wouldn't you say that God heard the prayers of that little orphan boy, decided to intervene, and began nudging all kinds of people toward him? But no one came.

That would mean what God urgently wanted to

happen on that winter morning in Johannesburg didn't happen. Someone—perhaps dozens of people in different places during the preceding days—said no to Heaven's nudge.

## A door marked "Yes"

In the opening chapters of this book, we've seen that each of us was created for nothing less than a miracle-filled life. It's not a special existence reserved for the select few but is for everyone.

We've seen that a life marked by the miraculous is not just possible, not even just desirable, but is at the very center of God's will for every one of us. When we settle for less, our lives lose delight, fulfillment, and purpose. Personal needs of people we meet get overlooked. Extreme needs in our communities and around the world go unmet.

**When a whole generation settles for less, the character and motives of God get called into question. His shining presence seems to fade in the world.**

When a whole generation settles for less, the character and motives of God get called into question. His shining presence seems to fade in the world.

But you were born to be a living link between Heaven and earth. You were born to be God's ambassador in the Everyday Miracle Territory, making Him visible in unforgettable ways.

The miraculous touches of Heaven that God wants

to accomplish will come in all sizes, but mostly they'll be of the personal, everyday sort that you can be a part of. Why? Because God passionately desires to show Himself strong for you and through you, and because every person you meet has a significant need that only God can meet.

In the coming chapters I'll show you how to step into a lifestyle of miracles. You begin by picking up and putting to work four keys to a life of predictable miracles.

The first key is the simplest and the most profound. You'll find it at a door marked "Yes."

# Part 2

---

# FOUR KEYS TO A LIFE
# OF MIRACLES

# Introduction to the Miracle Life Keys

All seven miracle keys I talk about in **You Were Born for This** describe specific actions that unlock the miraculous in our lives. Each key is based on powerful biblical insights about how Heaven works. And each leads to a breakthrough in our potential to partner supernaturally with God in His work on earth.

The seven keys fall into two groups. Special Delivery Keys (Keys 5–7) apply to specific needs. They are external actions we take that lead to a miracle breakthrough for another person. We'll look at these in part 4.

The Miracle Life Keys (Keys 1–4), which I talk about next, describe internal actions that prepare you for a life of miracles. Each Miracle Life Key can become a habit that will radically change how you see the world and how you partner with God in the supernatural realm. Without these keys we would stand in the middle of Everyday Miracle Territory totally unaware of how to tap into the supernatural as a way of life.

Here's a brief preview:

> **The Master Key** is an urgent prayer to be sent by God on a miracle mission. Your request alerts Heaven that you are more than just available; you're committed to respond whenever God nudges you. It's

called the Master Key because your urgent plea opens the door to a life of miracles.

**The People Key** readies you for the inevitable moment when Heaven's agenda collides with your own. When you apply this key, you put yourself and Heaven on notice that you have decided to make God's heart for people your own. Because you now share His passion for people, you'll be prepared to deliver miracles to whomever He asks whenever He asks.

**The Spirit Key** prepares you to cooperate with God's Spirit, especially in regard to His supernatural power. The action of this key releases you from any false assumptions about your ability to do a miracle and aligns you with the supernatural power that's always required to accomplish a miracle outcome. As you learn more about how the Spirit works through you, you will come to rely on Him with increasing confidence.

**The Risk Key** shows you how to intentionally live in such a way that you take risks of faith, relying on God to accomplish what He wants done. You act in dependence on God despite feelings of dis-

comfort or fear, trusting that He will
bridge the gap between what you can do
and what only He can do through you.
When He bridges that gap with a miracle,
His power and glory are on display.

These keys are practical, doable, and biblical. They
position you to experience God's supernatural power
on a regular basis. And obviously, they will enhance
your relationship with God as well.

Which brings us to an important question. Why
did I include these four keys and not others?

Naturally, spiritual disciplines like Bible study, regular fellowship, acts of service, and prayer—along
with consecration and obedience—are indispensable
to Christian growth. But I chose these four keys
because they specifically unlock, or make possible, a
person's potential to partner with Heaven to do God's
work on earth. The priority I have given them is
based on the teaching of Scripture, considerable
research, and my own ministry experience.

I'm not suggesting these are the only possible
actions that influence our miracle potential. Other
people could come up with valuable alternatives or
additions. But these keys have proved essential and
profoundly meaningful to me and many others over
the years, and I'm confident they will prove the same
for you.

You might particularly notice that I don't list
prayer as a key. Prayer certainly plays an important

part in miracle delivery, as you'll see numerous times in this book. But I chose not to make it a key for several reasons. First, be-cause so much has already been written on this subject (including my own works **The Prayer of Jabez** and **Secrets of the Vine**). Second, because many use prayer indirectly to **avoid** taking action. For example, when we say, "I'll keep you in prayer," we often mean we don't intend to respond further. And third, the all-important focus of **You Were Born for This** is on what happens when God answers someone else's prayer by sending us to deliver a miracle.

None of the Miracle Life Keys alone is a guarantee that you will experience the miraculous. But the fewer of these keys you activate, the less likely you'll be to experience miracles. And conversely, the more you apply these powerful keys to align yourself with the way Heaven works, the more you will not only recognize miracle opportunities but also ask God to send you.

Taken together, these first four keys unlock a life of miracles. And by the time you combine these principles with the practical advice of parts 3 and 4 of this book, you'll have everything you need to begin delivering personal miracles.

# 4

# The Master Key

## You were born to be sent on miracle missions

On a steaming-hot Georgia night, as I was driving home from visiting my mother, I made a request to God. It's one I've made many times in my life. Right there in my car, I pictured myself walking into the courts of Heaven, kneeling before the throne of God, and asking, "Please, Lord, send me to do Your work. I want to serve You this evening."

Minutes later I came to my next freeway exchange and took the off-ramp. That's when I noticed the older-model van up ahead, pulled off to the side. A man wearing a turban stood beside it, motioning for help.

I slowed down and pulled up behind him. By the time I had stopped, he was already at my window. "What's the problem, sir?" I asked.

"My van is broken down. I called for a tow truck,

but they'll only take cash at night. I don't have any. I've been here for hours." He was soaking in perspiration and visibly traumatized.

"Come on around and have a seat in my car," I said. "It's cooler in here." He got in, I handed him a bottle of water, and we talked about what to do. "You've really been out here for hours?" I said.

"Yes. And I've got small children waiting for me at home." He paused. "But what people have been shouting at me—that is the worst."

"Shouting?"

"Yes, as they drive by. I have never heard such filth. Racial slurs. Profanities. Curses upon my mother. They throw things . . ."

I knew then that my stop was not a coincidence or just an act of charity. The defeated man beside me was God's answer to my prayer only minutes ago. God had sent me, and He was nudging me to act on His behalf.

"I'm sorry, sir," I said. "Hours of that would be extremely painful." I turned to make eye contact. "If you'll allow me, I want to apologize for every disrespectful thing those people said." He looked at me in disbelief. "Please forgive us," I said. "That's not who you are. And that's not who everybody out there is either."

I told him I wanted to pay for the tow truck. I reached for an envelope in the daily planner on the seat beside me. "Here's something for the tow truck and a little more to get your van fixed. It's money I've been carrying for someone else. I have reason to believe He would want you to have it."

At first he was speechless. Then he thanked me profusely and asked for my address so he could pay me back.

"Nope. No need for that at all," I said.

He got out and walked toward his van. Then he paused, turned, and came back to my window. "Sir," he asked solemnly, "are you an angel?"

"Well, I was sent to you, but I'm not an angel."

"It was God who sent you, wasn't it?"

"Yes," I said.

Driving home, I was shaking my head in amazement at how God works. I had asked for a miracle appointment and taken my exit only minutes later, and there it was.

Have you ever asked God with all your heart to be sent on a miracle mission?

By "ask" I don't mean tell Him you're willing. I don't mean mention to Him that someday He could send you if He's really in a bind. I mean specifically, passionately, urgently plead with God to send you—and send you today!

I have seen a direct link in my life between that little prayer and extraordinary outcomes. Sometimes the appointments are on a small scale, like that night on the freeway. But sometimes they're larger. I've been sent to speak with CEOs of corporations, to negotiate peace between warring tribes in Africa, to help restore a marriage right before it ended in divorce, even to meet with presidents of countries.

What all these experiences have in common is this: they were initiated by a specific request on my part, and they ended with a miracle. When I asked to be sent, God sent me on miracle missions.

That's what the first key to a life of miracles is all about.

## The kind of "yes" God is looking for

Your urgent request to be sent on a miracle mission is exactly the kind of "yes!" God is looking for. I call this purposeful move on your part the Master Key because it unlocks the invisible door between you and the Everyday Miracle Territory. Your action opens it, you step through, and everything changes.

What was once just the terrain of your life has now become a landscape brimming with miracle opportunity. Turn this key, and you are now fully acting upon your new job description as Heaven's delivery agent. You are a sent one from God on a mission inside the Everyday Miracle Territory.

By contrast, every other key I'll show you unlocks your miracle potential once you're there.

**The Master Key is an urgent prayer to be sent by God to do His work. You enter the throne room of Heaven on a regular basis and ask God, "Please, send me!"**

If you know the Bible, you might be thinking, **But**

**why should I ask to be sent? Didn't Jesus already tell me to go?**

You're right. He did. Before He returned to Heaven, He passed His mission on earth to His disciples with an explanation. He said, "As the Father has sent Me, I also send you." Then He made that into a command: "Go into all the world and preach the gospel to every creature."[1]

But there's a problem. Have you noticed? Millions of Christ's followers already know what Jesus said. Millions agree that, since Jesus commanded us to go, it must be important. And millions are willing and available to go.

But so few go.

When you and I ask to be sent by God, we are taking His urgent, heartfelt **command** and turning it into our urgent, heartfelt **request.** We are coming all the way over to God's point of view on what we were born to do. We are declaring to God:

**I** hear Your command, but I realize that hearing and agreeing are not enough. Therefore, I am sincerely asking, God, please send **me** today on a miracle mission. And I'm letting You know in advance, when You send me, I **will** go!

When you pray this way, God knows that He can call on you, His highly motivated delivery person, at any time. Whether He reaches into your heart with a nudge or simply puts you at the scene of something He wants done (as He did with me that night on the freeway), He knows you have already committed to act on His behalf.

Why **wouldn't** He begin to send miracle opportunities your way?

I used to think only those who knew the details of their mission in advance (and liked them) would ask so urgently to be sent. Then I looked again at the well-known story of how the prophet Isaiah asked to be sent.

I invite you to listen in on a most revealing conversation.

## Eavesdropping on your future

In the book of Isaiah we find another account from a man who saw behind the veil of Heaven. Like Micaiah before him, Isaiah was permitted to eavesdrop on a conversation around God's throne. But unlike Micaiah, Isaiah didn't just politely listen and learn. He joined right in.

You might be familiar with what he wrote about his amazing experience:

**In the year that King Uzziah died, I saw the Lord sitting on a throne, high and lifted up, and the train of His robe filled the temple. Above it stood seraphim; each one had six wings: with two he covered his face, with two he covered his feet, and with two he flew. And one cried to another and said:**

**"Holy, holy, holy is the Lord of hosts;
The whole earth is full of His glory!"**

**And the posts of the door were shaken by the
voice of him who cried out, and the house was
filled with smoke.**[2]

What a scene! The courts of Heaven filled to bursting—filled with the Lord's robe, filled with smoke,
filled with the cries of strange angel-beings, filled
beyond all that with the wondrous presence of God.
Just another day in Heaven. But on this particular day,
a witness from earth has been invited to watch.

As you'll soon notice, what Isaiah sees in Heaven is
strikingly similar to what Micaiah saw:

- He sees that God is at work,
  focused on Heaven's agenda
  for earth.
- He sees that God is looking
  for a volunteer to carry it
  out.

**God is not
sitting back
while the
centuries tick
by, merely
listening to
angel choirs.**

That's why in the previous
chapter we described Heaven as
Mission Central. God is not sit-
ting back while the centuries tick by, merely listening
to angel choirs. Instead He is focused on dispatch-
ing miracle missions to meet needs on earth. Sometimes He sends angels. But for face-to-face work
in the physical realm, God looks for people who will
say yes.

A few verses later Isaiah hears God asking two questions.

**Also I heard the voice of the Lord, saying:**

**"Whom shall I send,**
**And who will go for Us?"**

**Then I said, "Here am I! Send me."** [3]

Notice Isaiah's immediate response. The Hebrew he uses is in the imperative. Isaiah so intensely desires to be sent that he almost commands God to send him!

Send him to do what? Well, it turned out that Isaiah was going to speak for God in the courts of kings and deliver striking visions that still inspire readers today. But at that moment Isaiah didn't know what he had ahead of him. He didn't ask either. I think Isaiah was so captivated by what he was seeing that he forgot he was still in Jerusalem. And instead of holding back, he cries out, "God, send me!"

Why can you and I be so bold with God? One reason: we're asking God to accomplish through us what He's already made clear He urgently **wants** and **will** accomplish. What father wouldn't entrust the tasks that are dearest to his heart to a son or daughter who demonstrates that kind of loyal commitment?

Look again at the two questions God asks that day as Isaiah listens: "Whom shall I send?" and "Who will go for Us?" He's not asking the same question twice;

both questions are important. For example, not all who are sent will choose to go. (Wait till you meet Jonah in the next chapter.) God is looking for volunteers who have committed without preconditions to go when He asks.

Isaiah's answer embodies the truth of the Master Key: **God is looking for men and women who want to do Heaven's work so much that they earnestly request to be sent. And when they ask, He will act.**

> **I've noticed something reassuring. When we ask to be sent by God, He matches each of us with people we can help.**

## Match-ups for personal miracles

I've noticed something unexplainable and very reassuring. When we ask to be sent by God, He matches each of us with people we **can** help. He did so for me that hot night beside the freeway. He orchestrated an appointment for me with that stranded driver that was time, need, and resources specific. He'll do it for you too. Your chance of helping the people you meet is just as high as my chance of helping someone I meet. It's uncanny, and it's certainly not chance.

Recently on an airplane I had my Bible in front of me, and I asked God to send me to a person in need. A man on his way back from the rest room saw me reading and stopped to say, "Now, that's a good book." After we ex-changed a few words, he took the empty seat next to me. When I asked what I could do for him, he said, "Just before I walked back here, I was reading the book of Proverbs and begging God to tell me what to do. I need two miracles today. My construction company is in big trouble."

I couldn't believe it. He asked God specifically for two miracles! As it turned out, his problems were rooted in organizational and leadership issues that I have taught and consulted on for years. By the time we finished, God had answered his prayer. "Who would have thought God would answer my prayer so quickly," he said, "and as I was on the way back to my seat from the rest room!"

I share that incident to make a point: even when we're sure we have little to offer, God matches us with situations and people uniquely and for a purpose. Mission Central is **not** a haphazard operation. God will match you with different people than He would me. Yes, we both said, "Please send me!" But He will send us on different missions. They'll both have God's fingerprints all over them, though. And we'll both know we were set up for a miracle by the King of the universe.

## My Master Key U-turns

To activate the kind of remarkable partnership with Heaven I've described and to keep it flourishing as a lifestyle, most people need to redraw their assumptions about how Heaven works.

The A statements below represent what most people believe—and what you may have believed until now.

The B statements realign your beliefs with biblical truth so God can release miracles in your life.

### What I believe about being proactive
**Belief A.** God just wants me to be available and willing for Him to work through me in miraculous ways.
**Belief B.** God wants me to ask proactively to be sent on miracle missions.

### What I believe about who is responsible for God's miracle agenda for me on earth
**Belief A.** God's miracle agenda for me is completely His responsibility, especially when it comes to something only He can do. I don't have any responsibilities regarding miracles.
**Belief B.** God's miracle agenda for me is primarily my responsibility to fulfill by the power of the Spirit. I was born to partner with Heaven on miracle missions.

Where do you see yourself in these belief statements? Are you ready now to put down old misconceptions and grab hold of new, miracle-releasing ones? There's simply no way to step into a life of miracles while you're still shackled by false beliefs. And you don't have to be.

Say the new truths—the B beliefs—aloud to yourself right now, write them down in your journal, and watch what God does next in your life.

Unfortunately, for too many of us, the idea of being sent to do God's work can sound high-minded, super-spiritual, and out of reach. That's why I like to put it in everyday terms.

## Profile of a delivery agent

Picture this:

A parcel deliveryman comes to your door. He's holding a box. Your name is on it. Something inside the box is for you.

Or picture this:

A parcel deliverywoman comes to your place of business. She's holding a stack of oversize padded envelopes. Your name is on all of them. What's inside each one is for you.

What do you see in these two familiar scenes? A man and a woman on a mission. Each has been sent to you with a delivery. Each brings a particular package to a particular address and a particular person. They know you're most interested, not in them, but in the package. They're just delivery people.

Now picture this:

**You** are that delivery person. You are sent from Mission Central. Your job each day—maybe numerous times each day—is to deliver a package from God to someone else. What's in the package? You don't know exactly, but you believe that since it's from God, it is good—very good.

When you and I purposely ask God to send us to do His work on earth, we take on a completely different role in our day. We are now people sent from God, His delivery agents. We walk out the door knowing that He could have a miracle (a delivery through us) for anyone we meet. Why? Because, from God's point of view, everyone, everywhere, at all times is in need. God knows about every need, and He cares about each one. That's why He loves to send servants who are passionate about delivering visible proofs of His goodness and glory.

The life I'm describing is one that even longtime Christians rarely dare to imagine for themselves. But you and I were born to do more than imagine it—we were born to live it every day.

You might think that you must somehow make yourself more worthy before He would favor you with a miracle mission. But as surprising as it may seem, the opposite is the case. As you'll see in chapter 10, you are the one doing the "favor." It only makes sense that in a world of nearly infinite need, where most people say no to miracle missions, Heaven could have a backlog of divine missions just waiting to be delivered.

It only makes sense that when you and I enter into His presence and request with all our hearts, "Please, Lord, send me!" He will act.

Imagine, then, how God might respond if we asked to be sent, not just once, but on a regular basis.

## How to ask to be sent
Each of the keys discussed in this book reveals an action that needs to become a life habit if you want to be pro-

ductive for God in the Everyday Miracle Territory. But it all starts with the Master Key.

Here are simple steps you can take on a regular basis so that your yes to God becomes a way of life, not just a one-time event.

1. **Consciously enter the throne room of Heaven.** In your mind picture walking into the magnificent throne room where God the Father sits with Jesus Christ at His right hand. Consider this as an actual event that takes place in the courts of Heaven rather than just words you pray. Following the example of Isaiah, come with your urgent request in mind.

2. **Volunteer with the words "Here am I. Send me!"** Picture yourself asking God with all your heart to choose you for His service. "Here I am. Please send me on a miracle mission!" That's all you need to say. That's all He needs to hear. That's how Isaiah addressed God when he saw the way Heaven worked. The Bible uniquely honors the "**fervent** prayer of a righteous man."[4]

3. **Precommit to act when you are nudged.** Pledge to God, "As You lead, I **will** respond." Sometimes you'll say those words to the Lord, while at other times you'll simply reaffirm that commitment to yourself. But the point is, no matter how, where, or when God signals His will, you have decided in advance to act. In fact, you have decided in advance that the greater risk is not misreading His nudge but getting sidetracked by rationalizations, excuses, uncertainty, doubt, or neglect.

4. **Actively put your faith in God to deliver His**

**miracle through you.** Why? Because you'll be fighting fear before long. So exercise your faith by committing to God, "I trust You to deliver the miracle through me. Thank You that I can fully depend upon You!" Then you are done. Leave the throne room joyfully as a sent one.

Post it on your mirror, stick it on your dashboard or desk, or write it in your daily planner: "Today I am a delivery person for God. Please, Lord, send **me**!" The prayer is your signal to Heaven that you are on the alert and eager to serve.

Since you're now wearing the uniform of Mission Central, you can proceed on God's authority, confident about what lies ahead.

## What comes next?

Of course, it's only natural to wonder what happens next. You'll soon see that leaving the unknowns to God becomes part of the adventure. But if you're like most people, you immediately suspect that you left Mission Central without something—something very important.

Directions, maybe?

A name?

A few hints?

I have good news. First, you can expect miracles to begin happening in your life right away, even if you don't learn any more specifics about your mission. It's true! I've seen it happen many times. God just loves to work with a delivery person who is bold enough to say to Him, "Send me, Lord, whatever that means and however it happens. I trust You."

Second, you're now ready to discover God's agenda for your day and to share His heart for the beneficiaries of your mission like never before.

That's what the next chapter is about.

# 5

# The People Key

**You were born to share God's heart
for people**

**S**ome years ago, while boarding a flight to Los Angeles, I had nothing in mind but meeting a deadline. My book **Beyond Jabez** was about to go to the printer. This would be my last chance to make changes.

As I took my seat, I asked God to help me finish my work before we landed in California. (But honestly, my prayer meant "Please don't ask me to help anyone for the next three hours!")

Fortunately, I'd been able to upgrade to business class with frequent-flier miles, and I figured the extra room would improve my chances of working without distractions. And I had been seated next to a window beside an empty seat—even better. I breathed a sigh of relief and thanked God for hearing my prayer.

But just before the doors closed, I heard the voice of a loud and obviously drunk man entering the plane. My heart sank. He couldn't be headed to the seat next to mine, could he? Quickly I reminded God that the book I was working on was His book. **Surely You want me to get this done!**

Then the man came into sight, swaying down the aisle. His hair was dyed several colors, and his body had been pierced in numerous interesting places. When he paused at my row, the smell of alcohol seemed to fill the cabin.

"Hey, I think this seat is mine!" he announced.

"Yes sir," I said. "I wondered if it would be."

Once seated, Rainbow Metal Man accepted a drink from the flight attendant. Then he wanted to talk with me. We traded chitchat for a few minutes, then I made my move—a not-too-subtle turning of my attention back to my work.

He made his move too. He ordered another drink.

I happened to be proofreading a section of the book that included stories about our family's time in Africa. I worked, and Rainbow Metal Man kept drinking until the attendant suggested he'd had enough. The whole time, I kept my body turned away from my companion as much as possible. Meanwhile, I kept defending my choices. **Lord, You know I can't talk to this guy.**

**Don't let him interrupt me. I need to get these pages proofed!**

But after proofing so many pages about how Jabez asked to do more for God, I gave in. **All right, Lord,** I prayed. **Send me to serve You, even to this man. But let him start the conversation.**

I had no more prayed those words when Metal Man spoke up. "That's a @#!!@# good book!" he yelled.

"Uh, you think so?" I said. I didn't know quite what to say. It was the first time a person had ever sworn about one of my books (at least in my presence). "How do you know that?"

"@#!!@#! I've been reading it over your shoulder!"

I nodded, trying not to get tipsy from the fumes.

"But I have an important question," he announced. "Are you a priest?"

**Where on earth did that come from?** I wondered. I wasn't wearing black clothing, a clerical collar, or a cross. I was about to say no when a verse flashed into my mind:

**You are . . . a royal priesthood, a holy nation,
His own special people, that you may proclaim
the praises of Him who called you out of dark-
ness into His marvelous light.**[1]

"Yes," I stammered. "I guess you could say that I'm a priest. But what makes you ask?" I turned to him. "By the way, I'm Bruce."

Rainbow Metal Man was actually named Gary. He settled back in his seat, took a deep breath, and then told me exactly why God had sat him next to me. Of course, he didn't use those words, but that's what came through loud and clear to me.

"I'm flying out to Hollywood 'cuz I'm in charge of a sold-out rock concert at the Rose Bowl," he said. "But my best friend in the world was in an accident yesterday. He was killed."

"I'm so sorry," I said.

Gary sat in silence for a moment. "You know, when I went over and saw him dead, I couldn't help thinking, **If that was me, I don't know where I'd go after I die.**" He looked at me with bleary eyes. "I couldn't sleep all night. On the way to the airport, I said to God, 'If You are there, God, **please** send me a priest!'"

I laid aside my work then and picked up my miracle assignment. "How can I help you, Gary?" I asked.

## Anyone, anytime, anywhere

Do you believe that God can reach through a haze of alcohol if He wants to deliver a miracle? I do now. I'm so grateful God interrupted what I thought was important that day on my flight to L.A. If He hadn't, I would have missed Gary—the miracle appointment God had lovingly guided to the seat next to mine.

What would have happened if I had said no?

In the previous chapter we saw how the Master Key starts you in motion as God's delivery agent. If you've prayed to be sent, you're now ready to work for God in the Everyday Miracle Territory. But as my Gary story illustrates, being sent is just the beginning. What comes next takes nearly every delivery agent by surprise. I call them **collision moments,** and you will encounter them over and over in your life.

Here's how they happen.

You and I set out with the best of intentions to serve God. But we bring with us expectations and assumptions about what our new miracle life will look like—how God is going to work through us, when miracles will happen, what kind of people we'll serve, and how they will respond to us once the miracle has been delivered.

There's a problem with all that, though. In my experience, God's miracle agenda for me rarely matches my expectations and assumptions. And when the miracle appointment arrives, I'm often forced to choose—not between something bad and something good but between something good and something miraculous.

> **I'm often forced to choose—not between something bad and something good but between something good and something miraculous.**

If I'm not careful, I can miss my miracle appointment altogether.

Did you notice in my encounter with Gary how easily I mistook my agenda for God's? My plans sounded perfectly logical, even spiritual. I was working against a deadline on a book that could influence thousands of readers for God. Add it up: thousands of readers versus one inebriated, foul-mouthed Metal Man. No contest! I was 100 percent positive that I already knew Heaven's agenda for my flight, and it was spread out in front of me in black and white.

But I was wrong. Heaven's agenda for me was Gary.

Every miracle starts with a person in need. As obvious as it might sound, that fact is what makes this next key so critical.

**The People Key is how you make God's agenda and heart for people your own. You prepare for the inevitable collision between your preferences and God's by yielding your rights in advance. That way He can deliver a miracle through you to anyone at any time.**

I call it the People Key because God's entire agenda with regard to miracles can be summed up in a single word: **people.** This key unlocks several important understandings of God's purposes for sent ones:

- Our personal agenda must surrender to His.
- Our heart in any miracle must be His heart.
- Our role in any miracle must be to serve people—anyone, anytime, anywhere He directs.

Serving people according to Heaven's agenda was certainly Jesus' top priority. "I am among you as the One who serves," He told His disciples. On other occasions He said, "The Son of Man did not come to be served, but to serve, and to give His life a ransom for many," and, "I have come down from Heaven, not to do My own will, but the will of Him who sent Me."[2]

Jesus was sent by Heaven to serve—and you and I are too.

If we aren't passionately and deliberately focused on carrying out God's agenda with God's heart, we'll end up putting our own agenda first. We'll increasingly look for the kind of mission we enjoy most. We'll tend to ask God to bless our busyness for Him instead of asking Him to send us on the miracle mission of His choice.

The People Key releases us to be more available for miracle deliveries because we've already agreed with Him on some very important issues. For example, we have agreed in advance that the person, place, nature, and timing of a miracle are up to Him, not us. We have surrendered our perspective, our wisdom, our experience to one thing—His miracle agenda for us at any given moment. We have affirmed with God that His miracle opportunity, when it comes, will always be a person or persons in need. And we have said to Him that we understand that the person in need may not look to us like an opportunity at all.

Jesus knew exactly what an unexpected opportunity for a miracle might look like. For Him, as for us, the person in need of a miracle might look like

- an unpopular person (Zacchaeus),
- a social outcast (the Samaritan woman at the well),
- an unacceptable interruption (the lame man let down through a hole in the roof),

- a late-night visitor (Nicodemus),
- a desperate person clutching at us in a crowd (the woman suffering from a hemorrhage).

To put it another way, our delivery opportunity is likely to come at the time or in the manner we'd **least** prefer:

- during our kid's basketball game
- at the store when we're running late
- when every last bit of our energy is used up
- in the middle of important work we're doing for God
- when we finally settle in for a long-awaited Sunday afternoon nap

Which brings us to the action step in the second part of our People Key definition: knowing that God's miracle appointments for me will often collide with my plans and preferences, I precommit to yield my rights to Him whenever He asks and to serve those in need.

**If we go into our day wearing our Preferred People sunglasses, we'll miss a significant percentage of Heaven's miracle opportunities.**

Does this really mean we should be ready to deliver a miracle to any person we might meet? Yes. If we go into our day wearing our Preferred People sunglasses, filtering out the sight of those we'd rather not have to deal with, we'll miss a significant percentage of Heaven's miracle opportunities. Or we'll notice but say, "No thanks."

That's exactly what Jonah did.

## Mission unacceptable

You probably know Jonah from Sunday school or a children's picture book. But Jonah's story illustrates a grown-up truth: even though people are the reason God does a personal miracle, one of the biggest challenges to delivering those miracles is . . . people.

They can be so demanding and difficult, so unworthy and ungrateful. And of course **we** can be all those things too. Problem is, God doesn't seem to factor any of this in when He sends us on a mission. He certainly didn't when He sent Jonah.

Jonah was a prophet in Israel, so we know he had already said yes to being sent. But then came his collision moment. God asked him to go to Nineveh, the capital city of Assyria, with an important message: if you don't repent of your evil ways, God will destroy you. Now, the Assyrians were a notoriously violent nation of idol worshipers and were age-old enemies of Israel. In Jonah's opinion their destruction, not their repentance, sounded like the perfect plan.

So when God asked, Jonah said no and ran in the opposite direction.

Here are scenes from the YouTube clip of what happened next:

**A dusty road:** Angry Jonah stomps his way to the coast. His every step shouts, **No! No! No!**

**A busy port:** Angry Jonah buys passage aboard a ship.

**Storm at sea:** Ship plunges through huge waves.

**Stormier at sea:** Ship takes on water. Desperate crew throws cargo overboard.

**Stormier still at sea:** Ship about to go down. Desperate crew throws Jonah overboard.

**Calm day at sea:** No sign of Jonah.

But three days later there's an incredible turn of events—a big fish deposits Jonah, slimy but alive, onto dry land. What a shock! Instead of delivering a miracle **through** Jonah, God has done a miracle **for** Jonah—and it's a whopper.

Now is he ready to serve? God wastes no time in finding out:

**The word of the LORD came to Jonah the second time, saying, "Arise, go to Nineveh, that great city, and preach to it the message that I tell you." So Jonah arose and went to Nineveh, according to the word of the LORD.**[3]

This time Jonah obeys, and when he delivers God's message in Nineveh, Jonah witnesses his second whopper miracle—all 120,000 people in the city repent. God responds to their repentance by sparing them from destruction. Miracle mission accomplished for everyone.

Everyone, that is, except Jonah.

You'd think that two astonishing miracles in a row would have revamped Jonah's understanding about his role as a miracle delivery person. You'd think he would now be thrilled, convinced, and highly motivated to continue serving whenever and whomever God asks him to. But Jonah is not thrilled. The Bible says, "It displeased Jonah exceedingly, and he became angry."[4]

In fact, right through to the end of the chapter, Jonah argues with God about His plans and His motives. He's sure God has made a big mistake. Bottom line: **Jonah cannot accept that God's mission for him is to show God's compassion to people he doesn't like.**

It's easy to read the book of Jonah as an entertaining story of a stubborn prophet who would rather drown than let the wrong people know God loves them. But do you also feel the sadness in Jonah's story? He **knew** he was born to serve God. He **knew** he had been sent. And he **knew** beyond a doubt that God had showed up in his life with mercy and miracles. But it all seems wasted on him. I'd have to say Jonah failed the people test. Why? Because he refused to love others the way God loved him.

The apostle Paul wrote:

**God demonstrates His own love toward us, in that while we were still sinners, Christ died for us.**[5]

This is God's heart—while we were still unworthy and ungrateful, Christ died in our place. And this is God's heart too—if you're on the run from your miracle mission, God will patiently pursue you, right up to your last self-absorbed complaint.

The miracle power of the People Key lies in your choice to make God's self-sacrificing passion for people your own.

## Whom do you serve—really?

It's time to ask the important question: what does it take to bring God's heart for people into every miracle opportunity—not just for a while, but as a way of life?

If we're in this to serve only those we want to serve, we'll eventually wear out. Like Jonah, we'll start looking the other way when God nudges us toward a miracle appointment. We'll be tempted to call in sick, to say to God, "Could You send someone else today?"

I remember the day more than twenty-five years ago when I confessed to a mature friend that I was losing my heart for ministry. "It's just too hard," I told him. "Half the people don't like what I'm doing, and the other half don't even know I exist!"

"Well, why do you do it?" my friend asked.

"What do you mean, 'Why do I do it?' God tells us to serve one another!"

"Yes," he replied, "but is that all He tells us about serving people?"

I didn't understand what he was getting at.

He continued. "Bruce, if you're determined to serve

people for the sake of people, you'll eventually burn out and quit. And you'll quit for a very good reason."

"What is that?" I asked.

"Serving people just isn't worth it."

I was shocked. I had no idea that such a mature and highly respected Christian leader could feel that way. But he wasn't finished.

"Look, you have been called to serve God—and that's always worth it. But one of the ways you serve Him is by serving others. You have to keep your eyes on Him, because otherwise you won't last. Once you're focused on serving and pleasing God, the rest becomes irrelevant."

Then my friend reminded me of an important verse for servants:

**Whatever you do, do it heartily, as to the Lord and not to men . . . for you serve the Lord Christ.[6]**

Remembering whom you serve lies at the heart of the People Key. See in every face the face of Christ. Serve Him in "the least of these."[7] Put His heart and His agenda for people first. That's how sent ones stay in motion for a lifetime with the right motives and right priorities toward the right destination for God.

## Heaven's right of way

If the People Key unlocks a sustainable life of delivering miracles, what keeps so many from picking it up?

I can identify at least three common wrong beliefs that stop well-intentioned sent ones from getting far in the miracle life they want. See where you find yourself in each set of statements:

**Choosing the appointment God has for me**
**Belief A.** If I'm busy doing good things, I'll be less likely to miss my miracle assignment.
**Belief B.** Since I can easily miss my miracle assignment even while I'm busy doing good things, I need to stay alert for God's direction.

**Understanding the people problem**
**Belief A.** I should serve others if they are worthy and grateful.
**Belief B.** I should serve others because I am serving God and showing His heart for people. Whether or not I feel they are deserving or grateful is irrelevant.

**Sustaining a lifestyle of miracles**
**Belief A.** Once I experience a miracle, my new way of life will sustain itself. I won't have to worry about personal motives and priorities getting in the way of God's plans.
**Belief B.** I can sustain a lifestyle of delivering miracles only by having God's heart for people, putting God's plans ahead of mine, and serving "as to the Lord."

I hope you have noticed a shift in what you believe. I hope you are adopting the B beliefs. You were born to serve others for God, in His way, with His heart.

You can make the People Key your own today with what I call a Declaration of Right of Way. Think of it this way: When you plead with God to send you to do His work by His power, your delivery van leaves Mission Central. You carry with you miracles known only to God for people identified only by Him. But now you know that between your front door and your delivery destination you're likely to encounter a collision moment—that point where God's agenda for you and your agenda for you will run into each other.

How can you prepare in advance to avoid these smash-ups? That's what the People Key is all about. You decide in advance to surrender your rights to choose your own miracles, make your own plans, and serve your own Preferred People.

You can do that by turning your new convictions into a personal agreement to yield your preferences to God before a collision even happens.

**Decide in advance to surrender your rights to choose your own miracles, make your own plans, and serve your own Preferred People.**

### Declaration of Right of Way

Since I know that my own plans and preferences will often be on a collision course with God's miracle agenda for me, I surrender my rights in advance to God.

- I willingly take up my role as a servant, following the example of Christ.
- I view every person I meet as a potential miracle opportunity, no matter how surprised or unprepared I feel.
- I agree in advance to yield to God the details of time and place for my next miracle appointment.
- I surrender my expectations, rights, and preferences.
- I put down my expectation that those I serve should be worthy or grateful, because I serve everyone "as to the Lord."
- I place my busyness for God and any other good work in second position to God's leading in the course of a miracle delivery.
- I commit to seeing others through His eyes and responding to them with His heart, not mine, asking the Spirit to help me.
- I take off my Preferred People glasses and choose instead to view those I serve—including those I find most challenging or unappealing—as Christ Himself, because "inasmuch as you did it to one of the least of these My brethren, you did it to Me."[8]

Therefore, I no longer own the rights to how I serve. Those belong to God.

_____

Name and date

## Where won't He send us next?

From God's perspective, the real miracle on my flight to Los Angeles was what God did in Gary's heart as we talked quietly about friends and death, Heaven and hell.

From God's perspective, the real miracle for Jonah never really happened. As far as we know, he never opened up his heart enough to let God's heart in. The four-chapter book of Jonah ends on a question mark. God asks Jonah, "Why shouldn't I care about your enemies too?"[9] We never hear Jonah's answer.

The promise of the People Key is that you and I get to write chapter 5 for our own "book of Jonah." By our action of exchanging our passions and priorities for God's, we place ourselves at the very center of what He cares about most. And what He cares about most is people.

Once we love people with God's heart, we line up our agenda with God's agenda. Imagine, then, how motivated God is to partner with us as often as possible to deliver as many miracles as possible to as many people as possible. Where won't He send us next? We have precommitted to accepting our next miracle assignment—whatever it is.

Now you're ready to cooperate with God's Spirit to accomplish what only He can—the miracle itself. That's what the next chapter is about.

# 6

# The Spirit Key

**You were born to partner with God's Spirit**

**B**illy Graham is coming to Caroni!" At least that's how we publicized the Friday night event around the village. Darlene and I were on the Caribbean island of Trinidad for a summer of ministry, and the small local church—built on stilts to catch the ocean breezes—had come up with a big plan: we had borrowed a projector and rented a Billy Graham feature for a free film night.

Each night leading up to the showing, church members gathered to pray that many would come. And each night one of the newest converts, a teenager named Radha, told us he knew his father would never come. "Jesus is not strong enough to bring my father," he said. We all knew that his father was the village drunk and despised followers of Jesus.

Friday night arrived. People kept filing up the stairs to the church. By the time we kicked off with songs and stories, we had a nearly full house.

Then we heard him—Radha's father standing in the street below swearing loudly at the church, everyone in it, and anyone named Billy Graham. There was nothing to do but proceed.

A fourteen-year-old girl stood to pray. She begged God to help Radha's father get through the door. No sooner had she finished than we heard someone climbing noisily up the stairs. Radha's father stepped in, scowled at everyone, and took a seat in the back row.

I smiled at Radha, then introduced the film. But when I flipped the switch, the unthinkable happened.

Nothing. Only minutes before, the projector had been working perfectly.

I began sweating profusely and praying for God to help. Several of us tried but failed to make the projector work. Then, as we fiddled with the machine, Radha's father stood, swore a blue streak, and stomped into the night. Soon after, his distraught son left too.

What should I do—keep working on the projector or deal with Radha? The Spirit's nudge was clear. **Go see Radha.** Leaving the projector to another person, I went outside.

I found Radha underneath the church, leaning against a stilt. He was sobbing. "I knew it!" he shouted at me. "I knew my father would never find out the truth about Jesus. Now he's gone forever!"

Despite the turmoil I felt, I sensed the Spirit leading me to take a bold step. "Radha," I said, "God was powerful enough to bring your father to the church the first time. He is powerful enough to bring him back. We are going to pray right now and ask the God of the universe to bring your father back, not only to watch the movie, but to meet Jesus tonight."

My throat tight with emotion, I prayed a simple prayer of faith for Radha's father. Then the two of us walked back into the church.

But one look at Darlene's eyes told me we were still in trouble. The projector had been given up for dead. People were getting ready to leave.

If ever we needed a miracle from God, it was now. Walking to the front, I apologized for the disappointment. Then I felt nudged to pray one more time. "God, it's Your turn," I prayed. "We can't fix the projector, but You can!"

Then, feeling foolish and afraid, I reached for the On switch. Suddenly the projector whirred to life! Everyone raised a shout. God had demonstrated His power in a way we would never forget.

And He wasn't done. A few minutes into the movie, we heard footsteps on the stairs. It was Radha's father. Without a word he walked in and took his seat again.

When the movie ended an hour later, I gave an invitation. "If you want to put your faith in Jesus Christ like Billy Graham has explained, then would you please stand and come forward?"

The first to stand was Radha's father. With tears streaming down his face, he walked into the out-stretched arms of his son.

**Ministry without the Spirit of God is merely our best efforts. Ministry with the Spirit of God is the stuff of miracles.**

That night a roomful of witnesses watched as the wind of the Spirit moved in our midst. We watched as He contended mightily with unseen powers and worked in the heart of an angry man to bring him to new life in Christ. And we watched as He showed His love and power to a doubting young man named Radha.

Ministry without the Spirit of God is merely our best efforts. Ministry with the Spirit of God is the stuff of miracles.

## "Without You, I can't . . ."

With our next key, the process of unlocking a lifestyle of miracles will become more apparent.

First, the Master Key. You ask God to send you on a miracle mission.

Next, the People Key. You ask for God's heart for His agenda—people in need.

But now that you have been sent and share God's agenda, you will come face to face for the first time with a daunting question: how, exactly, are you supposed to deliver a supernatural event when you are so completely human?

That brings us to the Spirit Key. When you put this

key to work in your life, you are formally aligning your-self with your heavenly partner—the Holy Spirit—to do God's supernatural work through you every day. You are telling God, "Without You, I can't do what You have sent me to do."

**With the Spirit Key, you partner with the Holy Spirit to deliver a miracle by God's supernatural power. You precommit to cooperating with the Spirit at every opportunity to accomplish God's work.**

The fundamental fact of the Spirit Key is that while you and I can **deliver** a miracle, only God can **do** a miracle. In fact, it's impossible to accomplish anything in the Everyday Miracle Territory without Him. And God works through us by His Holy Spirit.

But—have you noticed?—no other Person of the Trinity raises more confusion and disagreement among churchgoers. Some think of the Spirit as a benign but impersonal force, like gravity. Others count on Him for intense emotional experiences. In recent years much of the teaching on the Spirit has focused on His work inside us—His comforting presence, for example, or His role in making us more like Christ.

This chapter focuses purposely and exclusively on something else: the vital part the Spirit plays in our work as God's miracle delivery agents. We want to know, how does the Holy Spirit go about God's work in us and in the person we're talking to? And how do we cooperate?

If you have spent most of your life hard at work for

God in the Land of Good Deeds, all this talk of partnering with an unseen person may seem like mere spec-
ulation. But it's not. The Spirit of God is a real and
knowable Person in our world. And you and I were
born to partner with Him for a life of miracles.

## The Helper sent from Heaven

I often ask this question of people I meet: "What would
you rather have: Jesus living as your next-door neighbor
or the Holy Spirit dwelling in you as He already is?"

Did you hesitate? Many do, perhaps because it feels
as if it requires them to choose between God and . . .
God!

Others just go with their gut. "Well, Jesus, of
course!" Why wouldn't a physically present God the
Son be far better than an invisible God the Spirit?

It might shock you to know that Jesus already
answered that question for us. We read about it in His
conversation with the disciples the night before He was
arrested. He reassured His friends that, although He
would soon be leaving, He would send a Helper, the
Spirit of Truth. Notice the reason Jesus gives:

> **It is to your advantage that I go away; for if I do
> not go away, the Helper will not come to you;
> but if I depart, I will send Him to you.**[1]

Disciples' question: "Jesus, You're saying we're better
off if You leave us?"

Jesus' answer: "Yes, it is to your advantage."

Then Jesus explained the roles the Helper would have in the world. He would bring comfort, He would guide the disciples into all truth, and He would glorify Jesus.[2] Everywhere present in the world, God's Spirit would be released to do the work of Heaven. In all times and places, He would communicate with people's hearts, convicting them of their need of salvation, changing their destiny forever.[3]

It didn't take long after the coming of the Holy Spirit for the disciples to experience the astonishing advantage of the Spirit as their divine Partner. One day Peter said to a lame man, "In the name of Jesus Christ of Nazareth, rise up and walk." When the man jumped to his feet, an astonished crowd came running. But Peter was ready with an explanation:

**Men of Israel, why do you marvel at this? Or why look so intently at us, as though by our own power or godliness we had made this man walk?** [4]

"Don't misunderstand what just happened," Peter was in effect saying. "I'm not superpowerful. And I'm not superholy. In fact, I didn't and couldn't heal this man. God did it through me by His power, not mine."

What I want you to see is that today, centuries after Jesus' time on earth, we don't have less of God with the Holy Spirit. Whereas Jesus could be in only one place at a time, the Spirit is a gift to all believers all the time all over the world. Unlimited by a physical body, He dwells with us and in us at all times to testify of Christ. And only through His supernatural presence and power can we accomplish miracle missions.

What does partnering with the Spirit look like in someone's life? In the story about Radha and his father that opens this chapter, you saw just how inadequate I was in my own human power to accomplish what God wanted done. That meant I had to rely on the Spirit in many ways:

- to bring Radha's father to the event—and bring him back again
- to direct me to follow Radha outside rather than tend to the crowd and our technical difficulties
- to encourage me to pray boldly for Radha's father to return
- to nudge me to try to turn on the projector one last time
- to work in the father's heart to bring him to salvation
- to show Radha himself the power and goodness of our living God

But how can **you** partner with the Spirit?

## A message for Marta

Lauren, a young woman I know, was away on a two-week assignment for her New York–based company. For the duration of the project, she stayed in the same hotel. Besides tending to her work commitments,

Lauren found herself asking God to send her to do **His** work.

During her morning workouts in the hotel gym, she noticed a petite Hispanic woman who was always busily cleaning. When Lauren greeted her by name and asked how she was doing, the housekeeper always brightened. "Marta would look up at me, and her face would just beam," Lauren recalls.

Toward the end of her stay, Lauren stopped in at Target to pick up a few items. That's when Marta came to mind. God nudged Lauren to buy something for her to make her feel special. Unsure of what to do, but not wanting to miss out on what God might be doing, Lauren put together a small collection of feminine items, including lotion and scented bath salts.

Her last morning at the hotel, Lauren presented Marta with her gift. The housekeeper was surprised and delighted. "Thank you, thank you!" she said shyly. "You don't know how much this means. I am so tired at the end of the day. This is wonderful!"

Marta brought up the flowers that had been delivered to Lauren's room the previous day. "Oh, they are so beautiful!" she exclaimed. Lauren agreed that they were gorgeous.

Back in her room, Lauren was packing up to go when the Spirit nudged her again. This time it was about the flowers her husband had sent. **Those flowers are for Marta now. She needs to know that she is beautiful.**

Without hesitation Lauren went in search of Marta.

"These are for you," she told her, holding out the flowers. "God wants you to have them."

Marta gasped. She grabbed Lauren's hand and pulled her into a nearby room. "You don't understand why this means so much to me," she said, her eyes filling with tears. "No one ever notices me. They don't even say hello. The past two weeks I've looked forward to coming to work because I know you see me. And now you show me that God sees me too."

I have little doubt that the housekeeper will always remember the day God sent her two extravagant reminders of His love.

Did you spot the Spirit at work in Lauren's story? Lauren asked to be sent. Then God led Lauren to give the housekeeper a gift. Lauren had no idea of Marta's need, but the Spirit knew it precisely. And through Lauren, He was able to speak directly into Marta's heart: "I see you, and I want to give you flowers today."

Lauren's story shows the kind of heart-specific miracle that God can deliver through any one of us when we are sensitive to the direction of His Spirit.

## How the Spirit works

How do God's Spirit and God's servants work together, practically, to deliver a miracle? We focus on this in depth in the how-to chapters coming up on signals and steps. But for now, consider some ways the Spirit does what we cannot do during a miracle encounter:

**The Spirit knows the other person.** The Spirit, who "searches all things," has intimate, complete knowledge of everyone, including the people He sends us to help.[5] He knows what they were thinking when they woke up, what happened to them at work yesterday, and what secrets they plan to keep until they die. He knows what kind of gift or encouragement they're likely to refuse or deflect and what kind of gesture will go straight to their heart.

**The Spirit knows us.** The Spirit also knows our strengths and weaknesses, our fears and limitations, and leads us purposefully to a person in need. Not that God's Spirit is an impersonal force moving objects around on a chessboard. He is a Person. He knows everything about us, loves us perfectly, and can perfectly match us with the right person at the right time to deliver the right message.

**The Spirit guides us.** Jesus said, "When He, the Spirit of truth, has come, He will guide you into all truth."[6] How do we experience this guidance?

Lauren's story shows that responding to the guiding of the Spirit will usually be a natural process. To a person who is outside the process, being sensitive to the Spirit's leading may seem too mysterious to understand or trust. But during a God-arranged encounter—when you have asked to be sent and are passionate about partnering with God to accomplish His agenda—you will know what God wants. God's promise is this:

> **During a God-arranged encounter, you will know what God wants.**

> **I will instruct you and teach you in the way**
> **you should go;**
> **I will guide you with My eye.**[7]

For most people, God guides us more than we realize. We don't have to look inside for a special emotion or inner voice. The Spirit will guide us **while we are in motion** to serve God. The New Testament uses words like "led," "compelled," and even on rare occasions "were forbidden" to describe how the Spirit communicates God's purposes to His servants.[8] Our part is to begin doing as much as we know He wants from us and then keep expecting further guidance.

**The Spirit speaks of the Father and Son.** Everything the Spirit does is directed by God the Father, and it's for one purpose: to accomplish Heaven's agenda and to bring glory to Jesus, God's Son. When He works in the heart of the other person, He is communicating the truth to that person about his or her need, God's character, and the Person and work of Christ.[9] As you'll see in many instances in the chapters ahead, one of the most thrilling moments of a miracle delivery is when you look into the face of a person and realize, "God is here! He is at work. I am witnessing His work right before my eyes!"

**The Spirit empowers us.** Three times in Acts 4 the disciples are described as sharing the gospel with boldness. For example: "Now when [the religious leaders of Israel] saw the **boldness** of Peter and John, and perceived that they were uneducated and untrained men, they marveled. And they realized that they had been with Jesus."[10]

Remember, these were the same men who only weeks before had cowered in fear when Jesus was arrested. What changed? The Father had sent the Spirit, just as Jesus had promised, and they had experienced His power.[11]

You and I have that same Spirit working powerfully through us when we ask to be sent on a miracle mission. Yes, the task is too big for us. But we don't do it alone. We are in partnership with God's Spirit, and that makes all the difference.

**The Spirit does the miracle.** We are partnering with the most powerful force on earth—God Himself. And the Holy Spirit has been given to us so we can do good works by His power. He is our Helper. He is the only one who does a miracle. You and I are simply blessed to be invited into partnership with Him.

**But we do the work!** I like to say that although the Spirit carries the load, we should approach our partnership as "100 percent Spirit, 100 percent me." We are to do the work, and the Spirit empowers us to do it. So if you are guided to witness, to show compassion, to help the poor and needy, or to give of your resources, then your part is to open your mouth, your heart, your wallet—to get started. The Spirit will give you boldness, guidance, information, and everything else you need **in the process** of your obedience, not separate from it.

Given the power and promise of our divine partnership, what might be keeping you from taking up the Spirit Key and unlocking miracles in your life today?

## New thoughts about the Spirit

It's time to look at our core beliefs about the Spirit's role in miracles. Nothing changes what we do like changing what we truly believe. Since beliefs determine behavior, misconceptions about the role of the Spirit as our essential partner in a divine mission keep millions from ever getting started.

See if you recognize your beliefs or unstated assumptions in these common misconceptions:

### My understanding of the nature of the Spirit

**Belief A.** God's Spirit is too elusive, impersonal, and unpredictable for me to connect with in a practical way to deliver a miracle.

**Belief B.** The Holy Spirit is real, personal, and knowable, and I am invited to understand who He is and how He works, including in the area of everyday miracles.

### My feelings and the Spirit's purpose

**Belief A.** The primary purpose of the Spirit is to help me feel spiritual or close to God, especially when I worship.

**Belief B.** The primary purpose of the Spirit is to help me accomplish God's agenda on earth.

**My self-reliance versus partnership
with the Spirit**
**Belief A.** I can probably accomplish everything
God wants me to do today by my own faithful
efforts and discipline.
**Belief B.** I can accomplish everything God
wants me to do today only by partnering with
the Spirit.

**My suitability to partner with the
Spirit**
**Belief A.** God will probably not have a miracle
agenda for me today that would require my
partnering with the Spirit, because I'm not spe-
cially trained or gifted.
**Belief B.** The Spirit is available equally to all
who know Christ, and God may have a miracle
agenda for me today that will require my partnering with the Spirit.

If you see yourself in any of the Belief A misunderstandings, you need to take ownership of your thoughts
and change your mind. I can tell you from personal
experience that wrong beliefs will absolutely keep you
from using the Spirit Key to unlock a life of miracles.
(For example, you won't be able to respond to the next
key, the Risk Key, if you are following your own natural inclinations instead of walking in the Spirit.)

But when you change your thinking and start living
by the truth, your miracle life will flourish.

## Open letter to the Spirit

To take up the Spirit Key as transformative action in your life, first affirm your new, true beliefs from the previous section.

Then you may want to write the Spirit a letter of apology and commitment, as a friend of mine did.

### Open Letter to the Spirit About Our Partnership

Dear Holy Spirit, I now recognize that every miracle is Your doing. Therefore, I apologize for how often in the past I have ignored or misunderstood Your guidance. I have often sidelined You and depersonalized Your role in my life. I have delegated the work You do to "professionals" and spiritual leaders. I have highly valued human solutions where only a supernatural act on Your part could bring Heaven's solution. I've done my best not to need You—not to live in partnership with You.

I'm sorry. How could I have been so foolish? Please forgive me. Now I know the truth, and I want to change.

I precommit to cooperating with You and following Your guidance every day, especially in every miracle opportunity You bring my way. I open my mind and heart to You, and I ask You to teach me in the days ahead how to partner with You in practical, joyful, and effective ways that bring Heaven to others and joy and honor to God. In Jesus' name I pray, amen.

[signed]_____

## Becoming a skilled team player

Now that you have committed to partner with God's Spirit for miracles, you have signaled Heaven that God can count on you to do His work in His way to deliver a miracle.

Does this mean you should expect the Spirit to give you stunning visions as He did with His servant Isaiah and some other biblical figures? No. You're not them! God created you to be you. You can be confident that He will never set you up to fail. He will only ask that you take the next step He puts in front of you.

**When the Father has a miracle mission in mind, increasingly He will send you, one of His devoted team players.**

The exciting promise of the Spirit Key is that the more you purposefully partner with the Holy Spirit, the more He will release His power and intentions through you. When the Father has a miracle mission in mind, increasingly He will send you, one of His devoted team players.

In fact, prepare yourself to become one of God's favorite delivery people! Why? Because He knows you won't try to do the impossible alone. Instead, you will partner with His Spirit for miracle moments on earth.

# 7

# The Risk Key

## You were born to take risks of faith in dependence on God

**T**he traffic through downtown Atlanta went from slow to stop, and with it my hopes of catching my flight seemed to grind to a halt. What was I going to do? I was the only speaker scheduled for an important conference. As my departure time came and went, I prayed a desperate prayer you may have uttered as well: "Lord, please delay my flight!"

When I finally reached the terminal, well after the scheduled departure time, I ran up the escalator, feeling a little foolish even to be there. But blinking on the departures board was the word I'd hoped for: "Delayed."

At the gate I stared out the window and thanked God for what He had done. "Now I want to do something for You," I prayed. "Please send me a miracle appointment." I took a deep breath and turned around, believing, as I have so often, that the person God had in mind would become immediately apparent.

Standing next to me was a well-dressed business-woman who had also just arrived at the gate. "It looks like you are glad the plane is late too," I offered.

She nodded.

I took a risk. "How can I help you?" I asked.

"What?"

"No, really, what can I do for you?"

"You can't do anything for me," she said matter-of-factly. Of course, why would she expect help to arrive in such an unusual way? But from previous experience I knew to give the Spirit time to work.

We chatted about other things, then I tried again. "I know my offer was unusual," I said, "but perhaps something's bothering you. Is there anything I can do?"

The woman seemed to calm herself, then to reach deep into her heart. "Actually, I'm flying home to divorce my husband," she said.

"I'm sorry to hear that," I said. "That must be why I'm here."

As we talked, her resistance began to melt. Her name was Sophie, and her professional manner and wardrobe couldn't hide her pain. Tears welled up in her eyes as she began to talk. Her husband had been unfaithful. Even though now he wanted to make things right, she had had enough. In her mind the marriage was dead.

But as we talked, I was already reaching for a miracle key that you'll learn more about in part 4 of this book.

When our call came to board, we were the last to walk down the ramp. Sophie seemed concerned. "We aren't done talking about this yet," she said.

"Don't worry," I said. "We will sit together on the plane."

"What do you mean?" she said. "You don't even know what seat I have."

"I don't," I said. "But God does, and He'll put us together."

"God?" she exclaimed.

"If you were God," I said, trying to sound calm, "wouldn't you want us to sit together so we could finish this very important conversation?"

She shook her head in disbelief.

We compared boarding passes. We were five rows apart, and the flight was full. Now I was on the spot . . . and so was God.

Sophie took her seat, but as I got ready to take mine, the man in the seat next to her turned around and caught my eye. "I'll trade so you two can keep talking. I hate middle seats."

I'll never forget that flight. God showed Himself so strong and compassionate. By the time we landed, Sophie was a changed person. Even she could hardly believe what had happened. She had experienced a powerful miracle of forgiveness and had recommitted to giving her marriage another chance.

## The indispensable step of risk

Now that you know the happy ending, I'll tell you that as I followed Sophie onto the plane, I wasn't brimming with confidence.

You see, I had taken a huge risk when I told Sophie, "God will get us seats together." I believed that God wanted us to continue our conversation. Still, I had no guarantee that He would act on the matter of seating. If He didn't, I'd look foolish, and any thought on Sophie's part that God was revealing Himself in her life might vanish.

You might be wondering, then, why I took such a risk. Couldn't God meet Sophie's needs in some other way?

My answer goes to the heart of this key. Twice I took an action that proved necessary to the miracle Sophie experienced. What were those actions? I purposefully **exercised my faith**—first when I asked how I could help her and again when I told her God would seat us together. I was asking God to reveal His goodness and compassion to Sophie in a miraculous way, and I proceeded in the faith that He would.

I took **risks** of faith.

You know what faith is—most people do.

"We believe!" we shout at ball games, meaning we can win this one if we just have faith. But this is faith in ourselves or in the team we're rooting for.

"Have faith in God," we say to each other, meaning we can entrust our lives and hopes to a good and powerful God. But this faith is usually passive, inwardly focused, and comforting. As important and wonderful as these faith expressions are, they are not the kinds of faith that I want to talk about in this chapter.

The faith I'm talking about here is directly related to how we partner with God for miracles. This faith is what we **do** because we believe God. That's why I describe it as active, outwardly focused, and usually very **dis**comforting. Knowing that we are sent and to whom we are sent, we take deliberate risks that place us in complete dependence on God for a miracle. By doing so, we declare to Him, "I believe You want to intervene in this situation, and therefore I will exercise my faith that You will. That way, when You act, Your goodness and glory will shine through."

> **Knowing that we are sent, we take deliberate risks that place us in complete dependence on God for a miracle.**

When God came through that day on the plane, that's exactly what happened. Sitting in the seat next to me, surprise written all over her face, Sophie began to see that God had intervened in her day and that He deeply cared for her. We both knew that God would finish the miracle He had started. And He did.

In the previous chapter on the Spirit Key, you learned that God plays an indispensable part in every true miracle and that we must partner with His Spirit for a miracle to happen.

In this chapter you will discover **your** indispensable

part. You must precommit to acting in faith, depending on God for a miracle. I call it the Risk Key.

**The Risk Key is a purposeful action you take, in spite of discomfort or fear, to exercise your faith during a miracle delivery. Faced with an unbridgeable gap between what you can do and what God clearly wants done, you take a risk to act anyway, depending on Him to come through. When God supernaturally bridges the gap, He enables you to deliver His miracle and demonstrates His glory.**

How necessary is this key in the miracle realm? For example, if we don't take a risk of faith, will a miracle even happen?

These questions lead to an important observation. Perhaps you thought that God could do a miracle through you anytime He wants. But the truth is, He can't—or at least doesn't. How can I say that? Of course God is all-powerful. But Jesus Himself clearly stated that our faith has a direct impact on whether or not a miracle happens.

Sometimes, in fact, we prevent a miracle that God wants to do.

## The connection between your faith and God's response

When Jesus' disciples asked Him why they couldn't do a particular miracle, He told them that they were limited because of their unbelief. Their unbelief, in other words, had literally stopped a miracle from occurring.

By contrast, He told them that if they had faith the

size of a mustard seed, "You will say to this mountain, 'Move from here to there,' and it will move; and nothing will be impossible for you."[1]

What astonishing statements! Jesus' words reveal at least two important truths for sent ones about the role of faith in the miraculous:

- The amount of our faith is directly related to the likelihood that we will deliver a miracle.
- The amount of our faith is directly related to the size of the miracle we will deliver.

Notice also that Jesus doesn't say if you have a seed-sized faith in God, you **can** say to a mountain, "Move." His point is much more extraordinary. He says if you have a seed-sized faith, you **will** say to a mountain, "Move." Jesus is using the pictures of a seed and a mountain to help His listeners grasp the power of faith to exponentially impact the outcome. We might restate His teaching like this: real faith in God so radically changes what you know is possible that it **will** change what you attempt **and** what you accomplish for Him.

Christ's amazing promise of faith should lead us to wonder, **What is hindering us from delivering great miracles? What other power pushes faith so far out of the picture that God does not even act?**

Jesus revealed the answer to that too. For example, we read that He didn't do miracles among people in His hometown of Nazareth "because of their unbelief."[2] Do you see the link? He wanted to do miracles; He encountered unbelief; He didn't do miracles. This cause-and-effect relationship shows how unbelief acts

**We must name our unbelief in our all-powerful God, wherever it lies, and reject it.**

like a corresponding negative power to faith. Unbelief is the opposite of faith—and Jesus showed that it has the power to put a stop to miracles.

Clearly, if you and I want to pursue a lifestyle where God works through us in supernatural ways whenever He chooses, we must take action. We must name our unbelief in our all-powerful God, wherever it lies, and reject it. Then we must **exercise** our faith. Why? Because there is a direct connection between what we initiate with faith and how God responds with His supernatural power.

One of my favorite pictures of the difference between unbelief and belief in action, between passive faith and risky faith, is the well-known story of Peter taking his unlikely step from a solid boat to . . . nothing but water.

Do you remember the scene? One blustery night the disciples were sailing across the Sea of Galilee through a storm. Suddenly a strange figure appeared, walking on the waves. The men were sure it was a ghost. But Jesus called out, "It is I; do not be afraid."[3]

In the next second (as far as we can tell), Peter got an idea. A very risky one at that. He said to Jesus:

**"Lord, if it is You, command me to come to You on the water." So [Jesus] said, "Come." And**

**when Peter had come down out of the boat, he walked on the water to go to Jesus.[4]**

That first step—what an experience! What a risk! You can bet Peter remembered what that step felt like for the rest of his life. And all he needed to get him out of the boat and onto the waves was Jesus' command: "Come."

Interesting, isn't it, that everyone else in the boat stayed put? They had all spent the same months and years with Jesus, seen the same miracles, listened to the same teachings. They all held to the same correct theology.

But only Peter took a risk of faith—and only Peter experienced a miracle.

In spite of heart-pounding fear, Peter stepped out in proactive dependence upon God alone, believing that his faith would bridge the gap between the boat and Jesus. When Jesus did bridge that gap with a miracle, everyone in the boat "worshiped [Jesus], saying, 'Truly You are the Son of God.'"[5]

If you're familiar with the story, you know I'm leaving out everyone's favorite part. Out there on his watery stroll, Peter takes his eyes off Jesus, gets an attack of fright, and starts to sink. "Lord, save me!" he cries.

**And immediately Jesus stretched out His hand and caught him, and said to him, "O you of little faith, why did you doubt?"[6]**

It's easy to read those words and conclude that Jesus was chastising Peter. I don't think so. I think He was pleased with Peter's exuberant expression of trust.

The picture that comes to my mind is of a father, arms out, watching his baby daughter taking her first steps toward him. Can you imagine the moment? Baby's ready—eyes big as saucers fixed on Dad, a goofy smile pasted on her face. Then with a giggle she lets go of Mom's finger and starts toddling across the wide, wide world toward Dad.

Suddenly Baby realizes she has no idea what she's doing. She glances at the carpet. Her smile freezes. She falters, veers, and then **plop!** She's sitting on her bottom, wondering what just happened.

Now, what do Mom and Dad do at that moment? They applaud, of course. How do they feel? Proud as can be of Baby and her first step. It's a day they'll always remember. "You did great, sweetie!" they say. And in a minute, "Wanna try again? Now, look at Daddy this time. Just look at Daddy . . ."

Do you recognize a pattern? A risk of faith requires that we exercise our faith in such a way that we attempt what we cannot do, depending on God to do what only He can. But a one-time exercising of our faith is rarely all that's required. Not in my encounter at the airport. Not for a baby toddling across the carpet toward her dad. And not for Peter. Risks of faith are required **throughout** the miracle experience. Peter initiated a miracle with a big risk of faith. But later, when he focused on the waves instead of Christ, he let his fear overwhelm his faith. (I'll show you how to turn fear to an advantage when we get to the alert signal in chapter 8.)

But here's the bottom line: no matter what you and I believe, no matter what we feel, no matter how close we are to God, we don't have risky faith—and we won't experience miracles—so long as we're still in the boat.

The way to succeed in miracle delivery isn't to stay dry. It's to keep our eyes on what God wants to do, not on the watery depths or raging storms that stretch between us and the miracle. Then take that thrilling first step.

## Change what you think about faith and miracles

For reasons we can only partly understand, God performs His greatest miracles when we act in complete dependence on Him. But let's be honest: almost everything about this kind of dependence goes against our instincts, our experience, and our common sense.

That's why, for most people, the Risk Key requires a significant change of thinking. Read these belief statements slowly and aloud to identify your old and new beliefs about the role of faith in your miracle life:

### How my faith is linked to miracles

**Belief A.** Faith for miracles requires me only to believe in God, not to act upon that belief.

**Belief B.** Faith for miracles requires me to exercise my faith. Specifically, I must take proactive risks based upon what I believe about God and what I believe He wants done.

### How risk unlocks a miracle opportunity

**Belief A.** In the course of a miracle mission, I should never put myself or God in a risky situation.

**Belief B.** During a miracle mission, my risk of faith is often necessary to unlock a miracle for another person.

### How I should respond to discomfort or fearduring a miracle opportunity

**Belief A.** When I feel discomfort or fear during a miracle mission, it is a sign that God must not be in it or that I am the wrong person for the job. Therefore, if I feel fear, I shouldn't proceed.

**Belief B.** I should proceed **in spite of** discomfort or fear. In fact, I should reinterpret those feelings as normal and even promising in the course of a miracle mission.

Each of the A beliefs describes a common assumption about how faith relates to miracle opportunities. And each one is an error and a trap. In fact, any one of them will significantly hinder your potential to partner with God's supernatural agenda in Everyday Miracle Territory.

By contrast, the B beliefs form the core truths of the Risk Key. Have you truly made them yours?

We are to hold tightly to the truth about the role of faith in a miracle. Our complete dependence on God—which we express when we take a risk of faith—makes more room for Him to act.

But there's still one enormous obstacle that prevents people from putting what they know about miracles into action. The tricky thing is, it looks exactly like fear. But it's not.

## Getting to the root of fear

All of us feel fear when we're about to do something that involves considerable risk. Risk, after all, means there's no guarantee of success. And usually when we feel fear, we don't proceed.

But fear is a fruit, not the root. The root is unbelief in our hearts. That's why the greatest obstacle to a life marked by miracles is not fear but unbelief.

Unbelief is our unwillingness to believe that God is who He says He is and will do what He says He will do. When we respond with unbelief, we are saying to God, "You are not trustworthy. Therefore, if I'm faced with a situation that depends on You to come through, I won't take a risk."

Think about what unbelief looks like from God's perspective. It could be illustrated by the boy who refuses to jump into his father's arms because he believes his dad won't catch him—and may not even want to. Or by Peter refusing to get out of the boat because he believed that if he started to sink, Jesus would not reach out to save him. Or by any one of us who has been saved, blessed, protected, provided for, and comforted by our heavenly Father, only to tell Him, "Yes, You have done all those things and more for me, and I know that You have my best interests at heart, but I still don't trust You."

> **We don't tear down unbelief by trying to muster up our courage or fan the flames of emotion. We tear it down by rejecting the lies.**

When the residents of Nazareth didn't have faith in Jesus despite observing His miracles firsthand, He "marveled because of their unbelief."[7] Why did Jesus marvel? Because they clung to their unbelief in the face of overwhelming evidence that they should have clung to faith.

The lesson for us is clear. We don't tear down unbelief in our hearts by trying to muster up our courage or fan the flames of emotion. We tear it down by rejecting the lies, claiming the truth, and acting on it. Then we take courage in spite of fear . . . and step out of the boat.

You can take action today to move from un-belief to active faith by applying five simple but profound steps:

- Affirm that God is who He says He is.
- Admit to God that unbelief is sin, and apologize to Him for breaking faith in your relationship with Him.

- Recount and remember how God has come through in the past for you and for so many others in the Bible and history.
- Keep your eyes on Christ, not the circumstances you find yourself in or the feelings you are experiencing.
- Precommit to purposefully exercising risky faith whenever it is called for in the course of delivering a miracle.

With these actions, you are intentionally resting your hopes on the record, character, and promise of God. And you have signaled to Him that you are now a prime candidate to deliver a miracle.

## The promise of risk

I hope you are beginning to grasp the indispensable part you and I play in whether or not a miracle will happen. The amount of our faith—and the actions we take as a result—can either limit or release God to act in a miracle situation.

The exhilarating promise of the Risk Key is that it enables us to successfully and repeatedly deliver miracles for Heaven to those who are in need. And each time we exercise our faith, it will grow. Of course, no single action of risky faith is easy. Which leads me to suggest Delivery Agent Rule #1 on Risky Faith: "If it's easy, I'm probably not taking a risk of faith." Followed, thankfully, by Delivery Agent Rule #2 on Risky Faith: "If my risk of faith is a little scary, I'm probably in line for a wonderful miracle."

I can tell you from years of personal experience that the proactive faith I've talked about in this chapter will radically change your life for the better . . . and you'll never want to go back. Paul encouraged the Thessalonians to take risks of faith when he prayed that "by His power" God would "fulfill every good purpose of yours and every act prompted by your faith."[8]

Every genuine act of faith expands your horizons for God. Before long you will find yourself actually looking for greater risk opportunities for Him because you know that the size of the risk also determines the size of the reward.

Part 3

HOW TO DELIVER
A MIRACLE

# 8

# The Five Signals That Guide a Miracle Delivery

**You were born to understand and respond to miracle-related signals**

**I**f you think about it, signals carrying important information come at you all day long, and you know what they mean. In fact, the message is so clear and helpful that you rarely stop to reflect on the signal:

- A man in a crowd waves his hand above his head. ("Look. Over here!")
- Your toddler bursts into tears while grabbing his knee. ("Mommy! Owee!")
- Red lights flash at a railroad crossing. A gate descends across your lane. ("Stop. Do not proceed.")

- You're standing in line for concert tickets when you feel a tap on your arm. ("Hey!")
- You ask your teen, "Where were you?" He looks down. (Uh-oh.)

Since we're talking in this book about partnering with God to deliver His miracles to others, wouldn't it be wonderful if you and I could count on the same kind of unmistakable, universally identifiable signals to guide us in our work for God?

> **Miracle-specific signals are being sent our way on a regular basis, and we can learn to read and respond to them.**

The good news is, we can. Miracle-specific signals are being sent our way on a regular basis, and we can learn to read and respond to them. These messages have always been there. And even though most of us routinely miss them, they are messages that sent ones must learn to recognize and respond to in order to cooperate with God for miracle outcomes.

In this book I identify five miracle-related signals: a **nudge,** a **cue,** a **bump,** a **prompt,** and an **alert.** You may have already noticed passing references to them. But now it's time to slow down, define them, and show how they work.

Using such simple terms to describe what the Spirit is up to in our world will probably be a new experience for you. But I promise you'll discover right away that putting miracle-related signals to work is not difficult.

You'll realize you already know more than you think. You just may not have named or defined what's happening until now. You'll find yourself saying, "I already do that!" or, "That makes complete sense!"

Once you put them to work in your partnership with God, your success rate as an agent for the miraculous will rapidly increase. You will experience the exhilaration of being truly alive to what God is doing in the Everyday Miracle Territory.

Unfortunately, common misconceptions in this area limit success. For example, most people assume that signals surrounding a miracle event must be too mysterious for an ordinary person to decode.

But that's not true. We serve a God who has gone to extraordinary lengths to communicate with us. He even sent His Son to earth with a message from Heaven. And today He makes His way known to us through the Bible, through His Spirit, and in other ways as we walk in daily dependence on Him to lead and guide. Of course, understanding what God intends for us at a specific moment won't be like getting a text message from a friend or seeing your name written in the sky. But God intends to connect, and He does. For example, God told Isaiah,

> **Your ears shall hear a word behind you,**
>     **saying,**
> **"This is the way, walk in it,"**
> **Whenever you turn to the right hand**
> **Or whenever you turn to the left.**[1]

God wants to and will guide and direct us—all the more so when we are committed to partnering with Him in the tasks He cares about most.

Another common misconception concerns how people communicate. Many assume that only the highly trained can read the verbal and nonverbal signals people send about what they really think and feel. But the fact is, we all do this already. The pages ahead are packed with examples.

The five signals help you navigate your way to and through the miracle God wants you to be a part of. For example, they help you

- identify the specific person God has in mind for your miracle appointment,
- determine which of the person's needs is the one God wants you to focus on,
- know when you are succeeding in opening someone's heart to receive a miracle,
- feel confident that God is leading you even when you are unsure,
- know how to interpret your own thoughts and emotions,
- receive and respond to miracle-specific information that comes to you from God and others.

Let's begin with a story.

## Richard and April's story

It was early morning. Richard had to catch a flight. But in his rush to get to the airport, he left behind one of those little things that are so easy to forget: his cell phone charger.

"On the way to the airport, I swung by the office to pick it up," he told me. "But it was before six, and the alarm system was still on. I stopped the car. Should I try to deactivate, then reactivate the system just for my phone cord? I was envisioning the alarm going off, the whole neighborhood waking up, police, missing my flight. I turned around and headed for the airport."

At his connecting airport in Dallas, Richard bought another charger for his phone. While he was waiting for his next flight, he walked the concourse, praying, **Lord, is there anyone You want me to meet here?**

Walking toward the store where he had earlier bought the charger, he noticed the salesperson who had helped him, standing by the store entrance. Richard was well past her when he had an unexpected thought: **Lord, that's the young lady You want me to talk to, isn't it?** He hadn't even considered that idea when he was making his purchase.

So Richard said to God, **If she's still standing there when I go back**—which would mean no customers in the store—**I'll talk to her.**

"Well, when I went back, there she still was, leaning against the glass window," said Richard. "I said, 'Hi, I'm the guy who bought the charger. I just called my wife.'"

"That's good," she told him with a smile. He introduced himself. Her name was April.

Richard hesitated. He sensed a pang of uncertainty about what he felt led to say next. Should he proceed in faith? He made his decision.

"April, may I ask you a question?" he asked.

"Sure."

"If you could wish for one thing from God today, what would that be?"

April's eyes suddenly brimmed with tears. "My baby is coming in three months!" Richard didn't understand, but he instantly sensed God telling him, **She needs you to pray for her.**

Tearfully, April placed her hand on her stomach. "The doctor says the baby may be born with serious health problems."

"You must feel very afraid. May I say a short prayer for you right now?"

"Oh, would you? I know God sent you!"

"Do you know the Lord, April?" When she said yes, he explained. "I want you to know that I was walking up and down this concourse asking the Lord if there was anyone He wanted me to meet here. It is you, isn't it?"

"Yes, it is!"

While people came and went around them, Richard prayed, asking God to comfort April, grant her a safe delivery, and allow her baby to be born healthy. When he was done, she seemed encouraged and calm. He told her that since he was coming back to the airport in a few days, he'd like to stop by and see how she was doing.

April said she'd love that. "Thank you so much. I know God sent you to me today."

Elated that God had led him so clearly, Richard headed to the gate to catch his flight. Suddenly it dawned on him just how God had brought the two of them together. **Lord,** he prayed, **You did not want me to go back to the office and get my phone cord, did You? Thanks for leading me to meet April.**

### Surfacing the signals

I share Richard's story because it's a good example of how a sent person who's paying attention to the signals can connect with the one person God wants to touch through him. With a little practice, you can recognize the subtle clues in a story like Richard's that make it more than an inspiring account of someone's good deed. Without these turning points, no miracle would have occurred.

Let's retrace what happened:

- Richard, a man in a hurry, leaves home in Atlanta (oops, forgot something). About the same time, April, a fearful young mother, heads to work in Dallas.
- Now in Dallas, Richard paces the airport, asking God to send him to a person in need.
- God in Heaven, intent on reassuring April, signals Richard—**That's the one. See her standing there?** In this book we call that a **nudge.**

- Before he asks his question, Richard feels suddenly uncertain, a little anxious. In this book we call that an **alert.**
- Richard asks April a question that opens her heart. In this book we call that a **bump.**
- April signals Richard: she bursts into tears and shares her need. In this book we call that a **cue.**
- God signaled Richard that April needed his prayer. In this book we call that a **prompt.** The source of a prompt is our unseen partner, the Holy Spirit.
- April experiences personal proof that God knows and cares about her and her baby. In this book we call that a successful delivery! (More about this in the next chapter.)
- Her despair relieved, she tells Richard, "God sent you to me!" Richard agrees. Without God, the whole thing wouldn't have happened. In this book we call that transferring the credit. (More about this in the next chapter too.)

In this brief exchange between total strangers, you can see all five signals we'll talk about: a nudge, a cue, a bump, a prompt, and an alert. Taken together, these signals help us find and accomplish the miracle work God has in mind.

If you haven't already, you'll soon realize how simple and intuitive these signals are. That's good news for all of us average folks who want to be part of extraordinary God-incidents on a regular basis.

Let's take a closer look at each.

## Signal 1
# The God Nudge
### How Heaven gets your attention and provides direction

A nudge is an inner push that directs us toward a person, a place, or an action. It is a signal from God that, no matter how faint, suddenly turns our attention to something or someone we weren't thinking about.

> A nudge is an inner push that directs us toward a person, a place, or an action.

God nudged Richard to see the salesclerk in a different light—as an appointment God had waiting for him. Nudges are almost always about a single act that God wants done soon.

The nudge might direct us toward a person in our line of sight. I call that a **visual nudge.** Our eyes are drawn to a person in a way that feels as if God is highlighting his presence, and we sense there might be an underlying reason. Most of us know very well what this experience is like. We just need to become aware of how often it happens.

More often we experience what I call a **nonvisual**

**nudge,** which means the person we're prompted to think about isn't around. You may have described this experience before with words like "I felt God leading me toward . . ." or "Out of nowhere Aunt Iris came to mind."

A nudge is simply one way God communicates His wishes to our minds. On rare occasions He also uses dreams, visions, angels, and other individuals. But the most common kind of communication is a small, interrupting thought to get our attention: **Call Aunt Iris.**

Of course, not every interrupting thought is from God. I don't mistake my sudden craving for cherry cobbler as a signal from Heaven. Still, we can and must become skilled at discerning and interpreting God's unique style of guidance.

Most of God's guidance is without words. In case you wonder if something is wrong with you, I assure you that few people hear God audibly. As we've already acknowledged, He makes His general leading known to us through His Word, His Spirit, other people, and our thoughts and feelings. As you've already seen demonstrated in this book, Heaven has no problem communicating with us, even if it is without words.

Regardless of the way God's nudges are communicated, they tend to have certain qualities in common.

**A nudge is unexpected and out of context.** Typically, you're not on your knees in prayer asking God to nudge you. Instead, you're driving to work or brushing your teeth when it comes: **Go talk to that man,** or **Stop here.** It's unexpected and out of context. A God nudge rarely comes in the middle of your thoughts about a given person, place, or event but rather interrupts your thoughts about something else. God wants it to be clear: **This thought isn't yours but Mine!**

**A nudge is subtle but clear.** God doesn't mumble, but then again, He rarely shouts. This means His nudge is clear enough that we have no doubt we received the message. We often wish it were more complete, had more details. But where information or an explanation is missing, God wants us to exercise faith and act on what we have received.

**A nudge is uncomfortable.** A nudge invites you to do something you don't want to do. That's another reason it is so easy to dismiss. We commonly rationalize, "If God is asking me to do something, I will always feel great peace about it." But the truth is often just the opposite. God's work almost always requires that we stop what we're doing or what we have planned and make His agenda our priority. That's why He's looking for volunteers who will say yes regardless of discomfort or inconvenience.

Discerning the nudge is a learned skill. A God nudge will always bear fruit. If a nudge I follow doesn't lead to a positive result, then I know to pay closer attention the next time.

Once you're sure you've experienced a nudge from God, act on it as soon as possible. Some of the saddest stories I've heard are from people who brushed off nudges from God, only to discover later that He was directing them toward a miracle appointment with someone in desperate straits.

## The Revealing Cue
### How people reveal a need God may want to meet through you

**A cue is communi-cated, often unknowingly, by someone's words or body language.**

While a nudge comes from God, a cue is a signal that comes from another person. It is communicated, often unknowingly, by someone's words or body language. In the case of the person you're connecting with for a miracle, cues will convey important information about how he's feeling, what he wants, how emotionally open or closed he is, and most important, what needs he may have at the time.

A cue can come as more of a shout than a whisper. How could Richard miss the fact that April had just burst into tears? And she didn't just start crying. She told Richard exactly what was bothering her.

More often than not, though, a cue is fleeting. It's easy to overlook or disregard. We have to reach out and capture it.

Cues come in two ways. A **verbal cue** conveys a message in words. A **body language cue** conveys a message through a person's posture, facial expressions, or gestures. Taken together, the two kinds of cues often present a more complete picture of what a person is feeling and thinking.

We all know more about cues than we realize. Take smiles. A smile is not just a smile, is it? One kind of smile tells us a person is happy. Another—say, a quick or forced smile that doesn't reach the eyes—means something else altogether. And the smile of a person in pain? That's difficult to explain, but we know it when we see it.

Without realizing it, all of us send out cues constantly. We telegraph to others whether we're friendly or hostile, paying attention or daydreaming, relaxed or feeling defensive, along with dozens of other emotions. Just as constantly, people around us pick up on them. Or they don't.

Give thought to the following cues and the needs they reveal:

- A teen girl, her face drained of color, gasps, "I can't believe she did that!" She feels shock now. What comes next might be hurt, anger, or betrayal.
- A dad stares at the floor and says sadly, "I'm not sure that my son even wants me to come." Is he feeling rejected? discouraged? like a failure?
- A female co-worker slouches in her chair and exclaims, "Why do these things keep happening to me?" She feels defeated. Life hasn't been fair.

- An elderly man stands by a window. He's holding a little dog like it's his last friend in the world. "I haven't been the same since my wife died," he tells you. His feelings are right at the surface, and his cues suggest he might feel lonely, abandoned, afraid, or angry.

Our ability to read and respond to cues, as with nudges, is learned. Salespeople, trial attorneys, counselors, diplomats, and people in social services—to name a few—take reading cues very seriously. They constantly strive to improve their ability to read them. Once you and I sign up to deliver miracles for God, we need to do the same. Fortunately, we don't need special training. We can easily find a crash course on the Web or in our nearest bookstore. Or just sit in a coffee shop or mall and practice people watching.

In fact, you can practice reading cues anytime you're around other people. Focus on how particular words, movements, and postures work together to instantly communicate a wealth of information. Train yourself especially to listen for words and phrases that convey emotion:

- "I'm so worried that . . ."
- "I wish that . . ."
- "I can't believe that . . ."
- "I should never have . . ."

If you keep at it, the day will come when you'll be able to read what ails a person's soul with surprising accuracy.

But what if the signals seem absent or those we get are confusing? Do we conclude that the other person doesn't have a need? Since we know that at all times and in all places everyone has a need that God wants to meet, it makes sense to be ready with a proactive step. That brings us to our third practical tool for detecting a personal need.

_____ **Signal 3** ___
## The Clarifying Bump
### How you use a question to clarify a person's need

A bump is something you do to another person to surface or confirm a need. A bump is usually a question. Richard surfaced April's need with a bump: "If you could wish for one thing from God today, what would that be?"

As with a cue, the purpose of a bump is to help us gain more insight into a person's need. We gently gather the needed information by asking the right questions. The person's answer or reaction will point us to the need that God desires us to meet in partnership with Him.

With the first two signals, we are receivers. With the bump, we are initiators. An easy way to think about the first three signals is this:

• A nudge comes to you from God.

- A cue comes to you from another person.
- A bump goes from you to another person.

**The purpose of a bump is to help us gain more insight into a person's need.**

As with nudges and cues, bumps are already part of our lives. We bump someone every time we ask, "How are you doing?" or "You okay?" The difference with a miracle-related bump is that we really want to know, because we're on a mission. We're looking for specific information that clarifies our understanding of a person's need.

A bump is not an intrusion or a question out of the blue. We don't suddenly have permission to be socially inappropriate. For example, you wouldn't walk up to a couple you don't know and ask how their marriage is going.

An effective bump is often based on information you've already gathered either by observation (nonverbal cues) or by careful listening (verbal cues). You're in a doctor's office waiting room. You notice that a mom with three young children looks exhausted. You catch her attention. "It must be stressful to wait for the doctor with several kids in tow," you say empathetically. "How do you manage?"

Might any thoughtful person ask the same question? Sure. The difference is, you're on a mission. You're looking for an opportunity for a miracle you can deliver.

The best bumps tend to be open-ended questions that can't be answered with a simple yes or no. This invites the person to share more helpful information.

In **The Prayer of Jabez,** I wrote about my favorite bump: "How may I help you?" I often call it the Elisha bump because the biblical prophet Elisha asked a similar question three times, and miracles followed each time.[2]

Here are some other clarifying bumps:
- "If you could change something about your life, what would it be?"
- What are one or two of the biggest problems your family is facing these days?
- If you could ask God one question, what would it be?
- What, if anything, has discouraged you lately?
- If Jesus were standing here, what do you think He'd say about this discussion?

The more you practice, the easier bumps will become. You'll learn how to phrase a question sensitively and specifically for the person at hand. Just remember to keep your bumps gentle, inviting, and purposeful.

And your purpose is simple. You are asking to be invited into the inner place where a personal miracle is completed—the heart.

# Reading Signs in the Desert
## Nudges, cues, and bumps in the Bible

If God can bring Richard and April together from different states for a miracle, do you think He could bring together two people from different continents for a miracle, using the same nudges, cues, and bumps we've just talked about . . . and leave a record of it in the Bible?

You might have read in the Bible about Philip's encounter with an African official, but I'm guessing you never noticed the signals that brought it all together. I've included the story here, inserting a few comments about signals to show you what I mean.

The miracle encounter, found in Acts 8:26–39, begins with a very unusual nudge, and things get only more exciting from there.

**Whopper nudge: An angel of the Lord spoke to Philip, saying, "Arise and go toward the south along the road which goes down from Jerusalem to Gaza." This is desert. So he arose and went.**

**Cue: And behold, a man of Ethiopia, a eunuch of great authority under Candace the queen of the Ethiopians, who had charge of all her treasury, and had come to Jerusalem to worship, was returning. And sitting in his chariot, . . .**

**Big cue: . . . he was reading Isaiah the prophet.**

In just three verses Philip has responded to a nudge and left town. Where to? He's not sure. **Just start walking toward the desert.** But surely as he walks along that road, he's giving every passerby a careful look. "Why do You want me here, Lord?" he asks. "Is there someone here You want me to meet?" Then a chariot approaches, one that stands out from all the rest. Clearly, the man inside is a VIP. **Hmmm.** And he's reading the Bible? **That must be the person!**

**Nudge: Then the Spirit said to Philip, "Go near and overtake this chariot."**

**Bump: So Philip ran to him, and heard him reading the prophet Isaiah, and said, "Do you understand what you are reading?"**

Nice leading question, don't you think? Friendly Philip. No wonder Philip's bump worked perfectly. Look at what happens next.

**Another big cue: And he said, "How can I, unless someone guides me?" And he asked Philip to come up and sit with him. The place in the Scripture which he read was this:**

**"He was led as a sheep to the slaughter;
And as a lamb before its shearer is silent,
So He opened not His mouth.
In His humiliation His justice was taken away,
And who will declare His generation?
For His life is taken from the earth."**

**And another big cue: So the eunuch
answered Philip and said, "I ask you, of
whom does the prophet say this, of himself
or of some other man?" Then Philip opened
his mouth, and beginning at this Scripture,
preached Jesus to him. Now as they went
down the road, they came to some water.**

**And yet another big cue: And the eunuch
said, "See, here is water. What hinders me
from being baptized?"**

But wait. Do you see what's really happening here? Philip is at work following God's nudges and using a bump. But behind the scenes is the real action. The Holy Spirit is powerfully at work in the Ethiopian's heart. We know that because his cues are constant and increasingly urgent. He literally begs Philip to help him find the miracle of salvation.

Philip asks just one more question—to validate the Ethiopian's sincerity—and the encounter reaches its climax.

**Bump: Then Philip said, "If you believe with all your heart, you may."**

**Miracle delivered: And he answered and said, "I believe that Jesus Christ is the Son of God." So he commanded the chariot to stand still. And both Philip and the eunuch went down into the water, and he baptized him.**

I hope you encountered this miracle story in an entirely different way than you have in the past. Surfacing the signals helps us become better students of what God cares so passionately about—delivering His saving goodness and power to people.

I also hope you see that the signals I'm describing are simply helpful tools to point out how miracle messages happen in normal life. I also hope you see why they're so important to understand and use in our partnership with God.

Now I want to show you the fourth important signal.

_____ **Signal 4** ___

# The Spirit Prompt
## How God provides you with insight during the delivery of a miracle

A prompt is a signal from God to you in the form of a sudden insight about the person you are seeking to help. The purpose of a prompt is to reveal information you could not otherwise know in order to help you deliver a miracle. Prompts usually occur while you're talking with a person (unlike nudges, which happen at the front end and help you identify your miracle appointment).

A prompt has much in common with a nudge, but the differences are important:

- A nudge is **directional.** God directs your attention toward a person or a place so you will connect with your miracle appointment.
- A prompt is **informational.** God drops into your thoughts a nugget of information about the person or situation that better enables you to deliver the miracle.

> **A prompt is a sudden insight about the person you are seeking to help.**

Thankfully, there is nothing spooky or magical about a prompt, even though it supernaturally links Heaven and earth. In fact, a prompt happens so quickly that you may not realize until later that you received one and were acting on it. Later you may wonder, **Where did that thought come from?**

At other times a prompt is more challenging. It may not make sense immediately, or it may convey something that can push you beyond your comfort zone:

- **Why should I ask about her grandfather when we're talking about her marriage?**
- **Why should I tell him to make his bed?**
(Remember Jimmy in chapter 1?)

In such instances you may feel tentative, uncomfortable, or even afraid. Why? Because you're being challenged to trust the information you're receiving. It requires you to take a step of faith, demonstrating that you trust the Spirit's guidance and His intentions.

That's why fear at such a point is rarely, if ever, a sign for you to turn back. The real purpose of fear is to alert you that a risk of faith is in order. (We look at the surprising usefulness of alerts in Signal 5.)

I just mentioned Jimmy from chapter 1. As you recall, he was talking to Nick, a man who desperately wanted to save his marriage. When Nick asked Jimmy what he should do, Jimmy was nervous. That's why he told Nick to get paper and pen—he was stalling because he didn't know what to say. And then God put the prompt in Jimmy's mind: **Tell Nick he should go home and make his bed.**

So the point is this: even though Jimmy was hesitant to say something he couldn't defend, he kept going, and God came through for both men, His miraculous hand clearly evident. Nick exclaimed,

"How did you know?" Because Jimmy trusted God enough to say what he did, Nick knew that God was intervening and cared about him and his marriage.

This next story is another helpful example because it was clearly initiated by a nudge, then the need was suggested by a prompt. Here's what happened.

One morning Toni asked God to send her to do His work that day. One hour later she noticed something ordinarily she would have missed. She was in a meeting when a woman she didn't know well made a passing comment about sons being a challenge. Something in her remark alerted Toni to a hidden ache.

"I don't think anyone else in the room noticed anything," she recalls. When Toni asked God to show her how she could help, she felt a clear nudge. It came in the form of a direction: **Write her a note.**

Toni didn't have much to go on. But she took out a pad and pen.

**Dear Sonya, your son is in a . . .**

What was she going to say? She didn't know.

Then God prompted her. A picture came into Toni's mind.

**. . . wrestling match with God. He's fighting hard, but it won't be long till he goes limp. God is going to hold him tight till he gives up completely. It will be the love of God that wins.**

When Toni was done, she folded the note, wrote

Sonya's name on it, and passed it down the row. She noticed that when Sonya opened the note, she began to quietly weep. Toni thought, **Oh no! Maybe I got it all wrong.**

But as soon as the meeting ended, Sonya came up to Toni with a question. "How did you know?"

"How did I know what?"

"My son is a wrestler. He loves to wrestle," she said, still tearful.

Then she told the rest of the story. "You're right. Lately he's been wrestling with God. In fact, in just one hour he'll be standing before a judge on an assault charge. My husband and I can't be there to help him, so we've been praying that God will be his advocate in that courtroom."

The women decided to go to lunch. Then just as their sandwiches arrived, the woman's son called. The court had dismissed the charge. "I know God was watching out for me," he told his mom. "I get a chance to start over—and I'm going to."

Isn't it reassuring that God **wants** to communicate with us when we serve Him? As you awaken your spiritual senses to what God is showing you, you can rest in the fact that God will lead you into the most meaningful experiences of your life so far. More and more, you'll experience a spiritual peace that confirms you are heading in the right direction.

Here's something else to consider: during the miracle delivery process, inner peace and surface anxiety will often coexist. You can be anxious about a prompt yet still experience peace and confidence that God's Spirit is at work through you.

And remember, a prompt is to help you deliver the miracle. It's not a revelation about the future or a message for another person. (For example, you won't find yourself saying, "God told me to tell you . . .") Rather, a prompt is an insight or information God gives you to act on in the moment so you can complete your miracle assignment with excellence.

## Signal 5

# The Fear Alert
### How we signal ourselves when to go forward in faith

A fear alert is a signal you receive from yourself. During a delivery the alert is a reliable indicator from your emotions that you should exercise your faith and move **through** your feelings toward the miracle.

**A fear alert is a reliable indicator that you should exercise your faith.**

Let's talk first about fear itself. Fear is like the warning light on your car dashboard; it tells you, "Pay attention!" We experience this normal human emotion in varying degrees many times a day, such as when we're trying to maneuver through rush-hour traffic, when we've been unexpectedly called into our boss's office, or when we realize we forgot to pay an important bill and the power may be turned off by the time we get home.

A fear alert occurs during the process of a miracle delivery because you are no longer in your comfort zone. You are taking a risk of faith. Since miracles rarely happen inside a delivery agent's comfort zone, a fear alert is actually full of promise and serves as a very different kind of warning light: "Pay attention! Exercise your faith! Miracle directly ahead!"

Of course, if you verbalized a fear alert to yourself, it might sound like this:

- "Who, me? I can't possibly be the right person to deliver this miracle!"
- "Do what? I can't succeed at that!"
- "What will they think? I will get ridiculed and rejected if I say that!"

Once we identify what's happening, we can be proactive about our response—and what we do next makes all the difference. Of course the human mind and body use fear signals to keep us away from danger. But in our work of partnering with God for a miracle, the very same alerts can become something else: **confirmation** that we are moving in the right direction (toward a miracle) and an **invitation** to overcome fear with faith.

This kind of active trust in God's Spirit is foundational to a lifestyle of predictable miracles because it activates the partnership and makes room for God to do what only He can do: the miracle. Instead of responding to fear in the normal way—by fleeing or postponing—you purposefully interpret the alert as a valuable signal that it's now time for you to exercise your faith and complete the very action you're afraid to do.

Take a second look at the story that opens chapter 2. I was in the middle of speaking to eighty men at a conference when I received a clear and very specific nudge. God wanted me to ask a man sitting four rows back on the aisle what I could do for him. I paused, walked down the aisle, and asked, "Sir, I feel like there is something unusual going on in your life. Is there anything I can do for you?"

I don't usually behave that way when I'm addressing an audience! Every step down the aisle, I was feeling uncomfortable, awkward, a little foolish. The man's reply didn't help. He told me in no uncertain terms that he was just fine, thank you very much.

I retraced my steps to the podium feeling even more uncomfortable, awkward, and foolish. But I had just picked up my comments where I'd left off when God nudged me again and even more dramatically.

This time the fear and discomfort alarm in my heart really went off! What was God doing? Hadn't I already tried that once without success? The men in the audience had flown in from all over the country to hear me speak on a particular topic. What would they think if I made a fool of myself again and wasted even more of their time?

I experienced fear alerts all over the place. But for

sent ones intent on doing what God wants done, a fear alert is not a signal to turn back but a signal to step forward. I decided to stop speaking and walk down that aisle again and—depending on God for a miracle—ask that man the same question a second time. The result was a huge miracle that radically altered the weekend for the entire audience and showed all of us in an unforgettable way the wonders of God's love and power.

More than with any other signal, misinterpretations of the fear alert short-circuit the miracle process. But it doesn't have to be that way. Fear and discomfort are just negative emotions. We shouldn't wait until those feelings go away but rather act in faith in spite of them. We don't have to blindly obey what they push us to do. Instead, we can look past our feelings and press forward to the miracle that is waiting to happen.

I've identified the most common times during a miracle delivery when your fear-alert caution light is likely to start flashing. For a helpful discussion on these, along with a summary chart of all five signals, go to www.YouWereBornForThis.com.

### "Now I can understand and use miracle-related signals"

When I first present these simple truths about miracle-specific signals to audiences, I notice two predictable cues.

One is heads nodding. That's body language for "Absolutely! You're right. That **is** the way it works."

Many come up to me later and confirm that I've read the cue correctly.

The other, which comes later in the session, is people staring thoughtfully into space, sometimes with their eyes closed. Or they'll look down pensively. I know from hearing from them later what that cue means too. It's body language for "O Lord, I must have missed hundreds of miracle opportunities that You have constantly, purposefully, lovingly brought my way . . . but I didn't recognize and respond to the signals."

What cue are you sending right now?

If you're sobered by what you might have missed, let me remind you of something: now that you know how signals work, your life can begin to change today. Reading signals from God, others, and yourself as they relate to a personal miracle is a natural and immediately usable skill.

I hope you've seen the promise of learning to recognize, receive, and send miracle-related messages. That's what you were born to do. God created you to partner with Him in a process that produces memorable miracle outcomes.

The result of your learning to read miracle-related signals will be astonishment, gratitude, and glory to God. The book of Acts says that after Philip and the Ethiopian parted, the official "went on his way rejoicing."[3]

You will too.

# 9

# The Five Steps That Lead to a Miracle Delivery

**You were born to know and follow
miracle-related delivery steps**

At the beginning of this book, I proposed that God chooses to partner with ordinary people for His supernatural agenda. For such an extraordinary role, I said, no previous experience was required. No special degree, talent, or qualification either.

But for that to be true, wouldn't there have to be skills we could learn and an approach that would bring success—not just once but regularly—in our new life in Everyday Miracle Territory? Of course, Heaven's part in delivering miracles would still be full of mystery, just as you'd expect, but our part would have to be very down-to-earth.

Thankfully, a simple, self-evident approach to delivering miracles does exist. In fact, the ideas can be understood by a ten-year-old. And why wouldn't that be the case if delivering personal miracles is part of God's agenda for each of us? How else could we explain the fact that God has been using people to deliver personal miracles for centuries?

The process I want to teach you begins with the five parts of every personal miracle. These parts are present even if we can't see them. If you were to revisit the stories you've encountered so far to identify elements that always appear, I think you'd come up with a similar list.

For a personal miracle to take place, we must have
- a person (the recipient of the miracle),
- a need (the purpose for any personal miracle),
- an open heart (the place where a personal miracle is completed),
- a delivery agent (the means for getting the miracle where it is needed),
- God (the Person who **does** the miracle and receives the credit).

As motivated delivery agents, we can get from these basic elements of a miracle to a job description in no time. For example, the five parts suggest a series of steps we can follow to partner with God successfully. The steps are universal, learnable, repeatable, and aligned with how Heaven actually works in a miracle situation.

I call them the Five Steps for Delivering Personal Miracles:

1. Identify the person.
2. Isolate the need.
3. Open the heart.
4. Deliver the miracle.
5. Transfer the credit.

When we put these elements in the order in which most miracles unfold, we have a set of action steps that we can learn and use. For the miracles we focus on in this chapter, a step sometimes appears to get skipped or the order of steps unfolds differently. But I think the reasons for this will be clear to you as we look at them together. What you can count on is that all five steps play an important role in every personal miracle.

In the next section of the book, which deals with three special delivery miracles, the sequence of the steps becomes even more important. When taken in order, they will help you guide a conversation toward a specific, known miracle outcome.

Don't think of these steps as a rigid formula but as a basic framework. My goal is to be helpful without diminishing in any way the grandeur and leader-ship of God in the process.

You'll see that the five-step pattern brings together all the big ideas you've learned so far: now you are a **sent person** (Master Key) who **shares God's heart for people** (People Key) and who **intentionally partners with the Spirit** to do God's work (Spirit Key) through **acts**

**of proactive dependence on Him** (Risk Key) in delivering His miracle to others.

My intention is to describe what I've learned through Bible study, extensive research, and personal experience over many years so you can deliver miracles for God in increasing numbers in your life.

## Step 1
### Identify the Person

If God is going to meet a specific need for another person through us, then we need to find and connect with that person. That's step number one. To put it in delivery agent terms, we begin by asking, "Where am I taking this package? Who is it for?"

> **To put it in delivery agent terms, we ask, "Where am I taking this package? Who is it for?"**

One of the best ways to find our answer is to respond to God's nudges. A nudge directs us to that special person who will be our appointment.

With Owen, I received a very specific nudge not once but twice. In my experience, God generally doesn't repeat a nudge if we willfully ignore it. But if we genuinely need further guidance, He may nudge us again.

The fact that a nudge seems out of context or surprises us is a help in identifying our person with confidence:

- **Give the waiter one hundred dollars.** (my encounter with Jack)
- **Show Marta My heart for her.** (Lauren and Marta's story)
- **Look. The woman from the phone store.** (Richard and April's story)

As the stories in this book demonstrate, God leads us to appointments in different ways. But a process that might sound vague to a person who doesn't understand miracle missions shouldn't sound vague to you by now. You see the world very differently than you used to. Where before you saw a waiter, a co-worker, or a neighbor, you now see people with needs—needs often known only to God, needs that He may want to meet today through you.

Sometimes we'll assume an encounter is about one thing, only to suddenly realize, **Oh! God has something else in mind.** Sometimes the person finds us and declares in so many words that he desperately needs a miracle. Think back to Jimmy in chapter 1. His first clue that Nick might be a miracle appointment came when Nick started talking about his troubled marriage.

I always encourage people who are just getting started with delivering Heaven's miracles not to get hung up on wondering, **Is this the person?** in every conversation. You don't make your miracle appointment; God brings it to you through His nudge, through causing you to see their cues, or through your initiation by means of a bump.

Especially during your early days as a delivery agent,

God will make your appointment obvious. Your job is simply to grow into your new role as Heaven's ambassador and to be awake to Heaven's agenda for your day.

In the meantime you're not doing anything socially unacceptable if you approach a person and start a conversation. If in doubt, proceed—all you risk is being friendly.

### Step 2
## Isolate the Need

Of all the possible needs the person you've identified may have (and we all have many needs), you now need to isolate the **specific need** God wants to meet through you at this time. Remember, God isn't asking you or me to meet every need or even necessarily to meet a person's greatest need. We're looking for the need that is at the top of God's agenda for us and for the person we've identified.

> **We're looking for the need that is at the top of God's agenda for us and for the person we've identified.**

Of course, sometimes you can't miss the need. But more often it takes a little sleuthing to uncover the urgent need God wants to meet. As we discussed in the previous chapter, a lot of information about needs is signaled to us by tone of voice, body posture, circumstance, expression of emotion, and words. We have described this as watching for cues—verbal and nonverbal messages that show or suggest what's happening inside the person.

Bumps also help to surface the need or to confirm that you have identified the right need. This is where a bump question like "How may I help you?" can be effective. You are taking a risk to make yourself available, depending on God to be at work in the other person so that he or she reveals the need God wants to meet through you. The best bump gets you past all the chatter, posturing, and surface conversation to focus directly on the need.

In my interaction with Owen, after two strong nudges it was clear to me that I had the right person. But getting Owen to open up about his need was challenging, to say the least. I bumped him in a personal and direct but open-ended way: "I sense that something is deeply troubling you." It wasn't until I risked a second bump that Owen's story, including his need, came tumbling out. Now I understood his crisis and had information that helped me steer him toward the miracle God wanted.

Of course God can work through us when specifics about the need are few or absent. You've probably already experienced this. You did something for another person without realizing that God was in it, and when you did, the recipient said, "I can't believe you did that. I've been asking God for that very thing!"

But what God **can** do doesn't change our responsibility in this step—to surface the need He wants to meet. Our role is to look for the need patiently and sensitively. More information can suddenly show you what God wants to do or why God chose you for the encounter. You're still relying on God's guidance, but now you can partner with Him more completely to meet the need at hand.

I've noticed that when I have the right need in view, I feel a sense of peace. Still, I often confirm that I have the correct one by asking the other person, "Is this need the one area that's bothering you most right now?" If it turns out that another need is the real one, I don't hesitate to switch focus.

Here's a practical reminder: if a glaring need surfaces in a conversation that we **can** meet with our own resources, we should respond. It's never right to ask how we can help if we have no intention of helping unless God does a miracle. James warned us against falling into this sort of smug spiritual detachment:

> **If a brother or sister is naked and destitute of daily food, and one of you says to them, "Depart in peace, be warmed and filled," but you do not give them the things which are needed for the body, what does it profit?** [1]

Now you're ready for the third delivery step, which goes to the place where a personal miracle is completed: a person's heart.

————————— **Step 3** ——
## Open the Heart

When it comes to personal miracles, the heart is where the action is. How often Jesus reached past a surface request to the deeper human need—for relationship, forgiveness, a sense of meaning, salvation. Yes, a miracle often does involve some kind of material provision. So by all means feed the hungry and clothe the naked, but miracle delivery agents don't stop there. We want to partner with God to get inside their heart. Only when a provision changes how the recipient sees and responds to God is the personal miracle complete.

Not surprisingly, our role in preparing another's heart to receive what God wants to do is a critical part of the delivery process. We want the person to let us in, to show us what really matters, in some cases to acknowledge with us that the need is real.

> **When it comes to personal miracles, the heart is where the action is.**

Do you remember in chapter 2 how tightly Owen's heart was clamped shut? In my recounting of what happened, I didn't detail all my responses. But while Owen poured out his reasons for quitting ministry, I was actually very responsive:

- To show him that I empathized with his pain, I slowly nodded in agreement and said softly, "I understand."

- To let him know that I was actively listening, that I really did care, I responded with "Hmmm"—the universal word for "I'm right with you!"
- To show him my acceptance of him as a person, my body posture was open and relaxed, not rigid and judgmental. I tilted my head to the side to let him know that I was concentrating on genuine understanding.

In other words, I was both sincere and intentional. In fact, if I hadn't already identified Owen as a miracle appointment and purposed to draw out his heart, things might have proceeded very differently. For example, I simply might have encouraged Owen to reconsider his plan to quit his ministry, or I might have asked the other men to remember him in their prayers—both caring, Christian responses, you'll agree, but not very helpful in opening his heart. And, without his heart open, a miracle in the making might have been thwarted.

Note that I wasn't trying to change Owen's mind about anything. I was simply doing my part and believing the Spirit was doing His part to prepare Owen's heart for the miracle I was now convinced God had brought me to deliver.

Opening a heart can happen naturally, with almost no effort. As we've seen in several stories, sometimes people throw their heart wide open to you as soon as their need is isolated. This is especially the case when they are in a lot of pain and the emotions are already near the surface. I think that before my friend Richard had even finished his bump ("If you could wish for one thing from God today . . ."), April's emotions were already rising to the surface.

But if a heart seems closed, how do you open it? We know we can't force it open. A heart tends to respond best to gentle and sincere invitations from the heart of another. Here are some tips on how to speak the powerful, universal language of the heart (some I've already shown in my conversation with Owen):

- **Maintain eye contact.** Eyes really are the windows to the soul.
- **Soften and lower your voice.** We talk about our feelings at a slower pace, with a deeper tone, and at a softer volume than we use to debate ideas, discuss the news, or tell jokes.
- **Slow down and practice pausing.** In this way, you're inviting the other person to carry more of the conversation. You're saying, "What you have to say is very important."
- **Relax your posture.** Our bodies speak volumes without words. So make sure your posture and gestures are conveying openness and safety. You sincerely want to be invited into the other person's most protected place—his or her heart.
- **Invite more heart sharing.** A head tilted to the side indicates you are in a listening mood. A quiet "Hmmm" shows you're really paying

attention and you care. Nods indicate you understand and are interested. When a verbal response is in order, use a gentle bump like "How does that make you feel?" or "What does your heart tell you at a moment like this?" Or even use a straightforward question: "What is happening in your heart right now?"

- **Practice Empathy.** Empathy means you put yourself in the other person's shoes. In the Master Key chapter, I told you about my encounter with a man in need alongside the freeway who had been taking verbal abuse from passersby for hours. I was practicing empathy when I said, "Hours of that would be extremely painful. If you'll allow me, I want to apologize for every disrespectful thing those people said." That expression of genuine understanding opened his heart wide for the miracle that followed.

You already know so much of what I just told you, don't you? You've been practicing the language of the heart since you first opened your eyes. For example, you already read cues about whether a person's heart is open. You sense a connection or its absence. You pick up on whether a person is focused or scattered, vulnerable or defensive. Body language signals mood and intent to you. If a person wants to talk, and if you're paying attention, you don't have to think about how messages are being sent—you just know.

As God's delivery agent, you simply get to be more

intentional about what is already a second language to you.

## Step 4
## Deliver the Miracle

In this step in the process, we actively partner with the Spirit to deliver the miracle for God. Our role is to facilitate and invite, responding to the Spirit's guidance. That's why I say that even though the miracle itself is God's work, the step of delivering the miracle is our responsibility.

> **Even though the miracle itself is God's work, the step of delivering the miracle is our responsibility.**

Until now in the delivery process, our role has been like John the Baptist's—preparing the way for God. Through circumstance and miracle-specific signals, we have been led to both the person and the need God has in mind. And we've done our part to open the person's heart.

Now it's God's turn to act. Thankfully, He desires to deliver miracles through us even more than we want Him to. That means we can relax. We don't have to try to understand exactly how our unseen partner works. We only have to trust that He **will** and that we have a necessary role in the event. In this step of the process, God often guides us to do or say something important during the miracle delivery process that we wouldn't have thought of otherwise.

So there you are, God's delivery person, standing at the door of a person's life. The heart is open. What comes next?

Here is a sequence I find helpful:

**Take your thoughts off yourself and place your faith consciously and directly in God's Spirit to lead.** Continue making eye contact with, and focus completely on, the other person. What needs to happen next will depend on the kind of miracle that is in order. What does God want to happen? Does the person need to:

- receive something?
- let go of something?
- make a choice of the will?
- experience a breakthrough of insight about an important life issue?

**Search for the emotional obstacle or limiting belief.** Watch for the tender spot (the rise in emotional temperature) that indicates a need or injury. Often all it takes is the right question from you for the tender spot to suddenly appear.

**Speak to the heart.** God will guide you to say the right thing, so you don't need to get overly cautious or start second-guessing yourself. Jesus told His disciples not to be anxious ahead of time about what to say in a difficult situation when they were asked to speak for Him: "For the Holy Spirit will teach you in that very hour what you ought to say."[2]

You might find yourself quoting a Bible verse you didn't even know you'd memorized or suggesting a solution that hadn't been in your thoughts a second ago. Plenty of times you won't even realize what you said or why it mattered until later. Sometimes you won't notice, but the other person will—"I think God must have sent you!"

**Give God time to act.** You'll know when this is a good idea, because at the time you won't know what else to do! You need to get out of the way. God will begin to work in the heart in one way or another. Purposely slow down. Stop talking. Use more pauses. Consciously depend upon the Spirit, and pray silently.

I remember doing exactly that as I spoke with Owen that night. It was obvious that it would take a miracle to set Owen free. Keenly aware of my inadequacy, I'd raised all of my spiritual antennas to receive God's direction. What I sensed Him leading me to do was to be very straightforward and not worry about anyone else in the room. I was careful in leading Owen to realize the truth for himself: **If God clearly called me into ministry, He will clearly call me out of it.**

Keep in mind, God could have been calling Owen to quit, and He could have brought me to that room to help him do it. I didn't know. My goal was to help him find solid ground, then let God show us what to do from there.

As I challenged Owen about his decision process, I could tell that the Spirit was at work in his heart. I think everyone there that night could. It was visible in

Owen's posture, in his pauses, on his face. And it was equally clear the moment the miracle was delivered. When Owen declared, "I won't quit," everyone in the room knew for sure that God had done a mighty work in Owen's heart.

At that moment his heart language revealed a new truth: He wasn't fighting anymore. He wasn't angry and despairing. He had fallen into God's arms in complete and peaceful surrender. We could see freedom and relief written all over his face.

I want to add a few more thoughts here about the role of prayer in a miracle delivery. You may have noticed that many stories reveal the delivery agent actively praying:

- Richard prayed with April about her baby's health.
- John prayed with Terrence in prison, asking God to reunite him with his daughter.
- Jessica asked her friends for urgent prayers for Leila, who—unbeknown to Jessica or her friends—was at that moment attempting to take her life.

In each case, the prayer became strategic for the miracle delivery. Yet none of these events unfolded in quite the same way: April received God's comfort and encouragement from a stranger in the middle of an airport. Terrence received an answer to his prayer in the form of his daughter's visit—a week and a half after John led him in prayer. (Did John still deliver a personal miracle? Absolutely!) And Jessica wasn't present with her friend Leila when God led her to pray or when God intervened to save Leila's life.

All of our delivery examples show that this part of the process can look different in different situations. One wonderful constant, though, is that the recipient is nearly always the first one to know that a miracle has taken place. Often he will say something that lets you know this is the case: "Wow, that was an amazing breakthrough for me!" Or "How did you know?" Or simply, "That was a miracle!"

Which leads to the last step in the process: making sure that the Person who did the miracle, not the delivery agent, gets properly recognized.

_____ **Step 5** ____
Transfer the Credit

For delivery agents like you and me, our mission is not complete until we have shined the spotlight on what God has just accomplished. We intentionally do everything in our power to help the person make the all important leap between the wonderful experience and the wonderful source of that experience—God Himself.

> **Our mission is not complete until we have shined the spotlight on what God has just accomplished.**

To give God credit means showing gratitude. But thankfulness is just the beginning.

You might remember the story from the Gospels where Jesus healed ten lepers yet only one returned to give thanks. Notice how Luke records this man's response:

> **One of them, when he saw that he was healed, returned, and with a loud voice glorified God, and fell down on his face at His feet, giving Him thanks.**[3]

Thankfulness to God focuses on how we feel about His gift, whereas glorifying God focuses on what we now know to be true about the Giver. God is the ultimate source of the miracle. After a personal miracle, worshiping Him with gratitude, sincerity, thankfulness—and maybe even with a "loud voice"—is the ultimate acknowledgment that we really understand what just happened.

The closer we help the miracle recipient get to that kind of truthful response, the more completely we will have delivered the miracle.

You'll find that sometimes your encounters come to a close with a partial transfer (see how my conversation ended with the van driver, chapter 4). When you're dealing with people who don't seem to have an open relationship with God at the time, you need to bring their attention to a personal, caring God in a way that feels natural, not "churchy," to them.

Of course, sometimes a miracle unfolds in such a way that God's involvement is never in doubt. This is what makes prayer miracles such a great vehicle for revealing God's goodness and power. When God answers a specific request with a miracle, His hand is immediately evident.

Or take Owen's experience at the men's retreat. It happened in a setting where transferring credit to God came naturally. Every man present that night enthusiastically praised and worshiped God for His wonderful works.

How do we make sure God gets the credit?

I think the first thing is to help the other person put words to what just happened. Help him recognize that it was God who just showed up. But don't tell him that. If that's what obviously happened, help him reach the conclusion for himself. For example, you might begin by asking, "What just happened?" If God did something in his heart, he'll be quick to say something like, "That was God!" or, "I can't believe what just happened—it feels miraculous!"

It's so important for people to hear themselves saying in their own words what happened. That way the meaning of the event—not just the event itself—rises into their awareness and stays in their memory.

As with opening the heart, the step of leading a person to understand what happened and to respond to God is our responsibility. It's our work—and wonderful privilege—to link that person's heart to God's actions so that he or she can express appreciation to God. I typically move through this in three stages.

First, I help the other person **identify and describe the specific need that was met.** For this I might use leading questions like these:
- "You don't feel that fear anymore, do you?"
- "Do you see the cost of bitterness differently now?"
- "Something just changed inside you, didn't it? What was it?"

Second, I help him **express how he feels about what God did.** For example, I might ask:
- "How do you feel about what God just did?"
- "What did God show you about how much He really cares about you?"

Finally, I help him **transfer the appropriate credit to God.** I might say something like this:
- "Can you say a short prayer to God, thanking Him for that gift? Or may I offer a prayer for you?"
- "Don't you think God would like to know how you're feeling about Him right now?"

For many, what they say next will be the first time in their lives they have expressed glory to God for something He did for them personally.

I hope you're seeing by now that transferring the credit might sound optional—like the bow on top of a nicely wrapped present—but it's not. It really goes to the heart of what we're talking about in **You Were Born for This.**

Good people doing good works in the world is not enough to fully accomplish what God wants done. God seeks to reveal Himself in majesty and truth in our generation—and to do so through us. That's why a miracle just delivered and received is a one-of-a-kind opportunity to give Him the glory He deserves.

When your miracle appointment has fully transferred the credit to God through a heartfelt statement or prayer, it's time to celebrate. You've just completed a miracle delivery!

## Five words, another story to tell

You've seen a process described that God can use in your life. It begins when you get up in the morning as a person who has asked to be sent. Then it has you partnering with God for a personal miracle in an exciting sequence of events from "Hello" to "Mission accomplished."

When I teach seminars on this subject, people rehearse the sequence to one another: **Identify. Isolate. Open. Deliver. Transfer.**

Five words.

Five steps in the process.

Another miracle successfully delivered!

In the next section you're going to apply these five steps to three different kinds of personal miracles. In each of the three following chapters, I'll show you how to become increasingly skillful at partnering with God for miraculous results.

# Part 4

❖

# THREE KEYS
# TO SPECIAL DELIVERY
# MIRACLES

# Introduction to the Special Delivery Keys

In part 2 we explored the power of four big ideas we called Miracle Life Keys—the Master, People, Spirit, and Risk keys. Miracle Life Keys describe actions that consistently unlock and sustain our potential to partner with God for a life of miracles. These four keys are all about us—about an ongoing personal transaction between God and us.

Having learned the signals and steps involved in delivering personal miracles, we now turn our attention to the second set of keys. Each of these unlocks a miracle for a specific and universal human need. I call them Special Delivery Keys. These three keys are all about other people—about what God wants to do supernaturally through you to meet a specific need for them.

You've probably either sent or received a package marked "Special Delivery." The label means the delivery agent will handle the package with extra care to ensure it gets delivered in the right way to the right person. In a similar way, when Heaven sends an agent to deliver a special delivery miracle, a few extra guidelines apply. For example:

- A special delivery miracle usually begins and ends in the context of a conversation.
- The conversation surfaces universal cues indicating that God wants to meet a specific need in a specific way.

- The delivery agent applies biblical truths that reveal what must happen for the miracle to occur.
- The delivery agent follows in sequence the five steps to deliver the miracle.
- Because both the need and the outcome that God wants are known, the agent guides the conversation toward a predictable result.

The three needs we address—money, life dream, and forgiveness—not only are universal but also represent the kinds of personal miracles that seem to be needed the most. Further, they represent areas where most people suffer from misconceptions about the topic. Once we understand what the Bible teaches for each need, we can become intentional and increasingly skilled in delivering miracles to the people who need them.

Here's a preview:

**The Money Key** unlocks biblical insights that prepare you to deliver a miracle of financial provision to a person in need. The miracle happens because God sends you and His financial resources to connect with a person who has a specific financial need.

**The Dream Key** unlocks biblical insights that prepare you to deliver a breakthrough miracle to those who need to embrace and achieve their God-given life dream. When people who have misunderstood or discarded their life dream suddenly seize upon the truth and commit to pursuing it, their lives improve in dramatic ways.

**The Forgiveness Key** unlocks biblical insights that empower you to partner with the Spirit for miracle breakthroughs in the areas connected to wounds of the heart. When you identify the wrong beliefs that keep a person suffering from unforgiveness and also the right beliefs necessary to bring healing, God works through you to deliver a wonderful miracle of forgiveness and freedom.

**The three needs we address not only are universal but also represent the kinds of personal miracles that seem to be needed the most.**

Of course, these aren't the only areas where God wants to meet needs. But you'll find, as I have, that hardly a day passes when you don't meet people who are burdened by a financial need, confused about their purpose in life, or stuck in bitterness and resentment.

One of the best things about these miracles is that we don't have to wonder what God wants to happen. When He directs us to someone with one of these needs, we approach the person with confidence. We know that God wants the need met, we know the truth that brings life change, and we know how to partner with Him to deliver the miracle. That's why we call these the keys to special delivery miracles.

# 10

# The Money Key

## You were born to deliver miracles of financial provision

**O**ne late night after a speaking engagement in Johannesburg, my son, David, and I were suddenly attacked by the same desperate thought: we just had to have some ice cream. It's true. My son and I seem to share the double-strength dessert gene. We rushed back to the hotel where we were staying in hopes that the restaurant would still be open. We made it just in time.

When the waitress came to take our order, I said, "You have no idea how glad we are to find you! We've rushed back here from across town just for ice cream."

What she said next was heartbreaking. "I'm so sorry, sir. We just closed for the night. I can't serve you ice cream, but could I get you some coffee?"

David and I looked at each other. Had we hurried to the restaurant for nothing? I decided to ask again. "Sure, we'll take some decaf. But is there any way you could find some ice cream for two guys who would really appreciate it?"

She smiled. "I'll see what I can do."

As she walked away, I received an unexpected but unmistakable God nudge. In some way we were here for her too, not just for ice cream. The nudge was clear and specific: **Give her a big tip.** Actually, it was more like **Give her a very big tip.**

And we hadn't gotten any ice cream yet.

After I told David about the nudge, he said, "Dad, I was just thinking the same thing. A really big tip for what, though?"

We both laughed. But my laughter concealed the discomfort I was feeling. You see, I'd been to the bank recently and happened to have a large roll of rand (the South African currency) in my pocket. In my heart God had clearly linked the very big tip with that roll of bills. They seemed to be one and the same.

Well, I can tell you that God loves people who love ice cream. The waitress came back from the kitchen with two big bowls of it…and coffees to go with it.

As we were finishing, I took the bills out of my pocket, folded them into a bundle, and held it ready under the table. When the waitress walked up with the check, I said, "You were so kind to find us that ice cream when the kitchen was closed. We appreciate your extraordinary service and want to give you a tip that reflects that." Then I slipped the money into her apron pocket. I didn't even want David to see how much it was.

Can you guess what I was feeling at that moment? Not heroic, insightful, or generous. No, more like awkward. I didn't want to be misinterpreted. In a hotel in Johannesburg, like in many other places, the only reason a man would give that kind of money to a woman is if he's trying to buy her favors for the night. What was God up to?

Three minutes later the waitress came rushing back to our table. "You know Jesus, don't you?" she said, tears in her eyes.

"Yes."

"I knew it! This is a miracle!" she exclaimed. "I have a baby, and we couldn't pay rent, and the landlord was going to kick us out of our apartment tomorrow morning. I prayed to God on the way to work just this afternoon, 'Please, God, send us the money, or we'll be living on the street.'"

She wiped at her eyes. "Sir, this amount is exactly the rent I owe—**to the rand.** That's how I knew you know Jesus."

David and I walked out of that restaurant two happy men.

## Ready and willing

Do you see the signs of God at work in our ice cream adventure? We certainly did! To me it highlights several key elements of the miracle deliveries we've talked about:

- God is at work behind the scenes, orchestrating the place and timing for a miracle connection.
- God nudges a sent one to connect with a person in need.
- God arranges the event so that when the delivery happens, the re-cipient knows in her heart that God intervened specifically for her.

But that night God was creative. He nudged me to do something that felt excessive and foolish. I knew whom I was supposed to give the money to, but I had no idea why or how much she needed. While I could have bumped her to isolate the need, I didn't. Honestly, it didn't even occur to me. And I think I know why.

God wanted to demonstrate His abundant goodness in a most remarkable fashion. So He decided to use a couple of ice cream fanatics to bring an anxious mom a supernatural experience of His loving care in a way she would never forget.

**God intends for us to use our money to display His goodness and faithfulness in miraculous ways.**

How you and I think about and manage our money matters greatly to God. Jesus spoke of money often, and He spent most of His time with those who didn't have much. He fed the hungry, helped his friends deal with taxes, honored those who gave out of their poverty. Clearly, God wants us to be both thoughtful and generous with our resources.

But if we stop there, we miss a much bigger idea—

that God intends for us to use our money to display His goodness and faithfulness in miraculous ways.

The first special delivery miracle I want to talk about has to do with this area of universal interest and need: financial provision. Can you think of a greater concern for people all over the world today? How would your life change if God worked through you on a regular basis to miraculously meet the money-related needs of others?

**The Money Key unlocks a miracle of financial provision for another person. The miracle happens because God sends you with His resources to a person who has a need. Your miracle delivery is based on powerful Bible truths about how God works supernaturally through people on earth to meet a financial need.**

Like the two other miracles we'll explore in this section, the money miracle is unusually predictable. By that I mean, from the beginning of your miracle appointment, you know exactly why Heaven has brought you together, and you know that God seeks to meet a financial need through you.

Even though we commonly feel protective and even possessive of our resources, the promise of the Money Key is liberating and rewarding. You'll discover that the reward of partnering with God in practical, visible ways becomes an event you genuinely look forward to.

Financial miracles often begin with a nudge from God. That nudge is likely to take you by surprise. (Consider His plans for my roll of South African rand.) But they all have the same goal: a miracle that switches all the spotlights on God the Giver and causes someone to exclaim, "Wow! God sent you to meet my financial need!"

The Money Key miracle is rooted in a faith-filled application of Paul's advice in 1 Timothy 6, where he writes:

> **Let them do good, that they be rich in good works, ready to give, willing to share.**[1]

Notice especially the phrases "ready to give, willing to share." These words lay the foundation for miracle missions to meet the financial needs of others. We prepare ourselves to partner with God in a money miracle by applying these twin directives—willingness and readiness—to the way we approach our financial priorities. Our precommitment alerts Heaven that we are fully prepared to act when God brings a miracle opportunity our way.

In case you were thrown off by the big roll of bills in my story, let me reassure you that God does miracles just as easily with a five or ten as with a hundred-dollar note. But we won't get anywhere unless we understand God's agenda for money and how He actually gets a financial provision to a person in need.

## How God transfers money

How, exactly, does God move money around to meet needs on earth? Specifically, how would He do that for you?

Could Heaven somehow transfer cash into your account?

Could Heaven print some currency and drop it out of the sky onto your doorstep?

Could God, who owns the cattle on a thousand hills, as Psalm 50 puts it, take out a loan on His earthly assets to meet your need?

Could an angel deliver the money from the vaults of Heaven?

The answer may shock you. While He could do all those things, every indication is that He doesn't. God only gets funds to a person in need when another human being releases some of his or her funds for that purpose. When it comes to prayers for a financial miracle, Heaven depends on people for answers.

> **When it comes to prayers for a financial miracle, Heaven depends on people for answers.**

A verse in the Bible succinctly describes God's transfer process:

**Whoever is generous to the poor lends to the LORD.**[2]

Surprising, isn't it? And the verse doesn't say it is **like** a loan—it **is** a loan. The moment a generous person gives in response to a God nudge, a second, invisible transfer takes place in Heaven. With those same funds, the generous person "lends to the LORD." And now

God has funds to answer the person's prayer with a financial miracle.

Now look at the universal principle revealed in the second part of the verse:

**And He [God] will pay back what he has given.**[3]

Do you see it? Yet another surprise is linked to the first: a loan to God for His work will be paid back by Heaven. Jesus confirmed this principle of divine repayment many times. In fact, He said that even a cup of water will be credited to the giver.[4]

After understanding how this process occurs, you can understand why God loves to initiate miracles with money. Let's revisit the sequence of a financial miracle from human need to supernatural provision:

- A person has a real financial need.
- Heaven either hears his prayers for help or recognizes his unstated needs.
- Heaven decides to answer the financial need with a specific amount and identifies an optimum situation and time for delivery.
- Heaven nudges a person who has the funds and opportunity to meet those needs.
- The delivery person gives the money to the one in need, preparing the way for the Lord to receive full credit and appreciation.

When you consider how many people need a financial miracle and how few people respond to a God nudge that's related to finances, you begin to see why so many opportunities await anyone who wants to partner with God for a financial miracle.

If that's you, where could you start today? Let me show you.

I want to introduce you to one of my favorite practical tools for inviting financial miracles. One thing that makes it so powerful—and enjoyable—is that you're giving money that isn't yours.

I call it the God Pocket.

## What is a God Pocket?

The God Pocket is a specific location in your wallet or purse where you keep money you have devoted to God so you can give it to someone in need as soon as He nudges you to do so. In the same way the Elisha bump—"How can I help you?"—launches you into an exciting life of servant miracles, the God Pocket launches you into an exciting life of financial miracles.

The idea for the God Pocket was born out of the frustration that my wife, Darlene, and I felt about our giving early in our marriage. It's not that we weren't generous to our church and other worthy causes. We were. Yet when we gave to individuals, God didn't seem to show up very often in the process. The more we thought about Paul's advice to be "ready to give, willing to share," the more we realized that our problem might lie not in **what** or **where** we gave but in **how** we gave.

What would happen if we were "ready to give" **in advance** so we could respond tangibly and without hesitation to a nudge from God? The simple tool of the God Pocket became our answer.

To prepare for a God Pocket miracle, take these five helpful steps:

**First, decide how much money you are going to put into your God Pocket.** These funds aren't the ones you give to your church or other organizations but are additional and are specifically for God to use in delivering a financial miracle to others. If you're confused about how much to start with, ask God to help. He blesses most when you joyfully give a sum that is meaningful to you.[5]

> To devote something, in the biblical sense, means you are dedicating it in advance to God.

**Second, devote that amount of money directly to God.** To devote something, in the biblical sense, means you are dedicating it in advance to another person—in this case, to God. When you devote, say, your twenty dollars to God, you are expressing to Him, "From this point forward, this twenty dollars is Yours. I will carry it in Your name until You show me who it is for."

**Third, deposit your devoted money into your God Pocket.** Choose a special spot in your wallet or purse where you won't get it confused with your other funds. The only money that goes into the God Pocket is money you have set apart in advance as belonging to God, not you. From now on, you keep only devoted money there. It is God's Pocket.

**Fourth, determine right then that when God nudges, you won't debate with Him or talk yourself out of the assignment.** Remember, you're not responding to apparent needs but to a God nudge. You are trusting God to meet a need He knows about and specifically reveals to you.

A good friend of our family's, Nancy, felt nudged to deliver her God Pocket money to a woman she didn't know well. But when Nancy drove up to the woman's house, she saw that it was nicer than her own. At that moment, Nancy told me, she felt strongly tempted to turn around. But she didn't. Once inside, she discovered that the recipient was in dire financial straits. For the woman in need, the God Pocket was an unmistakable miracle of provision.

**Fifth, consciously depend upon the Lord to nudge you when, where, and to whom He wants His funds delivered.** He will! You don't have to fret about who He has in mind or when He'll make His move. He might nudge you today or this week or next month. Meantime, you are free to go about your business as a sent person—"ready to give, willing to share."

What makes such simple preparations for a financial miracle so effective? Think about how many times you have been nudged by God, but in your confusion about what it meant or what to do, you talked yourself out of doing anything. The God Pocket changes that. If you're carrying money that is no longer yours—money that you've emotionally detached from—you're free to act when God nudges. And when you do, you'll do so with freedom, joy, and expectation.

Be careful to treat your God Pocket money with utmost respect. For example, just because you're carrying it around doesn't mean it's a slush fund you can borrow from when a need arises or when you're looking at a sale item you just can't pass up. It's not even money you'll put in the offering plate at church. Remember? The money in your God Pocket already belongs to God. So until He nudges you toward a particular person, don't touch it.

Sometimes the need God wants to meet is not only monetary but also deeply emotional. Through my God Pocket experiences, He has memorably demonstrated what He meant when He described Himself as "merciful and gracious, longsuffering, and abounding in goodness."[6]

And what exactly does "abounding in goodness" look like? Well, different in different situations. Here's what it looked like in a department store in the Rocky Mountains.

## "Somebody sent me"

On a trip out west, I needed a wristwatch in a hurry. (I've discovered that a visiting speaker who doesn't watch the time rarely gets invited back.) Standing at a counter in a department store, I was about to make my choice when I couldn't help noticing a shopper farther down the counter. She had been staring at a particular watch for some time, apparently trying to talk herself into buying it.

"That is a beautiful watch," I said. "It looks like it was made for you!" The turquoise trim on the watch matched her Native American attire perfectly.

"You really think so?" she replied.

"I do. Why don't you get it?"

She said, "Oh, I could never afford this watch."

"That's too bad," I said. "You might not find a watch quite like that one again."

She said, "I know," but gently set the watch back down on the counter. I was ready to try on the watch I had selected for myself when I received an un-expected but distinct God nudge. **Oh,** I thought to myself. **Her.** I was taken by surprise. **A tur-quoise watch? Right now?** But the signals were unmistakable.

I caught her eye. "Um, it's not hard to see you would really love this watch. May I have the privilege of buy-ing that watch for you?"

"What?"

"Wouldn't you like the watch?"

"Yes, very much. But you can't buy it for me!"

"No, I can't," I said, hesitating. How do you explain your God Pocket to a stranger? You can't really. But you can talk about the real owner of those funds.

"A special friend of mine instructed me to carry around some of His funds," I continued. "He asked me to keep my eye out for a person whom I think He would really want to help with His money. When I find that person, I'm supposed to use it. My friend would definitely want you to have this watch."

"Really?" she said, trying to process what I had just said.

"Oh yes. It's true. He'd really enjoy buying it for you." I motioned to the salesclerk for assistance.

"Oh my goodness!" she said. She stared at the watch, then at me. Then she said, almost to herself, "I had lost all confidence in mankind."

That's when I really noticed her face for the first time. It was heavily lined and bore an expression of deep sadness.

I said, "You have really been hurt, haven't you? You've been wounded many times."

"Yes, I have." Her eyes were tearing up.

"Well, Somebody who knew about your wounds sent me all the way from Atlanta because He wants you to know that He deeply cares about you. Might you know who that is?"

A light seemed to click on for her. "It's God, isn't it?"

"He does love you, doesn't He?" I said quietly.

She was brushing away tears as I made the purchase with my God Pocket funds and handed the watch to her.

But God wasn't finished. "Jesus knew sorrow more than anyone you'll ever meet. Every time you look at this watch, remember that God loves you and wants your heart not only to be healed but to sing!"

As I walked out of that store, my heart was singing too.

## The five steps of delivery for a financial miracle

You might have recognized a familiar delivery pattern—or at least recurring parts of it—in the stories in this chapter. That's because how you deliver a financial miracle follows a similar pattern to the other miracles we talk about in this book. The five-step process I'll apply next will help you intentionally partner with God to deliver a financial miracle.

**Step 1: Identify the person God wants to help.** With money miracles God leads us with a nudge. Take what happened when David and I were waiting for ice cream in Johannesburg: God nudged me clearly about the waitress. To overcome my uncertainties and fears, I had to purposefully exercise my faith and move forward, trusting the Lord to guide as He promised.

With the woman at the watch counter, God also initiated the process with a nudge. With a money miracle, that sequence seems to happen a lot; we are directed **toward** a person (the nudge), then often we recognize what we are to give the person during the process.

Especially in this area of finances, where we often encounter people in financial stress, we must remember that not every need is an invitation from God to use our God Pocket. Besides, external appearances are often unreliable, as our friend Nancy found out. Only God knows all the facts about someone's actual financial needs. That's why we must give His nudges higher priority than our own feelings or observations. That includes the cues we see.

The God Pocket is directly related to the God

nudge, not a cue or bump. In other words, the cue doesn't initiate the God Pocket; only the nudge does that. Why? Because our heart may go out to the needs of another, but that doesn't give us the right to make decisions about where and when and to whom God wants to distribute His funds. Of course, we always have the freedom to give our own funds to someone in need, just not from the designated funds in the God Pocket.

The cue may be an invitation for us to use our funds to help someone, but unless Heaven agrees with a nudge or some type of confirmation, then we must not make those decisions for God. Furthermore, we have a fixed amount of funds that are available for the God Pocket, and we don't know if God may want us to give His funds to someone else two hours later. If we empty His account for Him, we are assuming authority we don't have. The banker doesn't spend the depositor's money for him!

**Step 2: Isolate the need.** Once God has used a nudge to bring you to the person He has in mind for you to help, you may find yourself needing to use a cue or a bump to identify the particular need God wants to meet.

Recently I had a parking lot conversation with Charles, a hardworking man who appeared to have more than one significant need. He talked mostly about the struggles he was having with his teenagers and at work. But when he made a passing comment about his need to fix his front teeth, his expression changed. He became quiet.

"Do you have a dentist?" I asked.

"Sure," he said. "No insurance, though. And where our finances are at, my teeth won't ever get to the top of the list."

Suddenly I sensed why God had put me into this conversation. Among all the needs Charles faced, his obvious need for dental work seemed to cause him the most personal pain.

**Step 3: Open the heart and increase the desire.** With Charles, I sensed that the need I'd been brought to address was clear. I could tell by his tone of voice, facial expression, and body language that his heart was already opening.

An additional step I often take at this point is to help the person clarify and increase his desire for the specific miracle that God brought me to deliver. To accomplish this, I try to focus the person's attention on the single, isolated need, brushing away all other competing desires that might surface. Why is this so important? I want to guide the person to the firm conclusion that he or she indeed will use these funds for the identified purpose and not misuse the funds when I'm no longer present.

Another reason to clarify and increase the recipient's desire is that, at the moment the miracle is delivered, I want the person to have the strongest possible emotional response of thanksgiving to God. The more powerful the emotional response, the more credit and glory God receives and the more lasting the memory of His goodness will be in the recipient's heart.

That's why part of our role as a delivery person is to stir the desire of those who will receive the miracles. A simple question or two helps to get them more in touch with their deepest desires. Questions like "Why is that important to you?" or "If Heaven somehow granted that to you, how would you feel?" We are simply focusing their attention on the feelings of hope, pain, or despair that are tightly wrapped around the need.

I asked Charles, "If funds were available to get your teeth fixed or to be used for something else, what would you do?" I was asking him to put the degree of his desire into words.

Charles shook his head in disbelief. "Well, that's not going to happen." His voice got quiet and dreamy. "But if it did...I believe I'd be a new man. I wouldn't feel embarrassed all the time."

Clearly, the personal anguish caused by his dental problem was number one on his list, and the degree of his desire was intense.

"Well, Charles, I have some wonderful news I would like to share with you," I began. It was time for Step 4.

**Step 4: Deliver the miracle.** Perhaps by now you know what I said to Charles next: "A while back someone entrusted me with some money. This person told me that when I saw a need He'd want to meet if He were here, I should pass His money on for Him." As often happens, Charles's surprise and joy immediately demonstrated that he understood who was behind that miracle.

When you are delivering the funds, continue speaking to the other person's heart, relating directly to his need. Focus on his emotional response. Remember, the Holy Spirit is at work in his heart to draw him closer to God through this miracle. And a personal, powerful revelation of God's compassion is a very important outcome of any miracle we deliver for Him.

When we deliver the Lord's funds with excellence, the person's heart will open wide toward God. You've experienced this in your own life—God came through for you in such a way that you spontaneously poured out to Him your intense joy, thanksgiving, and praise. Heaven loves that kind of response!

Of course, the financial miracle started with God. But you asked to be sent, you asked for God's heart for the ones you will be sent to, and you invited His Spirit to do God's supernatural work through you. So when He leads you with nudges and prompts, you can be sure that He is actively at work in you and in the other person as you move forward in faith. Proactively and confidently depend on Him to guide you and to communicate His thoughts through you.

**Step 5: Transfer the credit.** You're trying to do God's work in such a way that He gets all the credit. God is the one who brought you and the other person together so His resource could be delivered. You just provided the hand-off.

Think of yourself as Heaven's bank teller, facilitating a heavenly withdrawal at the Owner's request.

Sometimes God's glory shines forth so obviously that everyone can see it. The waitress in Johannesburg happened to be a follower of Jesus Christ. And she was in such desperate straits that she prayed on the way to work for a miracle of provision. When she discovered what I had slipped into her apron pocket, she knew instantly—without any communication from me—that God had answered her prayer. Her praise and thanks flew immediately to Him, not me.

But if the recipient starts going on about what a nice person you are, it's time to help her get the picture back in focus. "Remember, this is not my money" is an important sentence. Another helpful statement is "The owner instructed me to carry it around until I saw someone who needed it."

Then gently lead the recipient toward her own conclusion about the source of the gift. To the woman at the watch counter, I said, "Somebody who knew about your wounds sent me all the way from Atlanta because He wants you to know that He deeply cares about you. Might you know who that is?" By then she knew who I meant, and that gave me a chance to tell her that God loved her.

You'll know you've hit a grand slam when the person is so absorbed with the fact that God has showed up dramatically to meet her need and show His love that she forgets you're there!

## Common questions, helpful answers

Over the years I've heard several questions from people who want to serve God with their money but hesitate for understandable reasons. Here are a few of the most common concerns.

**Aren't we supposed to give money in secret, not in public as with the God Pocket?** I applaud people who are honestly trying to live by Jesus' words in Matthew 6:1–4 about giving in secret. But this advice was aimed at people who were selfishly motivated to get the most public recognition possible for their giving. Jesus was confronting the prideful model offered by the religious sect known as the Pharisees, who were deliberately ostentatious in their giving.

But with the Money Key, we're being deliberate about something else entirely: bringing maximum credit to God. Inviting Him to reveal Himself through money always means deflecting attention away from oneself and toward God.

It's **God's** pocket, **God's** money, and **God's** miracle, after all. Our work for Him is successful only if people recognize what happened, not as a good work on our part, but as visible proof that God did something wonderful and we were merely His delivery agent.

In the Sermon on the Mount, Jesus commanded this direct approach: "Let your light so shine before men, that they may see your good works and glorify your Father in Heaven."[7] Jesus' command reminds us that we can give so creatively and purposefully that one outcome is assured: God receives great glory.

**What if I choose to give the money to the wrong person?** This could happen if you act without a nudge or misinterpret a nudge. God is so eager to give financial miracles to people who need them that He's going to clearly and unmistakably reveal to you the person He has in mind for you. In my experience, when a person first steps out to serve God with money, He leads with baby steps. With practice, our ability to sense His leading improves.

**What if the person uses the money for wrong things, like drugs?** This can happen, but in my experience it's much rarer than you might fear. Remember that a financial miracle is tailor-made by God to meet a specific need in a person's life. Ultimately, we trust that He will guide us to the right people and to the specific need He wants to meet. Of course, we also need to be wise and learn from our mistakes. I've made a few, but thankfully God can use a gift that might seem misdirected at the time to make an impact later.

## Taking God's gifts to extremes

While you and I are understandably cautious about giving away our resources when we see no apparent benefit or payback to us, Jesus isn't. Have you ever noticed? Consider His advice on how to serve up dinner:

> **When you give a banquet, invite the poor, the crippled, the lame, the blind, and you will be blessed. Although they cannot repay you, you will be repaid.**[8]

Jesus is telling us something breathtaking—and utterly life changing—about Heaven's view of giving. I would paraphrase it like this: now that you've signed up for a miracle life, don't play it safe. Give to those most overlooked or rejected by others. Give them a feast they'll never forget. By all means, risk getting nothing back, because now you know the truth: God repays those who lend to Him.[9]

> By all means, risk getting nothing back, because now you know the truth: God repays those who lend to Him.

Sounds extreme, doesn't it? But by now you should understand the powerful **why** of going to extremes—it's exactly this kind of giving that invites God Himself to become visible, to blaze in glory for an unforgettable moment in a person's life.

How could you throw a feast for someone in need today? Where would you start?

You could start by preparing in advance to give with a God Pocket. He has so many miracles waiting to be delivered through you. And you were born to reveal His extravagant goodness and generosity.

# The Dream Key

**You were born to deliver miracles
of life purpose**

**W**alking up to the lectern, I thought, **Well, this is a first.** The Mary Hall Freedom House on Atlanta's north side is a residential program for women from the streets who are alcoholics or addicts or both. For some reason, in a lifetime of speaking and teaching around the world, I'd never faced quite this kind of audience. But my main concern wasn't the audience. It was my topic. I was here to teach about big life dreams.

"Bruce, are you sure that's the best topic for that crowd?" a friend had asked before I went. "It almost feels mean to talk about big dreams to people who are in such a hard place."

If you ever want to clear your head about what really matters in life, spend a day at a rehab center. You'll come away inspired, humbled, grateful. Each one of the 150 women I met at Mary Hall proved to be a walking testament to courage in the face of cruel odds. A woman named Joyce, who said drugs had ruined the past fifteen years of her life, put things in black and white: "I knew my life would end if I didn't change."

But big dreams? These are women who just want to stay clean and sober for another day. Who long for the day when they can be reunited with their children. Who hope for the day when their boyfriend will stop beating them. Who dream about a safe place they could call home. Not one of them appears to be on the fast track to anything you or I would think of as a desirable life.

So why did I feel God leading me so strongly to talk to them about seizing their dream? It didn't take long to find out.

"I believe that you and I were created by God to pursue a big life dream," I announced. "Usually it's something we've been aware of most of our lives. It's not something we make up. It's just there."

Then I got straight to the point. "How many of you would say that you have a life dream? Maybe it's been forgotten, maybe it's been locked away, but you'd say to me, 'Bruce, I've **always** had a big dream of what I wanted to do with my life.'"

Hands shot up all over the room.

Think about this. Mary Hall Freedom House is a

halfway house for folks trying to get from nowhere to anywhere else. And still, at least half the women knew they had a big life dream!

I've seen the same response all over the world. Ask children in villages or cities, slums or high-rises, and they'll tell you they already know what they want to be when they grow up. They can already feel it and taste it—they're already there. Then ask adults around the world if they still carry a big dream in their heart, and most will say, "I think so…somewhere in there…yes."

Over the next few hours with those brave women, I laid out what the Bible teaches about what we might call the DNA of our personal life purpose. I showed them why they should never stop believing in their dream, how to reclaim it if it had gotten lost along the way, and how to discover what the next step should be in their pursuit of it.

"Your big dream isn't just about you, you know," I said. "Your dream is a one-of-a-kind part of God's larger Dream for the world. Maybe that's why He cares about your dream even more than you do. He made you not just to have your own big dream but to overcome all the obstacles in your way and actually live it."

And it's never too late to start. Or start again.

As I talked to the women, I saw tears of pain and regret at opportunities lost. But I also saw hope returning. Some who had thought a big dream was not for them understood for the first time that everyone has one—that a woman in a halfway house who has never believed in, much less pursued, a big dream has one too. For others, God was opening the secret rooms of their heart where they'd long ago hidden away what they knew they were born to do. They began talking excitedly about passion and purpose—a life that promised more than just surviving another day.

By the end of the day, tears had turned to laughter as the women worked together to identify the next important, doable step they could take to set out again on their dream journey. I was honored just to be a witness.

Have you ever watched someone wake up to the promise of his life? Have you seen a man, burdened by years of hard work and responsibility, rediscover the wonder and incredible significance of his personal passion? It's like seeing the desert bloom after rain into a riot of color.

That thrill can be your part in an unforgettable miracle, and it's what I want to prepare you for in the pages ahead.

## A big dream is the bull's-eye

What do I mean when I say big dream? Obviously, we all have numerous dreams over the course of our lives—dreams for our marriage, our children, our finances, and more. But when I say big dream, I'm referring to the driving desire to do something special, something that God put in your heart when He created you. He put it there for a very important reason. Follow your big dream, and you will pursue with passion the very thing He created you to do over the course of your whole life!

Let me ask, what percentage of the people you know

would you say are actually living their big dream? Ten percent? Fifty percent? Ninety percent? Most groups I talk to, professional counselors included, place the number at the very low end of the scale.

If that's true—and I believe it is—then the cost in personal and cultural suffering would have to be staggering. Wouldn't it help explain why so many people today feel trapped in unhappiness, depression, addiction, anger, or apathy?

A person who is pursuing his dream is energized by hope and purpose. His path may not be smooth, but he has direction. Even the challenges reveal a larger meaning to him. Why? The big picture of his life—his reason for being here—is clear.

Compare that to the person who thinks his life has no higher purpose, no big idea or goal. Over time his enthusiasm will fade. He'll lose his way. Without knowing quite why, he'll feel forgotten by God. To fill the emptiness inside, he'll tend to give in to excuses, passivity, or choices that harm himself or others.

Do you recognize yourself or anyone you know in these patterns?

Ultimately, we are happiest when we are doing what God created us to do. And He created us to do His work by His power. Living our big dream is the bull's-eye, the very center, of how we experience joy and

> **Ultimately, we are happiest when we are doing what God created us to do. And He created us to do His work by His power.**

purpose and how we contribute most to our world. The incredible promise of pursuing our big dream, along with the very real cost of not pursuing it, brings us to the Dream Key.

**The Dream Key unlocks a miracle of life purpose for others. God divinely connects you—a dream champion—with someone who is stuck or needs to know and fully embrace his God-created life dream. You deliver a miracle when God works through you supernaturally to help him take a crucial next step in his dream journey.**

Sent ones (the Master Key) who have God's heart for others (the People Key), who know how to partner with God's Spirit for a miracle (the Spirit Key), and who exercise their faith (the Risk Key) can champion the big dream in another person's heart. And because a person's big dream is so important to God, we can rely on Him to intervene in miraculous ways as we help others discover and pursue their dream.

Like the other two keys described in this section— the Money and Forgiveness keys—the Dream Key leads to a special delivery miracle. By that I mean we follow a special set of delivery instructions. For example:

- We apply a set of biblical truths and practical steps that we know must be embraced for a miracle to occur.
- We follow the five steps of the delivery process.
- We guide the conversation toward a pre- dictable outcome.

The opportunity for us as delivery agents is truly motivating. We know beyond a doubt what outcome God wants! That means, once we understand our part in the miracle, we can proceed with confidence and focused purpose to lead the other person to the miracle breakthrough he needs.

Whereas a money miracle is a provision miracle, I describe the dream miracle as a breakthrough miracle. When people who have misunderstood or discarded their dream suddenly seize upon the truth, their lives change in fundamental ways. Instead of confusion, they have clarity. Instead of apathy, motivation. Instead of being stuck, their lives show strong forward motion.

Invariably, they'll look back on their **aha!** moment with you as an unforgettable gift straight from God.

Helping others find or reignite their life dream might be something you already do with family or friends. You notice someone is struggling in this area, so you step in to guide and encourage. But as you'll soon discover, the Dream Key provides the understanding and the skills to be intentional with anyone you meet. It helps you be proactive about inviting God's Spirit to step in so that a breakthrough miracle occurs.

As you read this chapter, you may find yourself thinking about your own dream a lot—and that's what you should do! After all, you can't give away something you don't possess. Fully embracing your own life dream will bring you the fulfillment and sense of purpose God intends for you and, at the same time, will empower and motivate you to champion the big life dreams of others.

## The gap in God's big dream

Maybe you noticed that with the People Key I didn't have to convince you that people need help. Or with the Money Key, that so many face financial shortfalls. But with this key, I want to show you a cluster of related truths about our purpose in life that get overlooked by millions. When that happens, they don't just miss out on the big dream they were born to pursue; they stop believing they ever had one.

Look with me now behind the veil of Heaven to discover two of those truths: why everyone has a big dream, and where everyone's dream comes from. As we've seen in previous chapters, the more we understand and embrace how Heaven works, the better we become at delivering miracles for God.

In Jeremiah 1 we can listen in as God explains to His servant how he was created to be a prophet:

> **The word of the LORD came to me, saying:**
> **"Before I formed you in the womb I knew**
>     **you;**
> **Before you were born I sanctified you;**
> **I ordained you a prophet to the nations."** [1]

Notice the sequence of events in this intriguing sentence: "Before I formed you in the womb I knew you." What happened first? First, God knew whom He wanted Jeremiah to be—in his case, "a prophet to the nations." Then God formed him in his mother's womb, giving him a unique set of strengths and weaknesses to match the significant calling of his life. In other words, before Jeremiah was formed in his mother's womb, God imagined and designed him for a special purpose. First came the purpose, then the person.

That's how two doctoral students created a new way to get information. Larry Page and Sergey Brin started with a purpose: find a better way to organize the world's information and make it accessible and useful. From there they came up with a new method for finding and ranking search results on the Web.

Only then did they create Google, now the world's best-known search engine.

God reveals to Jeremiah that He created him in a similar way. God had something He needed to get done. (You could say He had the job description before He had the job candidate.) At a particular point in history, God knew He would need a prophet exactly like Jeremiah. Why? A prophet exactly like Jeremiah would be custom-made to accomplish an important part of God's agenda for that exact time and place in human history.

Imagine a line from one side of this page to the other, with a tiny section missing in the middle. Like this:

_____[ ]_____

The line represents time from eternity past to eternity future; the tiny gap represents Jeremiah's life. Suppose the whole line represents God's story. God needed Jeremiah to be a prophet at a particular time and place so His larger story would be complete.

Did God do the same thing when He invented you and me? Yes, He did. For each of us, God starts with one thing He needs done and then creates us with both the desire and the potential to accomplish it.

How many people does God make to accomplish that one thing? Only one. You and I have been created and put on earth now to complete our part of God's big Dream. That means, by the way, that everything about us is a gift from God—our unique strengths **and** our glaring weaknesses. **Who** He made us to be fits **what** we're meant to do with our lives…perfectly!

The psalmist beautifully describes God's purpose-directed creative process for each of us:

> **When I was made in secret**
> **And skillfully wrought…**
> **Your eyes saw my substance, being yet**
>    **unformed.**
> **And in Your book they all were written,**
> **The days fashioned for me,**
> **When as yet there were none of them.**[2]

These aren't just inspiring thoughts; they are life-changing truths. They declare something vital and opposite from what our culture declares. Consider:

- The world says you were born **without** a special purpose designed into your being. Therefore, you have to invent your dream if you want your life to have meaning.

- But the Bible reveals that your dream precedes you. God starts with His dream for you, and then He uniquely and lovingly forms you to desire the dream and to accomplish it for His glory.

Talk about a radical difference! That's why I can tell you that if a person sets out to pursue a life dream with doubts about its true origin, he's likely to end up cynical, sidetracked, and stuck. If he thinks that he (not God) invented his dream, why wouldn't he treat it as one goal that's no more important than some other goal? Under stress he'll be tempted to trade it away for something more convenient but much less fulfilling.

From one dreamer to another, I urge you to lay hold of these simple but amazing truths about the origin and importance of everyone's life dream:

> **Our dream is why God formed us. It explains who we are and why we're here.**

- Our dream is invented by God, not us.
- Our dream is why God formed us. It explains who we are (and who we're not) and why we're here.
- Our dream was never meant to be optional. It is an indispensable part of God's Dream for this time and place.
- Our dream was never meant to be just a remote possibility for us but a completed

achievement. God plans for each of us to accomplish our dream.

With these new paradigms in mind, we can become intentional about inviting a dream miracle with the people we meet, knowing that we are sent by God with this incredibly liberating and motivating message: **You were born to pursue and fulfill God's big dream for your life!**

We can ask God to lead us to people who don't know that or who have lost faith in God's dream for them. We can invite His Spirit to open eyes, make connections, and renew hidden hopes as we deliver a miracle breakthrough in life purpose.

### "All I ever wanted"

Now you're ready to look again at a foundational scripture we cited in chapter 2:

> **We are his workmanship, created in Christ Jesus for good works, which God prepared beforehand that we should walk in them.**[3]

We saw then that partnering intentionally with God on His miracle agenda for us is an important part of the good works we were created to do. As you might suspect, there is a direct relationship between the specific miracles God wants us to deliver and the big dream God has placed in our hearts.

Our dream—and all the passion, energy, and skills that go with it—is the powerful force or engine that

propels us toward the good works that God has prepared ahead of time for us to do.

What happens if we never unleash that powerful
force? never even realize it's there? Well, not only do we
lose out in terms of personal fulfillment and signifi-
cance, but critical tasks are left undone. A piece of
God's big dream remains blank. Individuals, families,
and communities can suffer tragic consequences.

That's what almost happened to Zack. From childhood he wanted to be in the marines. He used to turn
his family's backyard into an imaginary battlefield
where he could practice tactics and strategy. When he
got to college, he enrolled in an officer training program, where he excelled. He couldn't wait to get in uniform and be a leader of men in combat. And anyone
who knew Zack thought he was perfectly suited for the
task.

There was one problem—Zack has a slight but
unusual visual impairment. When he went to sign up,
he learned that his condition would limit his options in
a military career. That seemed to close the door for him.

"We watched Zack go through a difficult time,"
recalls his sister, Beth. "He felt forsaken by God. He
seemed lost. He tried other things, but nothing motivated him like his childhood dream. I remember the
day I asked him if he believed God had created him
for a military career. He said, 'Yes, absolutely. It's all
I've ever wanted.' So I told him if God had given him
that lifelong desire, there had to be a way for him to
pursue it."

Being reminded of the truth about who gave him his dream was enough to motivate Zack to try again. He called a recruiter who remembered him from the training program. The recruiter encouraged Zack to take the physical exam to see if he could pass the vision test. But Zack balked. He'd failed similar tests before.

"I encouraged him to go anyway," says Beth. "I said, 'If God created you to serve Him in uniform, He'll make a way even though there isn't a way at this moment.'"

And God did make a way. Zack passed the test. He's now serving in the marines, living the dream God created him for. And his sister witnessed the power of a reclaimed dream to shape a life.

When we set out each day as sent ones who know how important every person's big dream is and how many people are stuck or remain uncertain in this area, we place ourselves in very promising territory for miracles. It's a part of the Everyday Miracle Territory that our Creator cares passionately about, and we can expect Him to show up with power.

We are stepping out as volunteers with exceptionally good news. "You are not an accident. You are one of a kind. Your big dream is from God, and it's irreplaceable. And you were meant to seize it and celebrate it every day of your life!"

Let me show you what that might look like in your life.

## Profile of a dream deliverer

Once a person claims the truth of the God-invented dream in every heart and learns a few simple skills, he takes on great influence with others. I've seen it many times, and perhaps you have too. With a little practice, you'll be able to recognize a need in this area and speak to it with authority and insight.

My friend Joe is like that. He grew up in a missionary family where pursuing the dream was a big deal. Joe says his dad used to tell him, "Son, you can grow apple trees or fly jets. If that's what you were born to do, then it's the Lord's work for you. And I promise you there's no unemployment in the Lord's work!"

These days Joe's home is a favorite hangout for college students. For some reason they feel comfortable sorting through their hopes and dreams with him. I think it's because Joe has become a dream champion. He helps others see that their life was always meant to matter—a lot!

A goal of this chapter is to empower you to be another Joe or Beth, a sent one who knows that everyone is born with a life dream from God and who is prepared to help them pursue it.

Don't worry—being a dream delivery person for God is **not** the same thing as being a career counselor. We need those too. But what we're aiming for here is to prepare you to deliver miracles of life direction and purpose in many lives through God-directed conversations. That miracle dimension—where God shows up through us for the benefit of others and for His glory—makes all the difference.

One of my favorite examples of this kind of God-directed conversation is found in the Bible story of Abigail's meeting with David, the future king of Israel. We first see her at a low point in David's life. David is about to commit murder, and the man he plans to kill is Abigail's husband. Just imagine how that one act could have severely sidetracked the dream that God had placed in David's heart.

Along with the rest of Israel, Abigail knows that David has already been chosen by God to be king. Since she knows God's dream for David, she takes an enormous risk of faith, setting out to intercept David before he can carry out his plan. When they meet, Abigail brings David a generous supply of food and something even more valuable—a timely reminder of his destiny.

You'll find her dramatic speech in 1 Samuel 25, but a paraphrase might read something like this: "David, God has not forgotten you. You will become king as He has promised. In the meantime, don't do something foolish like taking vengeance on my husband. That would only jeopardize what's really important—God's amazing dream for your life."

David's response to her is so telling. Right away he recognizes that she is a sent person. He says:

**Blessed is the LORD God of Israel, who sent you this day to meet me! And blessed is your advice**

**and blessed are you, because you have kept me this day from coming to bloodshed and from avenging myself with my own hand.**[4]

If you had asked David, "Did a miracle just happen here?" he would have said, "Absolutely!" He knew God had intervened—that the miracle was directly from God. Before Abigail showed up, he was dead set on the wrong direction. Then, out of nowhere, a stranger appeared and delivered a message that put his whole life in perspective. That changed everything. His anger evaporated. In its place came gratitude, acceptance, and new hope for his future. What had Abigail done? Really just one thing. She had reminded him of God's big dream for his life when he had lost sight of it.

I point you to Abigail's story because in your new life of inviting God to show up in miraculous ways, you are called to do the same thing—and you can.

Do you wonder how Abigail knew what to say? For example, did she pull out a written speech that she had tucked into her saddlebag? I don't think so. I think she invited a miracle and opened her mouth and depended on God's Spirit to fill it. Obviously, David recognized every word as coming to him straight from God.

In the same way, we can relax as sent persons. Once we ask to be sent and we care about championing God's big dream for others, He will bring people across our path that He knows we can help. When we align ourselves with what God wants done, He will help us. He will bring us divinely arranged encounters, and He will show up to deliver a miracle through us.

## How to deliver a dream

Let's look at how the five-step delivery process applies to this new miracle key. As you would expect, you'll be able to apply much of what you've learned in the Money Key to this one too.

**Step 1: Identify the person.** You might be nudged by God or alerted by circumstances (as when Abigail realized that David was about to compromise his dream). But more than likely, you'll need to rely on cues and bumps to find the person God wants you to help.

If it's a cue, someone will say or do something that alerts you to the fact that he's struggling. You might pick up feelings of discontent, frustration, anger, or depression associated with how his life is going. You might notice an attitude of apathy or cynicism. These cues might be expressed in sentences you would have overlooked before:

- "My life is going nowhere. This isn't what I imagined for myself."
- "What I always wanted to do was…"
- "This job is the pits. I can't believe I'm stuck here."

Since people don't usually attribute their negative feelings to not living their big dream, you'll need to help them make the connection. My favorite clarifying bump in a dream context is this: "Are you living your dream, or are you stuck a little bit?"

It's informal, friendly, and positive, and it gets right to a big issue: most people think their big dream is out there somewhere, and they're just hoping it will come to them. That's where you come in. You know that their dream is closer to them than their own skin.

Did it strike you as odd in the Abigail and David story that a stranger could have so much influence on another person's dream? What I've learned is that people we don't know often have **more** influence in this area than those we do know. One reason is that those who are closest to us often can't see beyond the limits of our present experience any better than we can. I say this to encourage you to be willing to help anyone at any time to experience a dream breakthrough.

**Step 2: Isolate the need.** In my experience the vast majority of those you meet fall into one of two categories. Either they don't think they have a dream, or they are hindered from pursuing it in some way, usually by fear. And you can help both of these types of people.

For the one who doesn't think he has a dream, you now have a lot of truth to help you shape your questions. Do so conversationally. Keep your voice low, your statements personal and from the heart. You might start by saying, "You know, we all had a big dream when we were young. What was yours?" Or bring the conversation into the present: "If you had all the money and freedom you needed to pursue your big dream, what would your dream look like?"

You might learn that the other person stuffed his dream into a closet a long time ago. Or that he has never understood how important it is to pursue a God-given dream. With help from you and God's Spirit, he can have a breakthrough about what God wants—and what he wants too.

Ask those who know their dream, but feel stuck, to describe the dream. You'll find that many are afraid of what others might think or even of the dream itself. Some have never shared their heart on this matter with anyone. That's why revealing a dream to a receptive, nonjudgmental person can be such a powerful step forward. As they talk, ask God to show you what's holding them back.

The truth is, every dream from God **is** too big and too hard. That's why He gives us a lifetime to pursue it with His help. So the very fact that the person you're talking to feels afraid confirms that you are right on track. After all, we don't struggle with such fears when we stay in the same old rut or when we decide to do what everyone expects.

The fears each of us faces in pursuing a life dream tend to fall into two easy-to-remember categories:

- Fears about failure. The dream seems too big, or we feel disqualified to pursue it.
- Fears about rejection. The dream is opposed by others whose opinions we greatly value.

In my book **The Dream Giver,** I called these Comfort Zone fears and Border Bully fears. But the most important thing to do when you're isolating the need is to help others name their fears in their own words. You might ask, "If you were to describe the one biggest hindrance to your dream, what would you say?" You're going to find that simply helping a person put his finger on his fear is often enough to begin turning on the lights in his understanding. Let God guide your conversation. Now that you know the truth about big dreams, you're in the right place to invite a breakthrough for him by God's power and wisdom.

Once the fears are expressed, you're ready for the next step. Remember, isolating a need is different from solving a problem. You aren't a problem solver or life counselor. You are a planter of seeds of truth. You are a Heaven-sent dream champion.

**Step 3: Open the heart.** By this time you'll know if the person is open to thinking about his dream in a fresh way. When I think of opening a heart in the context of delivering a dream miracle, I imagine a single burning ember in a fire grate or campfire. My job is to find that ember, then get on my hands and knees and gently, persistently blow on it until it bursts into flame.

The ember is the person's big dream; your task is to reignite his desire for it. Here are some suggestions from my experience on how to do this with the people you meet.

Affirm that God does have a dream for them: "If you ask God to help you know your dream and discover your big purpose in life, He will help you find it."

Ask them to describe their dream and to describe what their life will be like when they are living it. Then ask them to describe what they are doing now. The comparison will increase their desire for the dream. You might say, "I've discovered that if I'm not pursuing my dream, my life just doesn't make much sense."

Help them see how important their dream is to God, and affirm its value for them. (That's what Abigail did for David.) They may feel embarrassed by it. More than likely, people close to them have dismissed it as impractical or impossible. So you might say, "I can see you doing that and really enjoying it. You'd be successful too."

Affirm their ability to live out their dream: "God wouldn't create you for a dream that isn't doable. It's impossible to do all of it at once, but if you keep moving in the right direction, you **will** see it happen. You just need to take the next step."

Ask them to go to the end of their life in their imagination, then look back: "What would make you really happy to have done with your life?" Or, "What do you think God would say to you if you've spent a lifetime really getting after the dream He gave you?" Or, "How would you feel if you came to the end of your life and discovered you hadn't done what you were created to do?"

To encourage them, ask them to tell about a time in

the past when God was faithful and good to them. What does that suggest they can expect from Him in the future?

Challenge them with the truth: "Would you say, then, that God expects you to pursue your dream?" If they say yes, then ask, "What could be a next step to getting you back on track?"

Remember that we never speak into another person's heart from our head. Rather, we connect from our heart to theirs. People have many longings attached to their dreams, and if they're not pursuing them, they have much pain and regret. As an ambassador of Heaven, you can help them see God's passion for their dream.

If you want to see God's heart on display on this issue of a life dream, read Paul's second letter to the young pastor Timothy. Paul is writing about Timothy's calling to be a minister, but the sentiments and values apply directly to any life dream. You'll find emotionally charged, dream-reigniting words like "Stir up the gift of God which is in you," and "God has not given us a spirit of fear, but of power and of love and of a sound mind."[5]

**When a person is feeling stuck, his dream will seem small while his fear will seem over-whelming.**

Paul knew that since you can't make someone's fear go away, the best thing to do is to build up his desire for the dream until it becomes stronger than his fear. When a person is feeling stuck, his dream will seem small while his fear will seem overwhelming. Our job is to set the forest on fire with his desire for his dream. And while we're doing our part, God will be at work on the inside, doing what only He can do.

**Step 4: Deliver the miracle.** Your precommitment to actively partner with the Spirit and to proactively exercise your faith in dependence on God are what prepare you for success in this step. Your part in a miracle is to prepare the person for the work of God; it is God's part to do the miracle. And remember how much God cares about the dream He put in each person's heart! While you encourage and inform, His Spirit will be at work in the person in numerous ways. He will take the seeds of truth you share and work in the person to bring about change. Without a change in belief, behavior cannot change. God stepping in here is the difference between your saying something helpful and a breakthrough that is miraculous.

We saw how God stepped into the life stories of Zack and David and the women at the Mary Hall Freedom House. Think of God's motivation to show up in that moment—to take a seed of encouragement and hover over it with His Spirit so that it flames up in their hearts and motivates them for years.

That's what we do. And that's what God does. Trust Him to do what you cannot do.

What does a dream miracle look like? You can always trace it to a change of belief—a paradigm shift—that results in the person's reaffirming his dream and acting on it in a way he couldn't before. For example:

- A person believes for the very first time that God does have a special and big purpose for his life and that he is precious and priceless.
- A person understands for the first time what his dream might look like.
- A person has a revelation about what is holding him back from beginning his dream.
- A person understands for the first time why he has felt stuck on the journey to his dream, and he resolves to step over or through the hindrance.
- A person who has abandoned his dream or hidden it away pulls it out of the closet, brushes it off, and moves forward in living his dream.

A miracle takes place by the Spirit moving in a heart. This doesn't mean our thoughts aren't involved; it just means that the miracle ultimately occurs in our heart and shows itself in our behavior. You'll know when it happens. The person's face will change. He may very well become emotional—dreams overflow with emotion and desire. He will seem lost in thought. By what he says next, you'll know that God has made His move.

Don't leave the conversation without leading the person to recommit to God to finish his dream. Perhaps you could say, "God loves you so much, and I believe He brought us together. His dream for you may look impossible right now, but if you walk toward it, God is going to help you. He created you so you could finish your dream. Will you commit right now to do that, whatever it takes?"

**Step 5: Transfer the credit.** Here's where you make sure the attention goes to the right person. The outcome you're looking for is David's exclamation to Abigail: "Blessed is the LORD God of Israel, who sent you this day to meet me!"

To direct the person heavenward, say something like this:
- "Do you sense that God was involved in our talk today?
- "I think God is up to something wonderful with you and your dream!"
- "There's no doubt about it—God is really behind the dream. He planted it in your heart. He will be with you as you achieve it with His power."

## More miracles for the road
My hope for you is that, with each step along your life journey, you will treasure and fulfill your dream more and more, and you will ask God to use you in miraculous ways to lead others to do the same. May you be like Paul, who even in his later years was still pursuing God's dream for him with all his might. In his last letter he wrote:

**I press on, that I may lay hold of that for which Christ Jesus has also laid hold of me. . . . One thing I do, forgetting those things which are behind and reaching forward to those things which are ahead, I press toward the goal for the prize of the upward call of God in Christ Jesus.[6]**

This is the liberating news we deliver to other dreamers God brings our way: "Your dream matters—to you and to God. If you find yourself sidetracked, start again. It's never too late to fulfill your destiny. God still wants your dream to come true!"

Be ready every day to invite a miracle into the life of a fellow traveler. Now that you know how to be a dream champion in other people's lives, I'm confident God will bring a dreamer in need of a miracle your way soon.

> **This is the liberating news we deliver to other dreamers God brings our way: "Your dream matters—to you and to God."**

# The Forgiveness Key

**You were born to deliver miracles
of forgiveness**

**W**hat if each morning you walked out
the door knowing you were carrying a
miracle key that could release someone from prison?

As dramatic as that might sound, it is the promise of
this chapter. I can't think of any area of the Everyday
Miracle Territory with more promise for immediate
personal change than what we're going to talk about in
this chapter. One reason the potential is so great is that
you and I are surrounded by sincere, law-abiding people who **are** those prisoners and don't even know it.

It was Christmas Day, and Darlene and Jessica and
I were out delivering meals for a local inner-city mission, asking God to send us to the people of His choosing. Our first delivery was to a family of seven. We

found the house at the end of a long gravel road, sur-rounded by junk and broken-down cars.

The mother and an adult daughter came out to greet us. As soon as the mom saw the seven meals we'd brought, she exclaimed, "We're so glad you came! We were praying someone would come." She told us that her husband had lost his job and was sick in bed. "We just don't have any food or money in the house."

No food on Christmas? None of us could miss such an obvious cue.

Nudge. **This is the family…**

She invited us in to meet her family. Her name was Mary Ann; her daughter's, Tess. While Mary Ann was introducing us around, she began to weep.

"Are you okay?" Darlene asked. Somehow we'd expected our delivery to bring more joy than tears.

"My baby drowned in the pool in the house behind us!" she said.

We could hardly believe what we'd heard. Instantly our hearts broke for her. "I'm so, so sorry," Darlene said. "I can't imagine what you must be feeling."

At that Tess started to cry too. We asked how it had happened. The mom told us she'd gone to work in the afternoon even though she'd felt strongly she should stay home. But her husband had insisted that they needed the income. While she was at work, her plan for childcare at home unraveled. The older son stayed in his bedroom, preoccupied with his music. Then the baby-sitter fell asleep on the couch. With no one to keep an eye on them, the two younger children wandered outside, then into the neighbor's backyard. By the time their absence was noticed, the youngest had drowned in the neighbor's pool.

"My baby drowned!" Mary Ann sobbed. "She was only two years old!"

By now Darlene had her arm around the mom, and my daughter and I were praying that God would show us how to bring His healing to such a devastating Christmas.

And that's when the conversation took a surprising turn.

"When did this happen?" one of us asked.

Tess looked at us through her tears. "Eighteen years ago," she said.

We were stunned. Until that moment we'd assumed that the accident had happened recently, maybe within the past few days. For Mary Ann, that's how it felt. But she and her family had been carrying their unresolved pain for eighteen years.

"You've really been through a lot, haven't you?" I said quietly to Mary Ann. "We're here for you. Would it help to talk for a while?"

Over the next ten minutes we heard a tale of almost unbelievable woe. In the years since the accident, Mary Ann had blamed the baby-sitter, her older son, God for not intervening, her husband for pressuring her to go to work that day, and especially herself. All that blame and bitterness had poisoned their lives. The marriage began disintegrating. Their son became an alcoholic. Tess had recently lost custody of her child to the authorities. The mom kept punishing herself for what had happened, but that hadn't helped either.

"Your whole family has suffered deeply, haven't they?" I said.

"We haven't been the same since that day," said Tess. "My mother used to laugh and smile. But not anymore. Not for eighteen years."

I turned to Mary Ann. "Would you say you have been in torment?"

"Yes, I guess I would," she said, wiping her tears.

"Would you like that to stop?"

"Well, yes," she said. "But how could that happen? We can't get her back!"

"Maybe that's why God sent us here today," I said. "Not just to deliver these meals but to bring a much bigger miracle. God is ready to set you free—completely, right here on Christmas Day in your kitchen!"

And that's exactly what happened. I gently led Mary Ann through the steps of forgiveness that we'll look at together in this chapter. She had a lot of old business to clean up—bitterness, anger, self-hatred, vengeance. But she took every step. And so did Tess. When we parted, mother and daughter were free for the first time in eighteen years.

Is it really possible that a heart wound left untreated could cause that much devastation in one life, in the lives of a whole family? Is it possible that an act as simple as forgiveness could be prized so highly by God that He releases miracles when it happens? And could His primary method of delivering this magnificent miracle be through willing servants like you and me?

In this chapter you're going to encounter a miracle key that has almost unlimited power for good in our world. Like the other two Special Delivery Keys, it requires a deeper understanding of several important biblical truths.

I'm talking about the Forgiveness Key.

**The Forgiveness Key unlocks a miracle of freedom for those who suffer as a result of unforgiveness. When God connects you with a person in need, you draw on powerful Bible insights and universal principles to lead that person to healing. As you partner with the Spirit, God works through you to bring about a miracle of forgiveness.**

In the next few pages, I'll show you why wrong beliefs about forgiveness keep so many people stuck in unforgiveness. I'll show you how Heaven views those wrong beliefs and what right beliefs God uses to bring freedom. You'll identify the simple steps every prisoner needs to take to break free, and you'll learn your part in delivering the miracle.

I often hear that, next to the miracle of eternal life, the miracle of forgiveness is the most powerful and precious experience a person can have.

## Why forgiveness can save a life

If we lived in a perfect world, no one would need to forgive. No one would injure another person. No one would be abused or treated unfairly. No one would sin.

But we don't live in that world. We live in a world where, despite our best efforts, we hurt even those we love. We injure others accidentally and sometimes intentionally. And others do the same to us. It happens between individuals, races, countries. Watch the news; the hurts have been piling up for centuries.

That's why forgiveness is such an important experience for all of us. Without it, we could drown in an ocean of regret, pain, anger, and bitterness.

But there's a catch: forgiveness is one of the most **un**natural responses in all of human nature. Think about it. Selfless giving is hard enough, but forgiving? That's like lavishing the best gift ever on the person who just robbed you!

Why should a mother forgive the drunk driver who killed her son? Or a husband forgive his wife for having an affair with his best friend? Or a teenager forgive the father who left when she was a baby and has never made an effort to see her since? Or a businessman forgive the partner who asked for his all, then betrayed his trust? At those times everything in us cries out for justice, retribution, fairness—**not** forgiveness.

> **When we don't forgive, it's as if we have chosen to leave dirt in a gash. Healing can't happen.**

We have to ask, though, what happens when we don't forgive? What happens to the hurt?

Picture it like this: You're walking along the seashore when you step on a piece of broken glass. Ouch! You limp back to your towel and try not to think about it. Later you limp around chasing a soccer ball. The next day you're out walking around your vegetable garden in your bare feet. The gash hurts, that's for sure. But won't it heal in time? You decide to ignore the pain.

You continue ignoring it. The wound becomes infected, and your foot swells. Walking is difficult, but you still try not to think about it. Infection spreads. You break out in a fever...

You get the picture. If you treat the wound with care—wash out the dirt, protect it from germs—your foot will heal. However the wound happened, God made your body to heal itself. But if you leave the wound unclean and untreated, infection sets in. The healing process is blocked.

God made our heart the same way. When we forgive after we've been hurt, the wound gets cleaned out, and the healing process can start. When we don't forgive, it's as if we have chosen to leave dirt in the gash. Healing can't happen, no matter how much we try not to think about it, no matter how much time passes. In fact, the more time that goes by, the more the destructive consequences spread.

I call it the Spiral of Unforgiveness—the descent into greater and greater misery that occurs when a person's heart wound is left untreated. The first level of pain is bitterness, which inevitably leads to resentment. Unaddressed resentment spirals into anger. Anger deepens into malice and then hatred. Eventually a person is consumed by vengeance. Vengeful people live with the overwhelming desire, not simply to see justice, but to injure those who injured them.

Once you learn to recognize the cues, you'll realize that the symptoms of unforgiveness are everywhere in our world. Often the signs of it are right on the surface. A man who was unjustly fired months ago walks back into his old workplace carrying a rifle. Or a family like Mary Ann's suffers for years from anger and harmful choices.

But sometimes the evidence is overlooked or misinterpreted.

I remember a confused young man who came to me for advice. He said he just couldn't seem to finish anything. "I've started and dropped out of so many colleges I've lost count. No matter what I do, I can't get my life together." He described his various attempts to find direction. "I thought maybe you could help me."

Actually, I thought I could. I asked, "So, how has your dad hurt you?"

"My dad?" He assumed I was changing the subject, but soon a painful story came spilling out. "I can never live up to my dad's expectations—he is a perfectionist!" he said. "I know he wants the best for me, but I've never once felt his approval. Anything I tried, he told me to try harder. Anything I did wasn't good enough. Since I left home, it's easier just to avoid him."

I helped him see that avoiding the problem wasn't going to make things better. I described the picture of the untreated wound. "Would you say your father has wounded you?" I asked.

"Yes. A lot," he said. His face and posture were changing. I could tell he was feeling the years of disappointment and rejection deeply.

"Are those wounds still there, still infected?"

"Yes."

We talked about how much a boy needs his father's affirmation as he's growing up. For a young man who's been injured by a rejecting, judgmental dad, decisions become difficult. Motivation dries up. He can't see who he is anymore or where he wants to go.

"You can begin to undo the damage right now," I told him. "But to do that, you have to forgive your dad. There's no other way. Are you ready to do that?"

He was tearful but ready. Taking the injuries one by one, I helped him to forgive. By the time we were done, he could say to me, "Before God, I have forgiven my dad of everything." He was a free man.

"Now will you help me with my future?" he asked with a smile.

"I just did," I said. I gave him my address. "If you want, in a few months send me a note. Tell me how you're doing."

A few months later he wrote: "All my old insecurity and indecision are gone. It's like something came into my head and blew out all that bad stuff." He had reconciled with his dad and was excited about his future.

I hope you're seeing the far-reaching power of forgiveness to reclaim our lives from the injuries of the past.

With the need for forgiveness being so great in our world, how important would you suppose forgiveness is to God? To help you discover that, I want to pull back the veil of Heaven again and show you God's perspective on the matter.

I think you will be amazed.

## How important is forgiveness to God?

The Lord's Prayer models how we should approach the heavenly Father. In His prayer Jesus reveals several things we can ask God to do—grant us provision, protection, and deliverance, for example. But you'll find just one thing that **we** are to do.

Forgive.

> **Forgive us our debts,**
> **As we forgive our debtors.**[1]

Jesus is telling His followers, when you pray—amid all your praises and petitions—be sure to affirm to the Father this one thing: that you are doing what He does. You are forgiving those who are your debtors and don't deserve your pardon.

In case His listeners miss the point, Jesus follows the prayer with only one commentary, and it's also about forgiveness:

> **For if you forgive men their trespasses, your**
> **heavenly Father will also forgive you. But if you**
> **do not forgive men their trespasses, neither will**
> **your Father forgive your trespasses.**[2]

Now, Jesus can't be referring here to what theologians call "salvation forgiveness." (That happens in Heaven and can't be earned—it is the gift of God to all who believe in Jesus Christ and His work on the cross as full payment for their sins.) He's referring instead to the flow of God's pardon in our lives on earth.

But clearly the stakes are high, or Jesus wouldn't have included these words about forgiveness. If I forgive, God will forgive me. If I don't, Jesus says, "Neither will your Father forgive your trespasses." Jesus leaves no room for confusion.

So I understand why Peter tried later to get Jesus to narrow it down to something a little more practical. He asked:

**Lord, how often shall my brother sin against me, and I forgive him? Up to seven times?** [3]

Peter must have thought he was being generous. My brother steals from me, and steals from me again, and again and again. How about up to seven times, Jesus? Wouldn't that be enough? Wouldn't forgiveness beyond that turn into a terrible mistake?

But Jesus said, in effect, "No, Peter. Forgive him without limit."

**I do not say to you, up to seven times, but up to seventy times seven.** [4]

How can any of us forgive somebody seventy times seven—or really, an unlimited number of times? Jesus' answer reveals the single most powerful motivation to forgive that you'll find as you deliver miracles to those locked behind prison bars of unforgiveness. That's why Jesus shares it—to give Peter the understanding necessary to actually forgive another person seventy times seven!

It's a story about a servant who gets deeply, hopelessly into debt to his king. To recoup his losses, the king decides he must sell the servant, along with his wife and children, into slavery. When the servant learns what's about to happen, he rushes to the king and falls on the floor, begging for more time.

Something about his servant pleading facedown on the floor melts the king's heart. Jesus says he is "moved with compassion."[5] On the spot the king makes a decision. He doesn't just give him more time. He forgives the servant of every debt, and the servant walks away a free man.

Can you imagine how that servant must have felt? One minute he's in disgrace, in crippling debt, and facing an awful fate. The next he's debt free.

But the servant doesn't take his king's compassion to heart. No sooner has he left the king's presence than he corners a friend who owes him lunch money. When the friend can't pay up, the servant has him thrown in jail until he pays back the entire debt.

Then the king gets wind of it. Burning with anger, he calls the servant into his presence and tells him:

**"You wicked servant! I forgave you all that debt because you begged me. Should you not also have had compassion on your fellow servant, just as I had pity on you?" And his master was angry, and delivered him to the torturers until he should pay all that was due to him.**[6]

Another stunning turnaround! From a blessed, free man one minute to a tortured prisoner the next. And only one thing will stop the torment—when he pays back everything he owes.

Don't miss who the king (also called master) is in the story. He is God the Father. We know that because Jesus is telling the story in answer to Peter's question about how often Christ's followers should forgive. Listen to what Jesus says next as He drives home the most shocking reason to forgive in the entire Bible:

**So My heavenly Father also will do to you if each of you, from his heart, does not forgive his brother his trespasses.**[7]

You want to know God's views on forgiveness? Jesus told us. God doesn't think of forgiveness as simply a nice idea or a mere suggestion. In fact, just like the king in Jesus' story, God gets angry when those He has forgiven everything refuse to forgive each other of comparative trifles.

And we now know that when we don't forgive, He

**will** act. Jesus clearly revealed that when He said: "So My heavenly Father also will do to you."

**You want to know God's views on forgiveness? Jesus told us. God doesn't think of forgiveness as simply a nice idea or a mere suggestion.**

What exactly will the Father do? He will deliver us "to the torturers." God the Father doesn't torment anyone Himself, but Jesus shows that He does turn people over to the painful consequences of their own unforgiveness.

For how long? Just as Jesus said—until from their heart they forgive others their trespasses.

Now you know why I asked Mary Ann that unusual question: "Would you say you have been in torment?" That simple question validates for you and me and everyone a deep need for a forgiveness miracle.

Over many years of delivering this miracle, I've never had people with unforgiveness in their heart reply no when asked if they are experiencing torment. In your miracle appointment, God the Father wants the person to be released from the prison of torment. Not only has He sent you to deliver the miracle for Him, but His Spirit has been actively at work in the person's heart ever since the moment the wound occurred.

And what does God want most from your encounter with another person locked up by unforgiveness? Not more suffering, that's for sure. He grieves with every wounded person that the injuries occurred in the first place. What God has always deeply desired for the wounded person is a supernatural deliverance from the prison of unforgiveness.

Freedom from the past starts when we grasp how strongly God feels about unforgiveness and when we initiate conversations knowing how strongly He desires to set people free of its misery.

## Five steps to the delivery of a forgiveness miracle

The delivery steps described here will train you to lead a person to break through to emotional freedom. The more you deliver this miracle, the more skilled you'll become.

Fortunately, you already know a lot. For example, you've already seen how Heaven partners with us to deliver miracles of many different kinds. And the five-step delivery process you encountered in chapter 9 applies directly and in sequence here.

**Step 1: Identify the person.** Sometimes a person will acknowledge right away that a grudge or broken relationship exists: "I don't speak to my mother anymore." Or you might notice that when a certain topic comes up, a person withdraws or becomes overly sensitive. You might notice displays of chronic anger. Or you might see more generalized attitudes that often cover up old wounds—attitudes like cynicism, defeatism, bitterness, judgmentalism, and distrust of relationships.

Any emotional wound that happened a long time

ago but still comes up in conversation or stirs out-of-context or inappropriate emotion is usually a giveaway. That's what happened with Mary Ann. She was experiencing an eighteen-year-old injury as if it were part of her life in the present. Whenever I see patterns of self-destructive behavior, I start with the assumption that unforgiveness could be an underlying cause. Whenever I see a difficulty in forming close relationships or confusion about life direction, I take these as important cues as well.

In your conversation, use affirmations, observations, and leading questions. Remember, you don't know yet if you're talking with your miracle appointment. You're simply using open-ended bumps to bring clarity:

- "That issue doesn't seem like it's been resolved. Are you still feeling unhappiness or pain because of what happened?" (You're observing an area of potential need, bumping for a sign of suffering or torment.)
- "Tell me about your family growing up." (A general question in an area where most of us experience hurts—more on this in the next step.)
- "That's a difficult subject for you, isn't it?" (The unspoken invitation is for the other to confirm his need.)
- "Do you ever feel like some painful things that happened earlier in your life are still holding you back?" (You're looking for signs of a pattern, confirming a need for forgiveness.)

Once you have begun to sense needs in this area, go to the most important bump for a forgiveness miracle—what I call the Unforgiveness Validator: "Would you say that you experience torment from time to time?" Then be quiet until the person has had time to think and respond.

You may feel uncomfortable the first few times you ask this validating question, but when you watch God working in person after person to immediately confess that to be true, you'll relax.

Once you are confident that the person you're talking to is your miracle appointment, you're ready to transition your conversation to the next step.

**Step 2: Isolate the need.** Obviously, God wants **all** unforgiveness to be taken care of. But rarely can people cope with all their wounds at one time. Count on God to reveal where and with whom He wants the breakthrough to begin. To isolate the need or needs that God wants to address, aim to bring focus in three areas:

- who hurt the person the most (the offender)
- what the offender did (the wounds)
- which injuries are the most emotionally distressing (the starting place)

Once you have your focus, don't stray to additional incidents or people.

Your intention is for the person who needs the miracle to have a clear list of grievances to work from—if not on paper, then in his mind. A clear list is all-important for the miracle to be effectively delivered. That's because unforgiveness is linked to the specific trespasses that caused the injury, not only to the person who inflicted them.

Keep in mind that a huge percentage of our hurts occur in our key relationships—a spouse, parent, child, sibling, close friend, relative, or an acquaintance at work or church. Bump with questions like "Think back over your life. Who hurt you most?" or "Would you share with me how you were hurt the most?"

You're in this conversation for one reason: to serve the person as a heart-wound physician who can facilitate the miracle of forgiveness. Be careful to remain sensitive and nonjudgmental as you are representing the Lord to the person and dealing with hurtful and at times even shameful areas that the person may never have shared with anyone before.

I've found that when we're partnering with God in this area, His Spirit is extremely active. He will bring specifics to the person's mind. Listen for expressions like "I don't know where this came from, but…" and "I had forgotten this…" That is the Spirit at work.

Now that you know who hurt the person most and have listed the specific, most distressing wounds, you're ready for Step 3.

**Step 3: Open the heart.** Jesus made it clear that release from torment can be granted only when a person forgives another "from the heart." The purpose of the third step, then, is to prepare a person to be emotionally ready to forgive the offender—not from the mind, not from the will, but from the heart. For that to happen, we must put him emotionally in touch with his wounds.

People can say, "Yes, I know I should forgive." But that doesn't mean they're ready to do it. A person can acknowledge compelling facts: "Uncle Robert hurt me badly. I have been devastated ever since. It continues to mess up my life today." But we still need to help that person become emotionally ready to let go of the injury.

Let go of what, specifically? Well, of a deep desire for justice. Of the need to even the score or get revenge. Of all the other powerful, entangling emotions that go with unforgiveness. And those feelings, no matter how toxic, can seem to the injured party like a necessary part of his identity. Strangely, to let go of them may strike the person as a loss, not a gain.

At this point the most powerful way to serve those who are trying to forgive is to share the story of Matthew 18, including the shocking revelation that they will be in torment until they open their heart and forgive. You've seen some of the most important truths in this chapter: the personal cost of unforgiveness, God's strong feelings and clear commands on the matter, and the very real promise of a complete end to torment—of escape from prison—once forgiveness is granted. Share these with the person who needs a miracle.

Try to identify the wrong belief that is keeping the

person stuck, and help him see the right belief. You can remember three important ones with three J's:

- Jesus: "Jesus forgave you. You can choose to forgive others."
- Justice: "Vengeance belongs to God, not to you or me."
- Jailer: "You are your own jailer. Your torment won't end until you forgive. Then it will end immediately. You will be free. And that is what God wants for you."

Keep the conversation focused on the person who needs to forgive, not on the one who caused the injuries. Again, your aim is to bring him to a point of readiness to forgive. Look into his eyes as you talk. You'll be able to tell when he opens his heart. The cues that his heart is open will be obvious—emotions, facial expressions, tone of voice, and often tears.

Now the person is ready to experience the miracle of forgiving.

**Step 4: Deliver the miracle.** At this point the person is ready to forgive, but with so many conflicting and swirling emotions, he doesn't have a clear path forward. In fact, he may even honestly say, "I really want to, but I don't know if I can." You serve as the human bridge from his "want to forgive" to his "did forgive." The Spirit of God will be leading you in this very personal process.

You can start by simply saying, "I'd like to help you do this. Would you be comfortable just repeating the words after me?" (Forgiveness between people is expressed not in a prayer toward God but as a statement of forgiveness toward the offender.)

If he agrees, gently lead him in a natural conversation, helping him to name and then forgive specific wounds that come to mind or that he has mentioned already: "I forgive my dad for telling me I'd never amount to anything...for walking out on my mom and me . . . for never being around . . "

In certain instances you may need to help the person with a few open-ended questions:

- "What else did your father do that hurt you?"
- "Is there anything else that comes to mind?"

You are trying to get to the pain of his wound. Be patient and thorough, gently encouraging him to get it all out—every kind of injury and every occasion—and then forgive each instance.

Don't hurry the person, and don't become uncomfortable with periods of silence, as it gives the Lord time to work. Remember, this miracle is God's to deliver. Don't worry that the person may forget to name some wounds. The Holy Spirit will be leading his thoughts to deal with the real injuries.

Of course you will expect the real pain to trigger emotions—tears, anger, anguish. That's good and natural. Your role is to be a patient, caring listener.

When the person seems to be finished, use the Forgiveness Test. Ask the person to repeat these words out loud:

Before God, I have completely forgiven _____
of every wound.

Then be quiet for a minute and see if God agrees. During those few seconds of silence, the person usually remembers something else. After each new round of forgiveness, try the Forgiveness Test again until nothing else surfaces. Then you know the forgiveness part of the miracle has been successfully delivered.

The torment ends when forgiveness has been genuinely granted. Expect the miracle to bring with it a sense of peace. If you notice it, bring it to the person's attention: "You look more peaceful already. Do you feel lighter inside?" Forgiveness is one of the most beautiful miracles you'll ever witness.

**Step 5: Transfer the credit.** Your final step is to help the recipient of the miracle focus on the One he has offended by not forgiving. I like to remind the person that God has been present in the conversation and that He is the healer of hearts and the terminator of all torment.

But to complete the full miracle of forgiveness for himself, he needs to receive God's full forgiveness. Remind him that God views unforgiveness as sin: "How do you think God felt about your unforgiveness and bitterness for all those years?" At this point the person's heart is so tender that he will easily admit God hasn't been pleased with his anger and bitterness. Often I continue the process of leading the person in short phrases he can repeat after me: "Dear God, I confess my sins of unforgiveness… I have held on to resentment, bitterness, hatred, and vengeance… I have offended You and broken Your heart… Please forgive me for not forgiving."

And now you have delivered two gifts: the person who brought injury has been forgiven, and a person who offended God by not forgiving has also been forgiven.

> Forgiveness can release healing in surprising ways. One breakthrough is often the beginning of restoration in other relationships.

In my experience, forgiveness can release healing in surprising ways. For example, one breakthrough in forgiveness is often the beginning of breakthroughs and restoration in other relationships, including a person's relationship with God.

## The man who came running

To close this chapter, I want to take you back to a scene from chapter 1. Remember Jack, the waiter and single dad? I told you about meeting him in a restaurant one fall evening in Colorado. On the way to work he'd told God he desperately needed a hundred dollars to cover an overdraft. Then, during dinner, God nudged me in a very unusual way to open my God Pocket and deliver the exact miracle he'd prayed for.

But the story didn't end there.

Our dinner group had parted for the evening, and I

was walking to my car when I heard someone call out, "Wait!" It was Jack, and he was bounding across the parking lot toward me.

"I just have to thank you again," he said. "That's never happened to me before."

He was done for the night and obviously wanted to talk. I reminded him that the money wasn't mine; it belonged to God, and I was just the delivery person. But I could see that what Jack was really trying to grasp was more than the fact of the miraculous provision. It was what that event **meant** that had him shaking his head—what the miracle said to him about God, about the meaning of his life.

As we talked more about his family situation, I felt that God wanted me to go further, so I asked, "Is God chasing you, Jack?"

Without hesitating, he replied, "Yes, He is."

"What about?"

He didn't answer. I could tell he was still trying to pull the strands of meaning together. But I thought I might know. I asked, "Has your ex-wife remarried?"

"No," he said.

"Have you remarried?"

"No."

"Are either of you in love with someone else?"

"No."

"Might God want you to get back together?"

"Oh, that's impossible," he said sadly. "I've said some terrible things and done some terrible things. And she's said and done terrible things to me." He stared off toward the mountains. "It would just never work."

But I didn't think that at all. And now that you understand how God sets up our miracle appointments, I know you wouldn't have either if you had been there!

I pressed forward. "If all that was worked out between you, what would you do?" I asked.

"Well, I'd ask her to marry me."

"Would you like to forgive her right here in this parking lot?"

Jack looked startled. "But that's impossible," he said.

"No sir, it isn't," I said smiling. "It won't even take very long."

And it didn't. As I led him toward a forgiveness miracle, Jack's heart was so open that he was straining forward at almost every step. You know what? From the moment I'd seen him running toward me across the parking lot, I knew he would be.

When we were done, he said with relief and a lot of conviction, "I'll be on my knees asking her to marry me by December!"

For Jack that night, one miracle had triggered another and another—like dominos falling. Not only did God meet Jack's financial need and set him free from unforgiveness, but He also became visible to Jack as a personal and loving God who still had a good future for his life.

I hope that, after reading this chapter, you never

again underestimate the power of forgiveness, the cost of unforgiveness, or the urgent need for a forgiveness miracle in almost everyone you meet.

People everywhere are in prison. God's heart is broken. And you and I have been given a key that brings freedom.

# Epilogue

---

# Welcome to
the Beginning

**I**f **you're like me,** you love nothing better than coming to the end of a successful adventure—unless it's starting a new one. Now that you've reached the end of this book, the best news is that it's only the beginning of your new life in Everyday Miracle Territory.

My hope is that you are not the same person you were when you read the first page. **You Were Born for This** was never meant to be **about** something; it was meant to **create** something—an unforgettable turning point in your life. Some may debate the terminology in the book or take exception to my interpretations. But that doesn't bother me much. What would break my heart is if you saw the wide vista of supernatural opportunity where God is inviting you to live…and you turned away.

Heaven's agenda in our world and in our daily lives is so much grander than millions of Christ's followers ever realize. But you have seen behind the veil of Heaven!

How many Christians have you met who realize that the flow of daily personal miracles for people in need is limited not by God but by people?

How many have you met who know that God is always looking for volunteers for His miracle missions, always sending signals about what He's doing and what He wants to do through us?

How many do you know who realize that partnering with God to do His work by His power is always possible?

My mission has been to awaken you to the largest, most promising life possible in your walk with God. He is, after all, the one "who is able to do exceedingly abundantly above all that we ask or think, according to the power that works in us."[1]

> **My mission has been to awaken you to the largest, most promising life possible in your walk with God.**

Have you encountered Him and His dream for you in a fresh way in these pages? I hope so.

If you have, you should already be seeing your life in radically different ways. Take a moment to measure how much your new beliefs have changed as you read the following statements:

- I used to see **miracles** as spectacular events from long ago or experienced these days by only a few. Now I see that God does personal miracles on a regular basis through ordinary people who know how Heaven works and who make God's agenda their own.
- I used to see **other people** in terms of what they appeared to be on the outside. Now I recognize that every person is someone with a need—perhaps known only to God—that He deeply wants to meet, very possibly through me.
- I used to see **Heaven** as a place where I might live someday. Now I recognize that Heaven is also a place where God is busy right now planning miracle appointments on earth and looking for people who will volunteer to partner with Him in delivering them.
- I used to see **myself** as someone who might experience a miracle someday. Now I see that God is ready to do miracles through me regularly to meet important needs for others. (And I'm on Heaven's list of reliable miracle delivery agents.)
- I used to see a **world** in which I was powerless to change much. Now I see a world where every urgent need or painful lack brings to

mind how God's desire from the start has
been to work supernaturally to meet those
needs through people like me.

- I used to perceive **God's Spirit** as a mysterious and invisible force that felt remote from
my daily life. Now I see the Spirit as a Person
who wants to partner with me in supernatural
ways to accomplish Heaven's agenda.

- I used to assume that a **miracle appointment,** should I have one, would be shrouded
in mystery and that my chances of success
would be small. Now I realize that identifiable signals and delivery steps can lead me
toward success in any miracle mission and
that God wants me to succeed even more
than I do.

- I used to see **today** as a day like any other day,
when God probably wouldn't intervene in any
noticeable way. Now I see every day as an
exhilarating opportunity to be sent on a
miracle mission to a person in need, and I can
expect success because His power will work
mightily—through me!

If you find yourself resonating with the truths of the
second sentence in each statement, congratulations!
You have taken the message of this book to heart. Now
you know that partnering with God in His miracle
agenda for others isn't just frosting on the spiritual
cake—it **is** the cake.

## Go through the roof

One of my favorite New Testament stories about delivering a personal miracle is the account in Luke of four friends who decided to bring a paralyzed man to Jesus for healing. Their timing couldn't have been worse. The house where Jesus was teaching was crammed with an overflow audience.

With every door and window blocked, how could the friends get the man on the stretcher to Jesus? They saw no possible way to make their miracle appointment. Should they turn back?

Luke tells what they decided to do instead:

**When they could not find how they might bring him in, because of the crowd, they went up on the housetop and let him down with his bed through the tiling into the midst before Jesus.[2]**

That sentence reads so innocently, doesn't it? But imagine the scene...

First, a lot of stomping and shuffling on the roof.

Jesus pauses in midsentence. Some of the listeners glance up.

Then dirt and bits of tile start tumbling down as a hole opens above their heads. Now everyone is staring up in disbelief. The owner of the house is outraged, the guests aghast. They jump to their feet, shouting at the scoundrels on the roof to stop or else!

But the four men don't stop. The hole yawns wider.

Then down comes a stretcher, lowered inch by inch with ropes. On the stretcher is a wretched shell of a man who comes to rest on the floor right in front of Jesus.

Everyone looks at Jesus. How will He react? If He's really God, **how will God react?**

And that's when they see that Jesus is still looking up toward the ceiling and into the faces of the four hopeful men.

How do I know that?

"When He saw their faith," the Bible says ("their" referring to the men on the roof), He turned to the paralyzed man on the mat and said, "Your sins are forgiven you.... Arise, take up your bed, and go to your house."

**Immediately he rose up before them, took up what he had been lying on, and departed to his own house, glorifying God. And they [the crowd looking on] were all amazed, and they glorified God.**[3]

From four friends with no opportunity...to mission accomplished and an unforgettable display of God's power and glory. How did that happen?

The answer is simple but not easy. When the friends couldn't see a way forward, they went forward anyway. They created a new way, refusing to be stopped by challenging circumstances. They also refused to be influenced by other people's expectations. Their desire to receive God's miracle for a friend was much greater than all that.

**You Were Born for This** is my best attempt to help you see that God can and will work through your faith to bring miracles to others. You don't need the perfect opportunity. You don't even need to be perfectly prepared. That's because you are already the perfect candidate to deliver a miracle.

Remember?

You are a **sent person** (Master Key) who **shares God's heart for people** (People Key) and who **intentionally partners with the Spirit** to do God's work (Spirit Key) through **acts of proactive dependence on Him** (Risk Key) to deliver His miracle to others.

So how does God see you right now? I think Jesus showed us. The same Lord who was passionate about delivering the gifts of Heaven to people in need is looking at you right now with pleasure and great anticipation.

## Thoroughly equipped

What are some personal decisions you could make today that would ensure your new miracle life continues to flourish? I recommend five.

1. **Commit.** Are you ready to "go through the roof" to make your miracle deliveries? In every miracle opportunity you'll come to a point where you won't know the **how** of your next step. But that's when faith that pleases God makes a surprising choice. When you

see no possible way to do what God wants done, you move forward anyway in confident dependence on

> **When you see no possible way to do what God wants done, you move forward anyway in confident dependence on Him.**

Him. In my experience those are so often the situations that lead to the miracle stories I never tire of retelling. Commit now to pursuing your miracle opportunities, knowing that God will show up in supernatural ways.

And here's a small but powerful action I en-courage you to take: sign in today with the growing online community at www.YouWereBornForThis.com. Why is this so important? I've noticed that two kinds of decisions rarely, if ever, result in life change: private decisions and postponed decisions. That's why publicly identifying and joining with others who share your new commitments has so much power.

2. **Act.** You can't master every principle in this book today, but you can ask to be sent to a person in need today. You can go through every conversation today newly awakened to what God might be bringing your way. You can respond to His nudge. You can watch for cues. You can bump. There's so much you already **can** do.

Which means that already **you can do your part** in the partnership with God. If you do yours, God will do His. You will find yourself standing in front of your miracle assignment with everything you need to know to cooperate with joy and success in a supernatural provision.

Ask God to show you what He's already prepared you to do. For example, your life experience, especially in an area where you've struggled or suffered, often suggests the kinds of people and situations where you will find the most opportunities. Ask God to bless you now with miracle delivery opportunities in the very areas where you have experienced pain in your past. Your life will have prepared you especially well for Step 3 of the delivery—"Open the heart."

Don't worry that God will ask you to do more than you're ready for, especially when you're just getting started. God loves beginners, and as you've seen, He perfectly matches each miracle opportunity with His best choice for the delivery agent.

3. **Grow.** Determine now that you will do whatever it takes to be ready for any miracle assignment God wants to send your way, even ones that seem completely out of reach to you now.

The most important way to grow your effectiveness is by studying the Bible for miracle ministry insights in addition to daily encouragement. God's Word has been given so that every delivery agent "may be complete, thoroughly equipped for every good work."[4] Since every miracle is a good work, think about the implications of that statement. **God has already made a way for you to be "thoroughly equipped" for every single miracle mission you were created for!**

The special delivery miracles presented in this book are just three that can and will happen when you apply biblical principles. Begin now to intentionally prepare for personal miracles in other areas such as troubled relationships, habitual sins, and a need for salvation, to name a few. And visit the book's Web site for Bible studies and other helpful resources for personal growth.

Another way to grow is to apply the basic principles and tools you're learning on a larger scale—in your family or another small group, for example, or even in bigger arenas in your community or around the world. Every principle or tool in the book works because it is based on how Heaven works. That means your miracle partnership with God has virtually no limit in where you can apply it for His glory. Take bold steps outside your comfort zone and watch what God will do.

4. **Multiply.** It is my deep desire and continual prayer that the truths in this book will liberate millions around the world to discover new ways of partnering with Heaven to serve the needs of humankind. But every movement starts with one person. So consider what you can do to multiply the message of the miracle life to others.

You know that Jesus commanded each of His followers to go and make disciples. But I'm always struck by what He didn't say. For example, He didn't command, "Go when you're ready" or, "Go if you're in professional ministry" or, "Go, but you don't have to make disciples if you just love people."

Here's the amazing truth: what Jesus commands you and me to do is nothing less than what God created us to do and will empower us to accomplish. When you make a priority of multiplying in the lives of others what God has given you, you'll find personal fulfillment and fruitfulness that you can't experience any other way.

Begin to multiply the message with the people God has already placed in your spheres of influence. Why not work your way through this book with your family? with your friends and co-workers? in your small group at church?

If you're a pastor, consider preaching through these topics to further equip your congregation to live in a miraculous partnership with the Spirit. Imagine what would happen in your community if the majority of your members learned how to depend on God's power for miraculous ministry results. Your church would be bursting at the seams with people who have witnessed what God can do through them and who can't wait to learn more.

Do you have a personal miracle story to tell as a result of reading this book? Go to www.YouWereBornFor-This.com, click on "My Miracle Story," and share what happened. You'll encourage others and give God credit for what He's done. The Bible is full of stories of how God intervened in time and space and what happened in people's lives as a result. Now it's your turn to share.

And that brings me to a final step every miracle delivery agent should take.

## Declaring His power

We live in an era that seems to have reduced much of the Christian life to two expectations: what God can do for us, and what we can do for God. But every page of this book has been intended to demonstrate to you a third and profoundly more thrilling expectation: what God can do through us for others.

And this brings me to my final encouragement to you.

5. **Declare.** Have you noticed how much of the Bible is devoted to recounting God's wonders? Scores of the psalms and major portions of both Old Testament and New retell God's miraculous deeds for all to hear. But in our generation, the wonders that God has done and will continue to do for us and through us are so often overlooked.

"One generation shall praise Your works to another," wrote the psalmist, "and shall declare Your mighty acts.... Men shall speak of the might of Your awesome acts, and I will declare Your greatness."[5]

**Will you join in reclaiming for our generation the reputation of our miracle-working God?**

Will you join in reclaiming for our generation the reputation of our miracle-working God? Will you reclaim for yourself and those you love your birthright to the miraculous as a normal way of life?

You and I were born for this...even if we have to go through the roof to do it.

# Acknowledgments

No project of this magnitude could have come together without a lot of help, and I've been blessed to receive it from so many. Because of the unusual nature of the topic, I tested the material before a wide range of ten different audiences, including churches of many stripes and an internationally representative gathering of ministry leaders in Hong Kong. On each occasion, audiences contributed valuable insights, and to all of you I am grateful. In particular I am thankful to those who attended a four-week teaching series organized by Bruce and Toni Hebel in Tyrone, Georgia. Your meaningful engagement with the content and your eagerness to put it into action have been a source of tremendous help and encouragement.

The publishing executives at WaterBrook Multnomah and the Crown Publishing Group have gone to extraordinary lengths to ensure the success of this project. I am grateful to Stephen Cobb, Ken Petersen, Carie Freimuth, and Lori Addicott in Colorado Springs and to Jenny Frost, Michael Palgon, and David Drake in New York City. Your enthusiasm and support, both personally and professionally, have been indispensable, and I do not take it for granted. Thank you.

The closer a book comes to a daunting deadline, the more authors require the skill and patience of the editorial and production teams. To Julia Wallace, managing editor; Laura Barker, editorial director; Mark Ford, senior art director; Kristopher Orr, graphic designer; Carol Bartley, production editor; Karen Sherry, interior designer; and Angie Messinger, typesetter—thank you for your perseverance and good cheer.

I'm already impressed by the creativity and energy of the marketing team at WaterBrook Multnomah and look forward to partnering with you for many successes in the future. To Tiffany Walker, marketing director; Allison O'Hara, marketing coordinator; Melissa Sturgis, senior publicist; and Chris Sigfrids, online marketing manager; and to all those who work with you—thank you so much.

It's been a pleasure to work again with David Kopp as my writing collaborator, and his wife, Heather Kopp, as our editor. Both of you have contributed extraordinarily to the vision and substance of this book. I am truly blessed by your abilities, creativity, and tenacity, and I'm grateful for your friendship. Thank you.

From early in the writing process, the writing team benefited greatly from the clear thinking and careful work of Eric Stanford, an informed reader and a superb line editor. Many thanks.

I owe more than I can say to my executive assistant, Jill Milligan, with whom I've worked closely for more than thirty years. As always, your enthusiasm and organ-izational talents turn impossible challenges into accomplished goals in record time. Thank you.

Finally, I express my deepest appreciation and affection to members of my family. First to my wife and closest partner, Darlene. Once again you supported, encouraged, and prayed me through to the finish. No man could ask for more than you are. And then to my daughters: Jennifer, your numerous insights and helpful reading of the manuscript helped shape the final product. Jessica, the weeks you invested as our editorial assistant brought great value to the book and treasured memories to your father. My deepest love and gratitude to each of you.

Atlanta, Georgia
July 2009

# 15 Frequently Asked Questions About the Miracle Life

**For answers and other resources, go to
www.YouWereBornForThis.com**

1. I've seen so few miracles in my lifetime. Are you saying it's in my power to change that?
2. Don't I need a special anointing or gifting from God to deliver miracles?
3. Bizarre things seem connected with some people who claim to do miracles. Could you suggest some cautions that would help me stay balanced and on track if I go down this road?
4. I've really blown it in the past, and I'm still not where I'd like to be with God. Am I a candidate to partner with Him for miracles?
5. What happens if I fail to deliver a miracle or someone turns away?
6. People say "God told me" and "God led me," but I don't have those experiences in my spiritual life. Is something wrong with me?
7. After reading about the risk of faith, I realize I suffer from a lot of unbelief. Any suggestions for what I should do about it?
8. Couldn't people go overboard on nudges and prompts and end up making foolish decisions? How can I tell if a thought is from God or me?
9. The five steps of miracle delivery are helpful, but

could you tell me more about that all-important fourth step: deliver the miracle?

10. Are there more keys to a life of miracles beyond what you've included in the book, or would you say this is the whole picture?

11. How can I be sure people will use my God Pocket funds in the right way?

12. So many are afraid to pursue their big life dream. Any more advice on how to help them overcome fear and take the next step in their journey?

13. Why do you say everyone needs a forgiveness miracle of some kind?

14. How could things change in our world if more people partnered with God in the supernatural realm? What could happen in churches?

15. I really want to learn more about delivery miracles. Do you offer other training materials, or could you recommend other helpful resources?

# Notes

**Chapter 1**
1. 1 Chronicles 4:9–10
2. **Merriam-Webster's Collegiate Dictionary**, 11th ed., s.v. "miracle."

**Chapter 2**
1. Acts 1:4
2. Acts 1:8
3. 1 Corinthians 2:1, 3–5
4. Ephesians 2:10
5. Ephesians 1:17–20

**Chapter 3**
1. 1 Kings 22:19–22, adapted
2. 1 Kings 22:22
3. 1 Kings 22:34–37
4. John 5:17, NIV, adapted
5. John 5:19–20
6. 2 Chronicles 16:9

**Chapter 4**
1. John 20:21; Mark 16:15
2. Isaiah 6:1–4
3. Isaiah 6:8
4. James 5:16, emphasis added

**Chapter 5**
1. 1 Peter 2:9
2. Luke 22:27; Matthew 20:28; John 6:38
3. Jonah 3:1–3

4. Jonah 4:1
5. Romans 5:8
6. Colossians 3:23–24
7. Matthew 25:40
8. Matthew 25:40
9. See Jonah 4:11

## Chapter 6

1. John 16:7
2. See John 16:7 (KJV), 13–14 (NKJV)
3. John 16:8
4. Acts 3:6, 12
5. 1 Corinthians 2:10
6. John 16:13
7. Psalm 32:8
8. Romans 8:14; Acts 18:5; 16:6
9. See John 16:8–14
10. Acts 4:13
11. See Luke 24:49; Acts 2:1–2

## Chapter 7

1. Matthew 17:20
2. Matthew 13:58
3. Matthew 14:27
4. Matthew 14:28–29
5. Matthew 14:33
6. Matthew 14:30–31
7. Mark 6:6
8. 2 Thessalonians 1:11, NIV, adapted

## Chapter 8

1. Isaiah 30:21
2. See 2 Kings 2:9; 4:2
3. Acts 8:39

## Chapter 9

1. James 2:15–16
2. Luke 12:12
3. Luke 17:15–16

## Chapter 10

1. 1 Timothy 6:18
2. Proverbs 19:17, ESV
3. Proverbs 19:17
4. See Mark 9:41
5. See Luke 21:1–4
6. Exodus 34:6
7. Matthew 5:16
8. Luke 14:13–14, NIV
9. See my book **A Life God Rewards** for much more on this topic.

## Chapter 11

1. Jeremiah 1:4–5
2. Psalm 139:15–16
3. Ephesians 2:10
4. 1 Samuel 25:32–33
5. 2 Timothy 1:6–7
6. Philippians 3:12–14

## Chapter 12

1. Matthew 6:12
2. Matthew 6:14–15
3. Matthew 18:21
4. Matthew 18:22
5. Matthew 18:27
6. Matthew 18:32–34
7. Matthew 18:35

## Epilogue

1. Ephesians 3:20
2. Luke 5:19
3. Luke 5:20, 24–26
4. 2 Timothy 3:17
5. Psalm 145:4, 6

# About the Authors

**Bruce Wilkinson** is best known as the author of the **New York Times** #1 bestseller **The Prayer of Jabez.** He is also the author of several other bestsellers, including **A Life God Rewards, Secrets of the Vine,** and **The Dream Giver.** Over the past three decades, Wilkinson has founded numerous global initiatives. He has developed a Bible teaching faculty of over thirty-two thousand in eighty-three nations, led a movement of eighty-seven organizations that recruited and trained seven thousand Americans to serve the former Soviet Union, published ten monthly magazines, developed numerous courses that have been taught in more than ten thousand seminars, and led thirty-six hundred Americans to address hunger, orphan care, AIDS education, and poverty in Africa. Bruce and his wife, Darlene, have three children and several grandchildren. They live outside Atlanta.

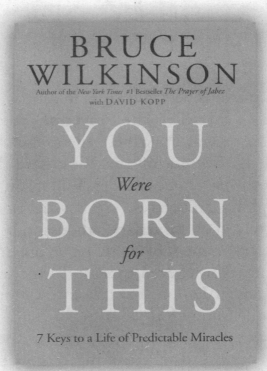

BRUCE
WILKINSON

Author of the *New York Times* #1 Bestseller *The Prayer of Jabez*
with DAVID KOPP

YOU

*Were*

BORN

*for*

THIS

7 Keys to a Life of Predictable Miracles

# Timeless Teaching
# from Bruce Wilkinson

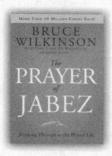

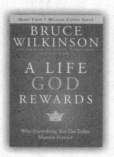

# Connect with Bruce online

To find out more about Bruce Wilkinson,
his books, and events, visit the website.

- Watch Bruce on video
- Share your life change stories
- Find upcoming events
- Get resources to deepen your faith

www.BruceWilkinson.com
www.YouWereBornForThis.com
www.Facebook.com/LastingLifeChange

# BUSINESS

# COMMUNICATIONS

INTERNATIONAL CASE
STUDIES IN ENGLISH

# BUSINESS

# COMMUNICATIONS

## INTERNATIONAL CASE
## STUDIES IN ENGLISH

## Drew Rodgers

School of Business, Oslo University College

CAMBRIDGE
UNIVERSITY PRESS

PUBLISHED BY THE PRESS SYNDICATE OF THE UNIVERSITY OF CAMBRIDGE
The Pitt Building, Trumpington Street, Cambridge, United Kingdom

CAMBRIDGE UNIVERSITY PRESS
The Edinburgh Building, Cambridge CB2 2RU, UK
40 West 20th Street, New York, NY 10011–4211, USA
477 Williamstown Road, Port Melbourne, VIC 3207, Australia
Ruiz de Alarcón 13, 28014 Madrid, Spain
Dock House, The Waterfront, Cape Town 8001, South Africa

http://www.cambridge.org

First published by St. Martin's Press, Inc. 1995

Reprinted 1998
5th printing 2002

Printed in the United States of America

Library of Congress Cataloging-in-Publication Data Available

ISBN 0 521 65751 2 Student's Book
ISBN 0 521 65750 4 Instructor's Manual

Acknowledgments are given on page 152.

*To Inger*

# PREFACE

## AUDIENCE

*Business Communications: International Case Studies in English* is intended for use in ESP-Business for advanced-intermediate to advanced students. The case study approach allows for the teaching of both language and communication skills by actively engaging the students in the solution of realistic business cases, thus requiring the constant use and development of these skills. The students are required to bring their knowledge of business to bear on the cases; thus, a business background is *not* a requirement to teach this course, as your students will be encouraged to share their knowledge to create the atmosphere of cooperation fundamental to this approach. Those cases which require the least amount of business background are:

*Case 1*: Preparing for Your Future

*Case 4*: Long-range Golf Equipment Seeks a Distributor

*Case 5*: Midland Heating and Cooling vs. the Primary Sheet Metal Workers of America, AFL-CIO

*Case 6*: Northern Electrical Services vs. the Environmentalists

*Case 7*: Commutair: Employee Motivation and Management Theory

*Case 8*: Unhealthy Leaders: Sterling Forklift

## THE CASE STUDY METHOD AND ITS APPLICATION

The case study method is based on the approach used in programs at Harvard Business School and other major schools of business. The cases in this book have been developed to teach ESP. This approach is better adapted to teaching ESP-Business than the traditional teacher-centered approach because it develops communicative competence by putting the students in the center of the action, where they can use language actively and practice communication skills.

The role of the teacher becomes that of facilitator, reference person, and provider of feedback, and *the classroom becomes a workshop in communication and language skill development*. After the cases are introduced, much of the class time is spent in group work in which the students prepare their roles.

The teacher aids this preparation by providing language input. The students will often ask for vocabulary and structures, which they will use immediately and thus internalize better than in rote memorization. The facilitator role helps create a *dynamic partnership* in learning between the teacher and students, thus greatly enhancing the learning experience. In the *active approach to learning* fostered by this method, the students will achieve *communicative competence* in English more efficiently.

Think about the traditional teacher-centered method, in which the instructor is the hub and all communication goes through him or her. Learning a language and communication skills requires active participation. If only one student can speak at a time, how much learning can be accomplished? With the case study method, on the other hand, students are allowed to communicate in their individual groups, thereby multiplying the opportunities to produce language and to be corrected, as well as to practice communication skills.

*This method allows the students to expand their repertoire of communication skills by requiring them to develop presentation, teamworking, and networking skills, as well as critical/analytical problem-solving skills, all of which are required in a modern business context characterized by a task force or team approach.*

This method does not exclude teacher-centered activities. Rather, such activities are integrated through the processes of defining and clarifying the cases or working on grammar and vocabulary. However, once these tasks are completed, the students should be allowed to communicate more freely.

If you have no previous experience in the case study method, rest assured that it is one of the easiest methods to use, once the proper mind-set is adopted. Such a mind-set requires ceding center stage to the students and assuming a support role. Instead of leading the class, the teacher's role is to provide the students with vocabulary, grammatical structures, and content feedback.

## OVERVIEW AND ORGANIZATION

*Business Communications* is divided into cases representing various fields of business, such as finance, marketing, business organization and management, and human resource management. The cases are arranged in a pedagogical order, which is explained in the Instructor's Manual.

*The cases are divided into two major groups: closed-ended and open-ended.* The closed-ended cases are at the beginning of the book (Case 1 to Case 9). All information needed to solve these cases is presented in the cases themselves (with the exception of Case 1: Preparing for Your Future, which requires some knowledge of local companies). The open-ended cases are a unique feature of this book as they are set in the students' local environment in order to encourage them to develop information-gathering skills and to apply their knowledge in real-life situations. If the class setting is Germany, for example, the students can look into local German conditions to solve the cases. If the class is held in an English-speaking country, the students can look into those local conditions to get a better picture of the business culture of that country.

Each case consists of

1. A cultural background section to explain cultural factors bearing on the case, which may be unfamiliar to non-native students
2. A description of the situation underlying the case
3. Discussion questions to help the student consider general aspects of the case
4. The case activity and roles to be played
5. Language mastery exercises to help prepare for the case
6. Written exercises as a follow-up to the case activity
7. Vocabulary and other support materials

Each case is a complete unit and is pedagogically segmented to provide a logical progression in the solving of the case.

In addition to the cases, three appendices are included:

*Appendix 1: Telephone English* is designed to help students develop telephone-related skills and language as well as accepted telephone etiquette.

*Appendix 2: Business Writing* provides models for letters, reports, and memos, as well as discussions of (a) proper tone and style and (b) audience-centered communication, to aid students in completing the written assignments in each case.

*Appendix 3: Electronic Communication Devices* provides a brief description of E-mail and electronic bulletin boards.

An Instructor's Manual accompanies this text. It provides an in-depth explanation of the rationale behind the case study method, the teacher's and students' roles, the progression from introduction to writing assignment in the cases, and tips relevant to teaching each individual case. Thus, no previous experience with the case study method is necessary to use this book successfully.

## ACKNOWLEDGMENTS

All the cases have been reviewed by experts in their respective fields, as well as by professionals in the field of education. I wish to thank the following members of the College of Business and the Labor Research Center at the University of Rhode Island for their suggestions: Dr. Kapil Jain, Dr. Chai Kim, Dr. Laura Beauvais, and Dr. Charles Schmidt. Thanks also to Grace Murphy, who served as my research assistant and provided necessary accounting documents and organization charts for the cases. A special thanks to Dr. Barbara Tate for a general review and to my editor, Naomi Silverman. Every author should be fortunate enough to have an editor like her. Finally, thanks to the reviewers who provided insightful suggestions that were incorporated into this book: Patricia Byrd, Georgia State University; Susana Christie, San Diego State University; Charles Cooper, Norwegian School of

Management; Lizabeth England, Eastern Michigan University; William H. Oliver, Evergreen State College; Miguel Parmantie, Universidad Pontificia Comillas (Madrid, Spain); Philip Vassallo, Middlesex County College; Kay Westerfield, University of Oregon; and Peter Cleaverley, Norwegian School of Management.

Drew Rodgers

# CONTENTS

**CASE** BUSINESS ORGANIZATION AND MANAGEMENT
**8** Unhealthy Leaders: Sterling Forklift    68

Cultural Background: Anglo/American Management Styles    69

**CASE** BANKING
**9** Smith Brothers and Florida Central    78

Cultural Background: Loan Applications    79

# Introduction to Open-Ended Cases

## CASE 13 INTERNATIONAL TRADE
## Competing Internationally    108

## CASE 14 BUSINESS ORGANIZATION AND MANAGEMENT
## Saturn: Can American Automobile Manufacturers Compete with the Japanese?    116

# BUSINESS

---

# COMMUNICATIONS

---

## INTERNATIONAL CASE
## STUDIES IN ENGLISH

# INTRODUCTION

## TO THE STUDENT

You are the key to the success of the teaching method behind this book.

You will be the focus of this method because it depends on your ability to play the roles assigned to you. You must actively share your knowledge of business in solving the cases. *You are the experts.* The more you share your knowledge, the better the class will be.

Although this book is designed for ESP-Business courses, the method will allow you to learn more than just English. You will learn many skills that are valuable in the business world, including:

1. How to make public presentations
2. How to actively share your knowledge of the business world so as to improve your marketability as a candidate for future jobs (a process known as *networking*)
3. How to work in teams
4. How to find necessary information
5. How to deal with foreign cultures, their values and ways of doing business
6. How to actively participate in problem-solving activities

However, in order to learn these skills, you will have to follow three basic rules:

1. *Be active* in all group and class work. You have to participate to learn.
2. *Speak only English* in class, except when you do not know a word and need to ask a fellow student or the instructor for a translation.
3. *Come to class prepared.* Remember, the role-playing on which this method is based depends on your preparedness and ability to play the roles assigned to you.

If you follow these three basic rules, you will not only learn English, you will also develop the six skills listed above, thereby greatly improving your chances in a competitive job market.

Some of the cases are set in an Anglo/American context, and all of them reflect certain Anglo/American values. Thus, a cultural background section is included to help you understand each case's cultural context. A language is a product of the culture of the people who speak it. Thus, both the cultural background sections and the solving of the cases will help you gain a better understanding of Anglo/American culture.

There are no right answers. Each group will have to work out its own solutions and present them in the role-playing. You will all be expected to solve problems, use your communication skills to present your solutions, and help each other by sharing your ideas. This approach is not only an excellent way to learn language and communication skills — it is also fun. Good luck.

## TO THE INSTRUCTOR

The level of this book is advanced-intermediate to advanced. It is intended for businesspeople and students of business in both non–English-speaking countries and schools of business in English-speaking countries. The accompanying Instructor's Manual provides an introduction to teaching with the case study method, detailed information on how to teach each case, advice on teaching vocabulary and grammar, the teaching sequence for each case (that is, how much time to devote to each part of the case), and secret position papers for the negotiation cases.

## OVERVIEW OF CASE LEVELS

Case 1: Preparing for Your Future — advanced-intermediate

Case 2: Portfolio Development — advanced-intermediate

Case 3: Larry the Liquidator vs. New England Wire and Cable — advanced-intermediate

Case 4: Long-range Golf Equipment Seeks a Distributor — advanced-intermediate

Case 5: Midland Heating and Cooling vs. the Primary Sheet Metal Workers of America, AFL-CIO — advanced-intermediate

Case 6: Northern Electrical Services vs. the Environmentalists — advanced-intermediate

Case 7: Commutair: Employee Motivation and Management Theory — advanced-intermediate

Case 8: Unhealthy Leaders: Sterling Forklift — advanced-intermediate

Case 9: Smith Brothers and Florida Central — advanced

Case 10: Penetrating the Market with Long-range Clubs and Bags — advanced-intermediate

Case 11: Costa de los Años de Oro — advanced-intermediate

Case 12: Industrial Pollution: Charting Pollution and Proposing Solutions — advanced-intermediate

Case 13: Competing Internationally — advanced

Case 14: Saturn: Can American Automobile Manufacturers Compete with the Japanese — advanced

# JOB SEARCH

## Preparing for Your Future

## CULTURAL BACKGROUND: JOB INTERVIEWS

Applicants for jobs in Anglo/American cultures are expected to sell themselves. They must show what they have accomplished and convince the interviewer that they will benefit the company. They should speak of their accomplishments and what they can contribute to the company, and they should be prepared to emphasize their strong points. To people from certain cultures, this may seem like bragging. In some cultures, employment is based on one's papers, and interviews are not even held. However, Anglo/American cultures emphasize the individual, seeking candidates with traits such as the ability to cooperate, communicate, and work in teams. Thus, the personal interview is important, and the personal impression a candidate makes may be as important as his or her educational background and work experience. Thus, the tendency in certain cultures to be modest and to understate one's qualifications may be a disadvantage. Instead, one must express self-confidence, and this is done by expressing one's accomplishments. In addition, direct eye contact, which may be considered impolite in certain cultures, is expected in an Anglo/American interview situation. In order to prepare for such interviews, candidates should do a personal inventory, discovering what educational background and work experience they have that are relevant to the job. Then they should express it in a practice interview before the real one.

# CASE

With increasing competition in the job market, any new graduate who hopes to get a job should have a plan worked out long before graduation day. The purpose of this case is to help you begin to develop such a plan. One important step is to recall and share past work-related experiences with one another (remember that one of the skills you wish to develop is *networking* — the sharing of information that can benefit all members of the group). The résumé and cover letter you write in this case will present you as the candidate you want to be by the time you graduate. In preparing this résumé and cover letter, then, you will be shaping goals to aim for in becoming this ideal candidate. This case will not only take you through the steps involved in getting a job, it will also give you tips on how to succeed in your job search.

2

## Start Preparing Now

What can you do now to ease the transition from student to professional? There are numerous ways to get your foot in the door (that is, to establish contacts with potential future employers) before you actually start looking for work. The more employers who know you before you start applying for a job, the greater your chance of being hired. Here are some tips that you can use to prepare yourself in advance.

1. Start files on companies you are interested in, so that you are well informed about the companies that may eventually be interviewing you.

2. Read professional journals, the business sections of newspapers, and business magazines. This will give you an idea of available jobs and the kind of education and experience they require. It will also help you tailor your courses and your experience to make you a competitive candidate.

3. Join clubs on campus that are related to your areas of interest, and invite potential future employers to speak to club members. Take advantage of the opportunity to establish personal contact with the speakers when they come to speak.

4. Connect your school projects with potential employers so that those employers can see you in action. If you do a good job, they will find you a more interesting candidate than someone they have never seen.

5. Informational interviews can also help you get a foot in the door. For example, in order to write an article for the school newspaper, you might interview directors of personnel about the present job market: expected trends, what they are looking for in a new graduate, what specialties are in demand, and so on. When you complete your article, send a copy of it with a note of thanks to the person you interviewed. You could use your studying of this case as a reason for arranging an informational interview.

6. Talk to friends working in your field of interest to find out what is happening in the job market. Let people know in advance that you will be looking for a job in the fall or spring of 20——.

# POINTS FOR DISCUSSION

1. Discuss job-finding strategies.
2. Brainstorm on techniques for getting your foot in the door.
3. Discuss the do's and don'ts of applying and interviewing.
4. Discuss ways in which the job application process in your country is different from the one described in this case.

# CASE ACTIVITIES

## Interview Preparation and Interviewing

Each group should begin by finding an advertisement in a newspaper or journal for a job that the group members are interested in, then doing some research on the company. If you cannot find an appropriate job in the newspaper, create a job description and write an announcement for a job within an actual company. If group members have such different backgrounds that, realistically, they would not all apply for the same job, create several different job descriptions, all within the same company. Each group member will be interviewed by the other group members. Thus, you will each play the role of both applicant and interviewer. The interview situation will rotate as group member A will be interviewed by the group members B, C, and D, then group member B will be interviewed by group members A, C, and D, and so on. Thus, all group members must know something about the company in order to ask intelligent questions as interviewers and to answer them as candidates. After all the candidates have been interviewed, each group will present to the class the candidate who obtained the job, explaining why this candidate was chosen and the others were not.

## Preparation

You will prepare just as if you were actually applying for the job. You will write a cover letter and a résumé (see Figure 1-1), and you will research the company. The best sources of information are annual reports and articles in newspapers and business journals. You want to have enough information so that you can answer questions intelligently and show that you know something about the company. The more you know about the company, the more you can present yourself as the candidate they are seeking.

You should have a friend give you a trial interview, using the standard questions below. The goal is not to have "canned" answers (answers that you memorize and repeat word for word) to all questions, but to have the chance to think through what you really believe and feel and to develop experience in interviewing so that you will feel confident when the actual interview occurs. You should have a ninety-second answer to the question, "Tell me about yourself." It is important that you give concrete examples. Don't just say that you are a hard worker. Give examples from your education or work experience or references.

## Standard Questions Asked during Interviews

These questions can be used during the trial interview, along with questions specific to the job and the individual candidate based on that person's résumé. Practice answering these questions in pairs prior to your trial interview.

1. Tell me about yourself (your background).
2. How would you describe yourself (your personality)?
3. What would you consider your greatest strengths and weaknesses?
4. What two or three accomplishments have given you greatest satisfaction?
5. How did you choose the career you have chosen, and what have you done to prepare for it?
6. What qualifications do you have to help you succeed in this career?
7. Why did you apply for a job with our company?
8. What do you think it takes to be successful in our company?

**Joseph Daniels**
2321 Park Drive
Providence, RI 02908
(401) 555-2365

| | |
|---|---|
| **Career Objective:** | A sales position in an international company where I can use my knowledge of languages and foreign cultures. |
| **Education:** | University of Rhode Island, B.A., 2002 Marketing/Spanish<br>• 3.25 GPA overall; 3.5 Marketing; 3.7 Spanish<br>• Dean's List, four semesters<br>• Relevant Courses:<br>International Marketing<br>Marketing and the Media<br>Business Spanish<br>The Business Culture of Latin America |
| **Work Experience:** | *Graduation Rings, Inc.*, 1998–present<br>• Marketed and sold rings, pins, and accessories on campus. Increased sales at URI by 25 percent.<br>• Allowed me the opportunity to design and test marketing strategies.<br><br>*Promotions, Inc.*, Summers, 1997–1999<br>• Layout, paste-up, and camera. Gave me insight into designing and visual presentation of advertisements. |
| **Organizations:** | American Marketing Association, President, 1997–1998<br>• Arranged the career day and a guest lecture series for marketing students. |
| **Special skills:** | Layout, paste-up, and camera<br>Fluent in Spanish<br>FORTRAN, Basic, Desktop Publishing |

**Figure 1-1**   Sample Résumé

9. Where do you see yourself in five years?
10. Why should I hire you?
11. How do you work under pressure? Give me some examples.
12. Are you willing to relocate?
13. What are the three most important things to you in a job?

## LANGUAGE MASTERY EXERCISE

### Using Power Verbs

Use power verbs (verbs that create a strong impression of action) such as the following:

| | | | |
|---|---|---|---|
| achieved | expanded | maintained | saved |
| administered | formulated | managed | solved |
| arranged | generated | motivated | streamlined |
| coordinated | implemented | organized | supervised |
| created | increased | planned | transformed |
| developed | initiated | prepared | utilized |
| doubled | launched | revised | verified |
| established | led | reduced | won |

Working in pairs, use some of these power verbs in sentences to describe your past accomplishments to a fellow student. After you have made a general statement, give an example and quantify it. For example:

I implemented a new accounting system [*general statement*] that reduced the time necessary to prepare the balance sheet by 30 percent, thus saving the company $30,000 each year [*quantification*].

Even if you do not have a lot of experience, try to invent the kinds of accomplishments that will allow you to use power verbs.

## WRITING: RÉSUMÉS AND COVER LETTERS

Write a cover letter and résumé to apply for the jobs your group selected. If you are currently a student, write the cover letter and résumé as if you had already completed your course of study. If you are already employed, write the cover letter and résumé to reflect your present status.

In addition to the advice given in Appendix 2 on Business Writing, consider the following tips.

Use quality paper (20–24 lb. bond).

Keep your résumé and cover letter short.

Always have someone proofread your résumé and cover letter.

Stress past accomplishments, promotions, and relevant skills.

Show, do not tell, and quantify results. For example, do not say "I am a hard worker." Instead state, "While maintaining a 3.25 average, I worked 20 hours a week as an on-campus sales representative for Graduation Rings, Inc., increasing sales by 25 percent over the previous representative.

## Résumés

The layout of a résumé is extremely important. Use bold type for headings, and use proper spacing to make your résumé easy to read. Arrange the layout to place your strongest areas at the top. If you have a strong academic career but not much work experience, place "Education" at the top of the résumé. Remember to include activities that show your initiative and skills, even if you were not paid for these activities. For example, emphasize responsibilities associated with campus activities or civic groups. Write concisely and clearly. See the sample résumé shown in Figure 1-1.

## Cover Letters

The cover letter should be addressed to a specific person, not just "Marketing Manager." The tone of your cover letter is extremely important. Once again, showing what you have done and quantifying your successes are excellent ways of presenting yourself positively without seeming overconfident. Present the relevant material, and let the receiver formulate a judgment. Do not tell him or her that you are the perfect candidate, but demonstrate your strengths through your accomplishments. An outline of a cover letter is provided below. You should review examples of cover letters that other people have prepared to help you develop your own.

FIRST PARAGRAPH: State why you are writing, what position you are applying for, where you heard about the position, and, briefly, why you would like to work for this company. For example, Joseph Daniels (whose résumé appears in Figure 1-1) might state that he heard a presentation of X company during a guest lecture in the series he arranged, was impressed by the company's success, and noted that they have several major accounts in Latin America.

SECOND PARAGRAPH: Discuss the relevance of your education, related activities, and projects to the job in question. Joseph Daniels might mention relevant marketing and Spanish courses, attempting to show how they help qualify him for the position. He could also mention his activities in the American Marketing Association.

THIRD PARAGRAPH: Discuss the relevance of your work experience. Joseph Daniels would emphasize his production, marketing, and sales experience and give any details that do not show up on his résumé.

FOURTH PARAGRAPH: Indicate your desire for a personal interview and your flexibility as to the time and place. A standard closing paragraph might be: I realize that a résumé cannot completely convey my background and qualifications. I would therefore welcome the opportunity to meet with you in person to present presentations will increase your knowledge of some of these instruments, as well as give you insights into how they can be exploited profitably.

It would be wise to do this case early in the class, because that would provide more time to chart the result of the portfolios and run a contest to determine the best portfolio in the class. Naturally, the length of the class will affect your investment strategy. But you might also state in your presentation that your strategy is based on a longer term than just the length of the class, and then go on to explain your portfolio in light of this long-term investment strategy.

## POINTS FOR DISCUSSION

1. Discuss investment strategies including:
   a) A breakdown of your portfolio in terms of the various instruments mentioned on pages 15 – 16. What percentage of your portfolio should be in stocks (and what types of stocks), precious metals, and so on? Why? [*For advanced students only.*]
   b) A strategy for a new investor with limited capital. [*For advanced students only.*]
2. What is the general attitude toward investment in your country? What are the most popular forms of investment, if any?
3. What sectors (such as oil and gas, biotechnology, auto industry, and so on) do you think will do well in the immediate future, and why?

## CASE ACTIVITIES

### Developing a Portfolio

You have $50,000 to invest (you can convert this to local currency if necessary). Meet with a fellow student who will act as a broker — preferably someone who has finance and investment as a specialty. Work out your investment goals and strategy and then develop a portfolio to meet these goals. You may use as many of the instruments (stocks, bonds, futures, puts and calls, and so on) as you feel will serve your goal. But remember the old adage, "Don't put all your eggs in one basket." Keeping this adage in mind, develop a portfolio. Your teacher will choose some of you to present your portfolios to the class and discuss why they are sound. Thus, you will need to do some research.

### Presentation

Those students chosen to present their portfolios will complete the following steps:

1. Explain your investment goals and strategies.
2. Present your portfolio and defend its soundness. For example, what types of investments were chosen, and what percentage of the $50,000 was allotted to each instrument (for example, 30 percent in stocks, 10 percent in precious metals, and so on)?

3. Explain your individual choices in detail. For example, provide the following information: (a) stocks (describe the growth potential, such as how much the price of the stock will rise); (b) dividends (how much interest, if any, will be paid on your investment); (c) the status of the company (as presented in its annual report); (d) the strength of the sector(s) (such as oil and bio-technology) that the company operates in, and so on. Provide information for mutual funds including the fund's past performance and the strength of the sectors emphasized in the fund, bonds, precious metals, and so on.

*Your presentation should be complete with overheads or flipcharts to represent your information graphically. Remember, at the same time you are presenting your portfolio, you are also giving your fellow students valuable investment tips and techniques for investment analysis and portfolio development.*

*Students with a limited knowledge of securities markets:* limit your portfolios to stocks. This will allow you to complete the exercise while not requiring a detailed knowledge of the securities markets.

*Students with a more in-depth knowledge of securities markets:* develop portfolios with several types investments. The following information should be given for each type of investment:

### STOCKS

Price/earnings ratio and other annual report data relevant to the soundness of the company

Dividends

Charts based on past performance to identify price trends and cyclical movements

Special details about the company that might make it attractive, including (a) technological breakthroughs and new products, (b) a prospective takeover, (c) estimated profits, (d) book value per share that is significantly higher than the trading price of the shares, and (e) the past and expected performance of the sector (such as oil and gas, biotechnology, or airlines) of your stocks.

### BONDS

Interest rates (fixed or not)

Whether or not the interest is taxed

Maturity date

Yield to maturity

The likelihood of the bond being called in

Par value versus present value

Bond interest rate versus its present price

FUTURES: [*For advanced students only.*]

### Currency Futures

Explain how the instrument works and why you have chosen the currency you have.

### Commodity Futures

Explain how the instrument works and why you have chosen the commodities you have.

PUTS AND CALLS: [*For advanced students only.*]

### Index Puts and Calls

Explain the instrument and why you have chosen the investment you have.

Give the market prognosis for the period up until the expiration date of your puts or calls. Explain the advantages and disadvantages with this type of investment.

### Individual Stock Puts and Calls

Give the same information asked for under Index Puts and Calls.

MUTUAL FUNDS

Explain the investment strategy of the mutual fund you have chosen in terms of the holdings of the mutual fund.

Discuss the advantages and disadvantages of mutual funds.

PRECIOUS METALS

Explain which instrument you have chosen (such as bullion, coins, certificates, or precious metals mutual funds) and justify this choice.

Predict the trend for this instrument over the period for this exercise and discuss factors that will influence this trend.

## LANGUAGE MASTERY EXERCISE

### Language Development: Stocks

Use the terms in the lists below to describe the fluctuations of the stock prices represented in Figures 2-1 and 2-2.

| Adjective | Noun | Verb | Adverb |
|---|---|---|---|
| a rapid | increase | to increase | rapidly |
| a substantial | rise | to rise | substantially |
| a steady | growth | to grow | steadily |
| a great | improvement | to improve | greatly |
| a slight | decrease | to decrease | slightly |
| a gradual | deterioration | to deteriorate | gradually |
| a sudden | drop | to drop | suddenly |

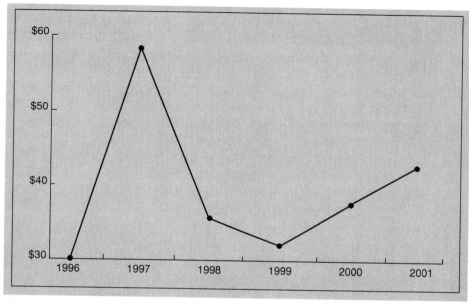

**Figure 2-1**   Transnational Financial Services Stock Price Fluctuation

| a slow | decline | to decline | slowly |
| a dramatic | fall | to fall | dramatically |
| a noticeable | change | to change | noticeably |

# VOCABULARY

The following vocabulary list should give you the basic vocabulary to solve this case. However, you should also get a copy of an investment guide to improve your understanding of investment instruments. One such guide is *The Wall Street Journal: Guide to Understanding Money and Markets* (1990), available from Access Press Ltd., 10 East 53rd St., New York, NY 10022. The *Wall Street Journal* has also produced a videotape version of *Understanding Money and Markets*.

## STOCKS (BRITISH: *SHARES*)

**blue chips,** *n.*   Stocks in large companies (such as AT&T) that are consistently profitable.

**common stock,** *n.*   Stock in a company that has second priority in terms of dividend distribution. **Preferred stock** holders receive dividends first and then the remainder of funds allotted to dividends (if any) is distributed to the common stockholders.

**dividend,** *n.*   A percentage of the profits of a company paid to stockholders. Stocks that consistently pay high dividends are known as **income stocks** and are generally considered a more conservative investment compared to **growth**

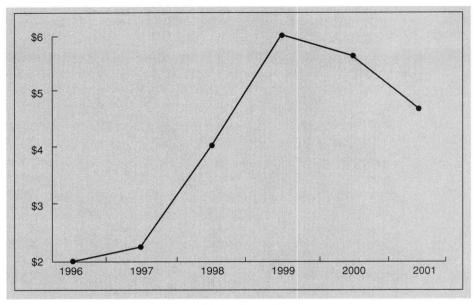

**Figure 2-2**   Wildcat Drilling Services Stock Price Fluctuations

**stocks,** which are bought in hopes that the price of the stock will rise. Growth companies often reinvest their profits and pay little or no dividends.

**fundamental analysis,** *n.*   An analysis of a stock based on the company's financial condition, products, and their sectors' growth potential.

**par,** *n.*   The face value of the shares at the time they were issued.

**penny stocks,** *n.*   Highly speculative, low-priced stocks for which the investment risk but also the profit potential is high.

**price-earnings (P-E) ratio,** *n.*   The ratio of the price of one share of stock to the annual earnings of the company per share. On the New York Stock Exchange, an average P-E ratio of about 18 : 1 or lower is considered positive.

**technical analysis,** *n.*   An analysis of a stock based on technical factors such as cyclical movement and price trends.

### BONDS

**asset-backed bonds,** *n.*   Bonds backed by assets. Examples are **mortgage-backed bonds** and **equipment bonds**.

**bearer bonds,** *n.*   Bonds whose owner usually claims interest payments by sending in coupons.

**bills,** *n.*   Bonds that mature in one year or less.

**bond rating,** *n.* Rating services such as Moody's and Standard and Poor's rate bonds on a scale of AAA (highest quality) to C (lowest quality). (Remember that if the issuing organization goes bankrupt there is a strong likelihood that you will lose your money.) Bond ratings will also affect yield, as bonds with high ratings usually pay lower interest rates.

**bond yield,** *n.* Not the same as the interest rate. At par value (say $1000) the interest rate and yield will be the same, let us say 8 percent. However, if the value drops to $800, the yield will rise, as the holder will still receive $80 (8 percent of the par value of $1000), even though the bond only costs $800 — producing a yield of 10 percent.

**callable bonds,** *n.* Bonds that can be **redeemed** (*v.*, paid off) prior to the due date.

**convertible bonds,** *n.* Bonds that pay interest but also give the right to convert the bonds to the company's stocks as a means of repayment of the loan. The terms of conversion are stated in the bond agreement. Of particular importance is the conversion price — how much will have to be paid for each share of stock when converting the bond to stock.

**coupons,** *n.* Attached numbered or dated sections of the bond, which provide a method of redeeming the interest due at various intervals.

**debenture bond,** *n.* A bond that is backed only by the credit of the organization issuing it and not by any assets guaranteeing its repayment.

**discount,** *n.* A bond that is selling for less than its par value.

**interest rate,** *n.* The percentage of the par value that will be paid to the bondholder on a regular basis.

**junk bonds,** *n.* A low-grade bond with high interest, a highly popular invention of the 1980s. Many of these junk bonds are now in default.

**maturity date,** *n.* When the loan will be paid off (that is, the bondholder will get his or her money back).

**par value,** *n.* The amount the bondholder will be paid at the bond's maturity.

**premium,** *n.* A bond that is selling for more than its par value.

**registered bonds,** *n.* Bonds registered in someone's name; interest payments to the owner occur automatically.

**T-bills (British: guilts),** *n.* Bonds issued by the United States Treasury or the Bank of England.

**zero-coupon bonds,** *n.* Bonds that pay no interest while the loan is outstanding; however, the interest does **accrue** (*v.*, to build up) and is paid out at maturity. To encourage investors to buy these bonds they are offered at **deep discounts** (prices much lower than their par value.)

## MUTUAL FUNDS

**diversification,** *n.* One reason to buy mutual funds. A mutual fund is a portfolio that is managed by professionals and spreads the investment across a wide number of stocks, allowing for **diversified investment**. A person who buys into a mutual fund buys a small part of an already diversified portfolio and receives professional management services at the same time.

**load funds,** *n.*    Funds that charge a commission (up to 8.5 percent) when you invest and withdraw money.

**no-load funds,** *n.*    Funds that do not charge sales commissions. However, *all* funds charge a management fee of from 0.5 percent to 1 percent, and some charge a withdrawal fee.

## FUNDS AND THEIR OBJECTIVES

**aggressive growth funds,** *n.*    Funds that invest in newer companies or companies with new management that the fund's managers feel can turn these companies around. The potential price rise is high, but safety is low to very low. The goal is maximum price rise.

**balanced funds,** *n.*    Funds that invest in a combination of bonds, and preferred and common stock. The goal is current income and long-term growth (price rise) and safety.

**fixed income and equity income funds,** *n.*    Funds that invest in stocks and bonds that provide high interest and dividends. The goal is high current income, but the disadvantage is low capital gains potential.

**growth and income funds,** *n.*    Funds that invest in companies with a solid track record and a record of dividend payment. Yield is both from **capital gains** (price rise) and dividends. Both the safety and potential income are moderate. Your goal is a combination of price rise and dividend income.

**growth funds,** *n.*    Funds that invest in common stock of settled companies. The potential price rise is high, but the safety is low. The goal is high **capital gains** (profit made by the increased price of your stock).

**money market and government money market funds,** *n.*    Funds that invest in short-term debt securities. The goal is current income and maximum safety. The disadvantage is no potential price rise.

## FUTURES

**commodities,** *n.*    Raw materials that go into the production of products. Examples are oil, pork bellies, grains, and precious metals (such as gold, silver, and platinum).

**futures contracts,** *n.*    Contracts made now for a transaction in the future. The main details of the future are the commodity to be bought, the future price, and the future date by which the transaction has to be exercised.

**to go long,** *v.*    To take a buyer's position.

**to go short,** *v.*    To take a seller's position.

**hedgers** and **speculators,** *n.*    The two major players in the futures market. *Hedgers,* such as farmers, for example, are just trying to insure getting a fixed price for their goods to insure a predetermined profit margin at a future date. Other hedgers could be manufacturers who will need commodities for future production and want to factor in costs now as part of their cost accounting. *Speculators* try to make a profit by guessing where various commodity markets are going.

**leverage,** *n.* Using a little money to control a much larger investment. For example, if you were going to buy 42,000 gallons of oil you would have to pay around $20,000 at today's price. But buying a future will give you the right to buy this amount at a future date. Let us say that the future to buy 42,000 gallons of oil at $22 a barrel costs $100. Let us also say that oil shot up to $25 a barrel and your future was worth $3 (actually, it would probably be worth more if people expected the price of oil to continue to go up). A barrel of oil is 42 gallons, so your one contract (see definition below) means you can buy 1,000 barrels of oil at $22 a barrel and sell it immediately for $25 a barrel, thus realizing a profit of $3,000 on a $100 investment. This is much more than if you had bought and stored the 42,000 gallons of oil. The disadvantage of futures is that if the price goes the other way, you can be forced to buy commodities at a higher price than the current market price.

**one contract,** *n.* Represents the right to buy or sell a specific quantity of a commodity. For example, one contract of oil = 42,000 gallons; one contract of wheat = 5,000 bushels.

## OPTIONS

**calls,** *n.* The right to buy a certain commodity, stock, or currency at an agreed price, called the strike price, up until an agreed time, called the expiration date.

**index options,** *n.* You can buy puts and calls on the index, which means that you are betting that the index will go up (*calls*) or down (*puts*). The standard index options in the United States are on the Standard and Poor's Index. Think how much money you would have made in October 1987 during the market crash if you had bought puts!

**options,** *n.* Like futures, options offer the right to buy or sell something at a designated date, but you do not have to exercise this option. If, for example, you have an option to buy a security at $20 and it is selling at $18 at the expiration date, there is no point in exercising your option. Thus, you don't, and you simply lose the money you have paid for the option.

**option premium,** *n.* A form of commission that the buyer pays the seller for this kind of transaction. However, the seller is committed to meet the terms of the transaction if the buyer chooses to exercise his or her option. If the option gives the right to buy a security at a certain price, the seller must obtain that security at the market price and sell it to the holder of the option at the price agreed upon in the option. For example, if the holder of an option to buy a security at $18 exercises the option when the security is at $20, he or she gains $2 per option at the expense of the seller, who must obtain the security at $20 and sell it at $18 to the holder of the option.

**puts,** *n.* The right to sell according to the same conditions described for calls.

# FINANCE

## Other People's Money:
## Larry the Liquidator vs.
## New England Wire
## and Cable

## CULTURAL BACKGROUND: FREE ENTERPRISE

The American play *Other People's Money* illustrates the extremes of a free enterprise system in which corporate raiders take over a company against the company's will and *strip* it (sell off or close down divisions of the company for quick profit). The play raises questions about how "free" a free enterprise system that lets a few rich people profit at the expense of the many who lose their jobs really is. It also raises questions about the need for more restrictions on the activities of corporate raiders. What has happened to the distinction between making an honest profit from investment and making a fortune by stripping a company?

# CASE

This case is based on Jerry Sterner's play *Other People's Money*, which has now been made into a movie of the same name. A prerequisite for solving this case is to have read the play or seen the movie. If you chose the latter, remember that Hollywood has naturally chosen a happy ending, whereas, in the play, the factory in question is shut down and all the workers lose their jobs — a more realistic conclusion to this scenario. As you will discover, Larry "the Liquidator" Garfinkle is a Wall Street raider who thrives on takeovers, usually hostile ones. He spots companies, such as New England Wire and Cable, whose book value per share far exceeds their stock price. He starts buying up the shares in a move to take over the company. His buy-up pleases the stockholders, who see him as the reason for the increased value of their stock and often support him in the takeover.

The negative aspect of Larry the Liquidator's activities is that his only real concern is the book value of the company; thus, once the takeover is completed, he is likely to strip the company, closing down unprofitable or marginally profitable operations and selling off other operations. As his nickname indicates, he liquidates companies to realize their book value, an operation which can result in quick profits. Another result, however, is unemployment and the ripple effect that it creates in the communities where factories are closed. The leveraged buyouts necessary to take over some companies can produce another negative effect as well. The resulting debt level makes streamlining of operations and modernizing the equipment impossible, because there is no capital available for this due to the high debt levels. Ironically, the streamlining of operations is often given as the reason for the takeover, but such streamlining is made impossible by the debt levels incurred in the takeover.

## POINTS FOR DISCUSSION

After having seen or read the movie or play, you should be ready to discuss the following topics:

1. Do you feel, as does Jorgensen, that the board of directors has a social responsibility to the workers and the local community? Or do you side with Garfinkle, maintaining that the directors' only responsibility is to the stockholders and thus to maximize profits? If you side with Jorgensen, how far are you willing to go in subsidizing jobs at a factory that is losing money?

2. After his buy-up is temporarily stopped by a court injunction, Garfinkle complains about the present state of capitalism. He rants on about lawyers and others who are destroying the capitalist system. He feels that anyone should have the right to buy out any company he wishes. He feels that the fact that he is not allowed to buy up and do whatever he wants with a company (including selling off part of it for a quick profit and even closing down factories, thus throwing people into unemployment) shows that the capitalist system is being destroyed.

   a) First, discuss Garfinkle's concept of a free market and whether or not you agree with it.

   b) Second, discuss whether it is government regulations, such as the injunction imposed on Garfinkle, or raiders like Garfinkle who pose the greatest threat to the capitalist system. Be specific about what restrictions, if any, you feel should be placed on raiders like Garfinkle.

3. Would Garfinkle's activities be allowed in your country?

## CASE ACTIVITIES

### Roleplay: New England Wire and Cable's Annual Meeting

Dramatize the annual meeting of New England Wire and Cable. Annual meetings give the stockholders the opportunity to voice their opinions on issues of importance to the company. In this meeting, the stockholders have to decide whether they support the current management headed by Jorgensen or the team headed by Garfinkle. One team of students will assume the roles of the present management, including Jorgensen, Coles, a representative from the workers, and a local politician. All of them will speak in favor of retaining the present board of directors. The second team will take on the roles of Garfinkle and his lawyers. After both sides have presented their cases, the stockholders, who will be played by the remaining members of the class, can ask questions of the two teams. Finally, the stockholders will vote for one of the two teams to assume the management of New England Wire and Cable. They can either be assigned the same amount of

# REPORT FOR THE STOCKHOLDERS MEETING*
February 27, 200__

## Market Prognosis

As loyal stockholders, many of you know that New England Wire and Cable has performed only moderately well for the past decade. However, we have survived these difficult times and have great plans and prospects for the future. We have survived numerous recessions, a major depression and two World Wars. To allow a company with such a history of survival to be taken over and broken up for its value by a man who cares for nothing but money would be devastating to this community and detrimental to the industrial infrastructure of our nation. Our industrial strength and manufacturing capabilities continue to be stolen and disbanded by these mergers and acquisitions specialists interested only in making money. They make nothing and contribute even less to our economy. At least the robber barons of old left something in their wake. These men leave nothing but a blizzard of paper to cover the pain.

Can you, in good conscience, allow this man to destroy this company just because its value dead is greater than its value alive at this point in time? While this may be true for now, are you willing to sacrifice the possibility of even greater future benefits for a single payment? The new $150 billion transportation bill has designated federal funds to be spent on rebuilding our nation's highways and bridges. This means a potential for New England Wire and Cable to operate with considerable profits. As you know, the parent company, New England Wire and Cable, has been operating with a loss recently, including a $3 million loss last year, while the remaining companies have been operating with significant profits, which allowed us to report a net income of $125,000. However, the construction activity that the transportation bill will generate will result, according to our prognosis, in a profit of $1 million already this year. The estimated profits for New England Wire and Cable based on the activity generated by the transportation bill <u>alone</u> will be $10 million over the next five years.

This possible takeover has also sparked us, as the management team, to examine our operations and determine what we can do to improve the op-

*continued*

---

*A report to the stockholders is an evaluation by management of the past year's performance of the company and a prediction of its future success.

*continued*

erations and profitability of our company. We have concluded that it will be entirely feasible for us to restructure and consolidate in such a manner that we will be able to save significant amounts of money through a reduction in operating expenses.

While the offer presented to all of you stockholders may be very attractive, I hope that you will be able to look beyond the immediate capital gains and vote for the future of New England Wire and Cable, our local community, and American industry.

ANDREW JORGENSEN
Chairman

shares or varying amounts of shares. After the vote is taken, students selected randomly will be asked to justify why they voted as they did.

The accompanying report states management's analysis of the company's present financial situation based on the balance sheet shown in Figure 3-1 and a forecast of future prospects. Naturally, it favors the present management's position.

Garfinkle's argument appeals to the stockholders on the basis of quick profit in that he will offer more money for each share than its current value on the stock exchange.

## LANGUAGE MASTERY EXERCISE

### Meeting Terminology and Procedures

The following statements include standard meeting terminology, which Jorgensen would use in *chairing* (leading) the meeting. Learn them in preparation for your dramatization of the meeting.

#### OPENING THE MEETING

I declare the meeting open.

#### APPROVAL OF THE ANNUAL REPORT

Are there any additions, corrections, or questions concerning the annual report and the accounts?

#### THE AGENDA

The main item on the agenda is the question of the election of a new board of directors.

# NEW ENGLAND WIRE AND CABLE
Balance Sheet
December 31, 20____

## Assets

**Current Assets**

| | | |
|---|---|---|
| Cash | $10,000,000 | |
| Accounts Receivable | 6,000,000 | |
| Inventories | 12,000,000 | |
| U.S. Govt. and other | | |
| marketable securities | 2,000,000 | |
| **Total Current Assets** | | **$30,000,000** |

**Property, Plant, and Equipment**

| | | |
|---|---|---|
| Land | $100,000 | |
| Equipment | 120,000,000 | |
| Building | 500,000 | |
| Accumulated Depreciation: | | |
| Equipment | 60,000,000 | |
| Accumulated Depreciation: | | |
| Building | 400,000 | |
| **Total PP and E** | | **$60,200,000** |
| **Total Assets** | | **$90,200,000** |

## Liabilities and Stockholders' Equity

**Current Liabilities**

| | | |
|---|---|---|
| Accounts Payable | $2,200,000 | |
| Accrued Taxes (other than | | |
| income taxes) | 250,000 | |
| Accrued Compensation and | | |
| Benefits | 50,000 | |
| Advances from Customers | | |
| on Contract | 2,500,000 | |
| **Total Current Liabilities** | | **5,000,000** |

*continued*

**Figure 3-1**   Balance sheet

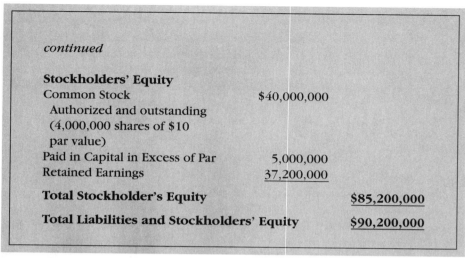

**continued**

**Stockholders' Equity**

| | | |
|---|---|---|
| Common Stock | $40,000,000 | |
| Authorized and outstanding (4,000,000 shares of $10 par value) | | |
| Paid in Capital in Excess of Par | 5,000,000 | |
| Retained Earnings | 37,200,000 | |
| **Total Stockholder's Equity** | | **$85,200,000** |
| **Total Liabilities and Stockholders' Equity** | | **$90,200,000** |

**Figure 3-1**    Balance sheet *(continued)*

### NEW ENGLAND WIRE AND CABLE

Combined Statement of Income
and Retained Earnings
For the Year Ended December 31, 20____

| | |
|---|---|
| Sales Revenue | $20,000,000 |
| Cost of Goods Sold | 13,750,000 |
| Depreciation Expense | 2,000,000 |
| Compliance Expense | 2,500,000 |
| Selling and Administrative Expenses | 1,625,000 |
| **Net Income** | **$125,000** |
| Retained Earnings Jan. 1 | 37,200,000 |
| Cash Dividends Declared and Paid | 125,000 |
| Retained Earnings Dec. 31 | $37,200,000 |

Combined Statement of Income and Retained Earnings

**OPENING THE FLOOR TO DEBATE**

After both teams have made their presentations, an announcement such as the following is made.

The floor is hereby open to debate.

### GIVING THE FLOOR

Having the floor means having the right to speak.

> Mr. X now has the floor.

### POINT OF ORDER

When someone questions whether proper meeting procedure is being followed, he or she is raising a point of order.

> Point of order, Mr. Chairman; I believe I was next on the list of speakers, not Ms. Y.

### POINT OF INFORMATION

Inserting a point of information allows someone the right to ask a question relevant to the present discussion without putting his or her name on the speakers' list and waiting for his or her turn.

> Point of information. I would like to know what Mr. Garfinkle intends to do with this factory here in Pawtucket if he takes over the company.

### KEEPING ORDER

If someone does not adhere to the proper rules of procedure for a meeting, the chairperson can rule that person is out of order.

> Order, order. Mr. W, you are out of order. It is not your turn to speak.

### MAKING A PROPOSAL OR A MOTION

> I propose that we. . . .
> I move that we. . . .

### SECONDING A PROPOSAL

Once a formal proposal or motion has been made, it must have a *second* — that is, one other person who supports the proposal or motion.

> I second the motion.

### CALLING FOR THE VOTE

When the chairperson or any other participant in the meeting with voting rights feels that an item has been discussed sufficiently, he or she can call for the vote. If there are no objections, then the chairperson can move on to the vote. If there are objections, a vote must be taken to conclude discussion. If over 50 percent of those present with voting rights vote for concluding the discussion, then they can go on to the final vote. If not, the discussion of the item in question continues.

PARTICIPANT: I call for the vote.
CHAIRPERSON: Are there any objections? [No objections are raised.] Hearing no objections, we will now proceed to the vote.

**SECRET BALLOT**

The vote will be determined by secret ballot, so please fill out your ballots and hand them in to Mr. Coles.

**THE RESULT OF THE VOTE**

The ballots have been counted and the results are: Mr. Jorgensen and the present board of directors,          votes; Mr. Garfinkle          votes.

**ADJOURNING THE MEETING**

After all business is completed, the meeting is *adjourned* (called to a close).

The meeting is adjourned.

All students should be familiar with the above terms. The person who plays Jorgensen will actively use all of them during the meeting.

# WRITING: RESPONSES TO THE ANNUAL MEETING

One group must take notes from the meeting and write a report summarizing the two presentations and the result of the vote to be sent to the stockholders. Another group can write a newspaper article about the meeting. The article should give a brief summary of the two side's positions, questions that were raised by stockholders, the result of the vote, and what the decision will mean for the local community. The teacher will assign these two writing projects to two groups prior to the meeting.

The competing factions should write up the presentations they gave at the annual meeting, and the remaining students should write a justification of why they voted as they did.

# VOCABULARY

**acquisition,** *n.*   The act of acquiring a business.

**assets,** *n.*   All things owned by a person or business that have some monetary value.

**book value,** *n.*   The value of an asset or group of assets of a business as shown in its account books.

**buy-out,** *n.*   The buying of the entire interest in a business.

**buy-up,** *n.*   The buying of as many of the shares of a company as one can buy, usually to get control of the company.

**capital,** *n.*   Accumulated wealth or property used in the production of further wealth.

**cash cow,** *n.*   A company which can be "milked" (take out as much money as possible).

**cash flow,** *n.*   Cash generated and used in operations.

**Chapter 11** (American), *n.* A provision in the federal bankruptcy law which allows a financially troubled company to postpone payment to creditors while it works out a plan to repay them.

**court injunction,** *n.* A court order prohibiting an action (in this case preventing Garfinkle from buying more New England Wire and Cable shares).

**debt,** *n.* The amount, usually of money, owed by one person or business to others, known as **creditors**.

**healthy company,** *n.* A financially sound company.

**hostile takeover,** *n.* Any takeover unwanted by the present management.

**in play,** *adj.* Used to describe a company which is a target of a takeover.

**junk bonds,** *n.* Low-grade bonds with high interest often used for leveraged buy-outs.

**lean and mean,** *adj.* Used to describe a company or organization that reduces its work force by getting rid of "deadwood" (unproductive employees) in order to be more profitable.

**leveraged buy-outs (LBO),** *n.* Buying a company with borrowed funds, using the company itself as collateral.

**to liquidate,** *v.* To sell off a company's assets.

**M and A,** *n.* Mergers and acquisitions.

**merger,** *n.* The combining of two or more companies.

**raiders,** *n.* People who look for companies that they can buy cheaply, often with the thought of stripping them.

**ripple effect,** *n.* The spreading effects caused by an event.

**shark repellent,** *n.* Something that makes a company in play less attractive to a raider. For example, if the board of directors substantially increased the dividend, it would encourage the stockholders to hold onto their stocks while reducing the capital in the company, thus making a raid not only more difficult but less attractive.

**to strip,** *v.* To buy up cheaply companies that are showing poor results, then sell off the assets one by one at a profit and close down the business.

**to take private,** *v.* A move by management to buy up the stock of its company so that it is not traded on the stock exchange. This is done to prevent a hostile takeover and is usually financed through a leveraged buy-out.

**takeover,** *n.* The act of gaining control of a company by making its shareholders a general offer, through an action called a **takeover bid**.

**tender offer takeover,** *n.* A hostile takeover not negotiated with the management of the target firm. The offer is usually made directly to the stockholders of the targeted firm.

**white knight,** *n.* A friendly acquirer who is sought by the target of a hostile takeover bid.

**working capital,** *n.* The excess of total current assets over total current liabilities. It represents the net amount of a company's relatively liquid resources and the margin of safety available to meet the financial demands of the operating cycle.

## REFERENCES

The following articles provide important information for the class discussion and the solution of this case. You should read them or similar articles.

Barlett, Donald L. and James B. Steele. "Simplicity Pattern: Irresistible to Raiders," In *America: What Went Wrong?* Andrews and McMeel. Kansas City: 1992.

Faltermayer, Edmund. "The Deal Decade: Verdict on the '80s." *Fortune* (August 26, 1991): 58–70.

# MARKETING
# NEGOTIATIONS

## Long-range Golf Equipment Seeks a Distributor

# CULTURAL BACKGROUND: CUSTOMS IN AMERICAN NEGOTIATION

Each culture has different ways of approaching negotiations. Being a negotiator in international negotiations requires an understanding of the way other nations' negotiating teams think and function. Books have been written on the subject of national differences in negotiating, but it is important to remember that even within a given culture, each negotiating team will vary from national norms. In negotiating, one must be aware of national traits and customs, while looking for individual variation. However, certain traits do appear, and the following list describes typical American traits.

**TIME:** Negotiations should begin on time. "Time is money" and thus negotiations should not take more time than necessary. This means that American negotiators are sometimes frustrated by what they may perceive as "Latin time," in which meetings tend not to start at the scheduled time. They may also be frustrated by the Arab tendency to want to establish friendship before negotiations can really begin or to allow negotiations to be interrupted by other business. Americans are very goal-oriented, set up time schedules, and hope to conclude negotiations within those time schedules; as a result, they can appear to be impatient or "pushy" (to pressure the opposite side to come to an agreement).

**CONTRACT:** Americans look at negotiations as a means of reaching a contract; thus they tend to stress legality and the binding nature of a written document setting out rights and duties that can be upheld in a court of law. Other cultures look at negotiations as a means of establishing a relationship which will be the basis of future business arrangements. For Americans, a contract is the sign of closing a deal, while for some cultures it begins a relationship. The American emphasis on a binding legal document may be interpreted by other cultures as a lack of trust.

**PROTOCOL:** *Protocol* refers to the formal aspects of negotiations. It includes such matters as how to address people (by first or last names), the use of titles, dress, gift giving, exchange of business cards, respect for age, the shape of the negotiating table and the placement of negotiators, and so on. Americans are informal and might overlook the importance of protocol, which can be interpreted as impoliteness.

**DECISION MAKING:** The decision-making process might be individual, authoritarian, or by consensus. While in American teams, the decision-making power often lies in the hands of individuals, other cultures emphasize group agreement, or *consensus*, which naturally takes longer.

**DIRECT OR INDIRECT COMMUNICATION:** Americans value directness and tend to say right out what they mean. For other cultures, especially those concerned with saving face, such directness can be embarrassing. Americans tend to ask direct questions and expect direct answers, whereas other cultures often respond through signs, gestures, and what may appear to Americans as vague comments.

**CONFLICT:** Conflict is not seen as necessarily negative for American negotiators; rather, it is often seen as an expected part of the negotiating process. Negative emotions are perhaps more acceptable to Americans than in some Asian cultures. Thus, American negotiators can appear more confrontational than their Asian counterparts.

**WIN-WIN VERSUS WIN-LOSE:** Win-win refers to a win for both sides, while win-lose describes a situation in which one side benefits at the other side's expense. The emphasis in the United States on winning may tend to push American negotiators toward win-lose strategies. Another factor is the U. S. tendency to emphasize the individual rather than the group, which can lead American negotiators to value individual interests more highly than collective interests.

**BODY LANGUAGE:** Americans look each other directly in the eyes, which may be considered impolite in other countries. On the other hand, if someone does *not* look an American negotiator directly in the eyes, the American may consider this a reason for distrust. Signs and gestures may have less importance in American negotiations than in negotiations from cultures where indirect communication is important.

# CASE

Distributing your products is one of the major aspects of marketing. Although it is possible to open up a sales office in foreign countries, most companies cannot afford the expense and choose instead to work with a foreign marketing agent. Dealing with an agent means that you can take advantage of his or her knowledge of consumer habits, advertising approaches, and existing distribution channels. However, this also involves negotiating contracts, which is the subject of this case.

Negotiating a contract for an ongoing business relationship is a delicate matter. Unlike selling a used car to someone whom you probably will never see again, an agency agreement must be mutually satisfying if you expect your agent to make a 100 percent effort to sell and distribute your products. Thus, pressuring the agent to give up $\frac{1}{4}$ percent on his or her commission might be like winning the battle, but losing the war. You win the $\frac{1}{4}$ percent, but weaken the business relationship. Naturally, you want to achieve the best possible result for your company, but at the same time you do not want to poison the ongoing business relationship on which your future success depends. Negotiations are a case of give-and-take, and good negotiators are sensitive to the priorities and requirements of the other side. Beating the other side into submission, even though it may give you a sense of victory, is certainly not the way to establish the atmosphere of mutual understanding necessary for an ongoing business relationship.

With this in mind, any contract preparation must take into consideration both parties in the agreement. Included in this case is a negotiation worksheet that you should fill out in advance of the actual negotiations you will conduct. What follows is a brief summary of how to go about filling out the negotiations worksheet.

## I. Goals

In this particular case, you are going to be negotiating rates of commission, an exclusive versus a nonexclusive contract, a fixed price contract versus a flexible price contract, and the covering of advertising, shipping, and storage costs.

You must determine which of these items are high priority, which are medium priority, and which are low priority. For items in the latter two categories, you must determine how far you are willing to go in making concessions and what you expect to get in return for your concessions. Some of your low-priority points may be used as trading cards to be given away in their entirety in return for concessions from the other side. However, you should have a clear notion of what you expect to get in return.

## II. An Assessment of the Balance of Power

Despite what was stated about the necessity of a mutually satisfying agreement, each side will evaluate the strengths and weaknesses of the other party involved in the negotiations in order to avoid being "steamrollered" (dominated by the other side). Assessment of the balance of power will help you in determining your strategy, including how much pressure you want to put on the other party (while not forgetting the importance of a mutually satisfying agreement). Some basic questions you have to ask are (a) How much do we need them, and (b) What alternatives do we have, and how viable are those alternatives? Naturally, you must also ask how much the other side needs *you*.

## III. Determining Your Strategy

Your strategy should be a result of your decisions on points I and II. You must determine where the *bottom line* is; that is, how far you are willing to go to obtain an agreement, and what do you ideally hope to achieve? The final contract will fall somewhere between these two extremes, and charting them will give you a tool to evaluate the result. Maybe you will achieve a result closer to your ideal contract. There is nothing wrong with shooting for an ideal result, as long as your goals do not appear unreasonable, and as long as when you do meet resistance, you do not maintain an inflexible position. Ultimatums rarely get you anywhere.

Determine your opening position and the mood you hope to create. As mentioned in the worksheet, there are degrees of positions from hard-line to softer stances. Remember, however, this opening position will determine the atmosphere for the rest of the negotiations. So choose it with care.

Determine what issues you want to negotiate first. This will help set the tone. If you take the low-priority issues first, you will create a tone of flexibility and good faith. You may be able to create a tone of flexibility on both sides, making it easier for you to get what you want on the high-priority items later. Your strategy here would be to suggest that you have shown good faith and that now it is the other side's turn.

On the other hand, starting with your high-priority items will let you know early in the negotiations what the other side's stance is on those items most important to you. Remember, the sensitive negotiator will constantly be listening for clues as to the other side's position and priorities. Starting with your high-priority items may give you necessary clues as to the other party's position. If you do not meet resistance, go for the maximum, and once you have attained what you want, you can be flexible on some of the other items to "sweeten the pot," thus creating an atmosphere of mutual satisfaction. Remember, while you are negotiating, you are constantly listening for clues as to the other side's priorities, as well as how they perceive the balance of power. Thus, in the beginning, you might "go fishing" just to see what "bait" interests the other side. Once you see what interests them, you may be able to formulate a clear picture of their strategy.

This has hardly been an exhaustive study of negotiation strategy, and you should study the subject in more detail and discuss your experiences and strategies. However, this should give you enough information to solve this case. So fill out the negotiations worksheet, determine your strategy, and be sensitive to possible clues during the negotiations.

## POINTS FOR DISCUSSION

1. Discuss any differences in approaches to negotiations within your culture in contrast to those described above. What problems could such differences create in negotiations with American negotiators?

2. Groups should be assigned a role as either Long-range or X YZ. Then each group should discuss strategies for the case individually, including the following:

   a) What tone would you set for the negotiations (hard-line or flexible) and how would you do it?

   b) What are the most important items to be negotiated (commissions, an exclusive versus a nonexclusive contract, and so on)?

   c) Would you start the negotiations with your "musts" (high-priority items) or your "trading cards" (low-priority items); why?

   d) What is your attitude toward the opposing side, and how will that affect your negotiations strategy?

## CASE ACTIVITIES

### Negotiating a Distribution Contract

Long-range Sporting Goods, Inc., of Elizabeth, New Jersey, has contacted XYZ Distributors as a possible agent for their golf clubs and bags in your country (if the case is solved in the United States, choose a country for XYZ). Long-range produces a mid-to-luxury range of clubs and bags. Their emphasis, however, is on the up-market segment, and they emphasize quality. Thus, they are very interested in pene-trating your country's market. Although a relative newcomer to the market, Long-range has enjoyed rapid success in the United States. By sponsoring some young and successful golf pros on the U.S. tour, they brought their sales from a modest $10 million in 1991 to an annual sales of $90 million last year. They feel that they have established their reputation in the U.S. market well enough to allow them to attempt a foreign market penetration. However, since their U.S. market is expand-ing and their profits are good, they do not wish to risk an expansion at any price.

XYZ Distributors is a medium-size distributor of U.S. sports equipment. They do not distribute any major brands of golf equipment, such as Wilson or Spalding. However, they have signed a three-year contract with Tiger Shark and Hurricane which expires at the end of this year. They have enjoyed much success with Tiger Shark and Hurricane and have captured 5 percent of the total market in your country. However, they are looking for an opportunity to get in on the ground floor with Long-range. They have connections with pro shops and up-mar-ket golf shops, but have avoided shops at the lower end of the market.

For this case, half the groups will represent Long-range and the other half XYZ Distributors. You can have as many negotiations going on at once as you have teams and space.

The basic items in the contract to be decided are the following:

1. *An exclusive contract versus a nonexclusive contract.* In an exclusive contract, Long-range would demand that XYZ distribute only their line of golf equipment, thus dropping Tiger Shark and Hurricane. However, if XYZ accepts this demand, they could in turn demand exclusive rights to be the sole distributor of Long-range clubs and bags in this market.

2. *A fixed price contract versus a flexible price contract.* In a fixed price contract, the price of the goods is fixed once a year. In a flexible price contract, Long-range reserves the right to raise the price of clubs in accordance with a rise in production costs. Naturally, the distributor could, and probably would, have to pass the rise on to the golf shops. This could lead to friction between the distributor and the golf shops.

3. *The rate of commission to be paid the distributor based on FOB (free on board) New York.* You can negotiate a flat commission, such as 7 percent on all sales, or a sliding scale, such as 7 percent on sales up to $10 million and 8 percent on sales from $10 million to $20 million, and so on.

4. *The covering of advertising costs and procedures for approving advertising campaigns.* Who should cover these costs, and who will have the final deci-sion about advertising campaigns?

5. *The covering of shipping expenses FOB, New York or CIF, your country (see vocabulary list) and storage costs in your country.* Who should cover these costs?

You should negotiate a contract that establishes the conditions for these five points.

### Presentation

Each group should be prepared to make a presentation describing (a) the contract arrived at, (b) their negotiating team's strategies and goals, and (c) how successful they were in attaining their goals in the final contract.

## LANGUAGE MASTERY EXERCISE

Use the following Negotiations Worksheet and Report Format outline to organize, and report on, your negotiations process.

### Negotiations Worksheet

**I. YOUR GOALS:** (A listing of the priority of the different areas to be negotiated.)

A. Decide on your high-priority items, and whether or not there is any room for negotiation concerning them.
B. Set bottom lines for those items that are negotiable.
C. Decide on "trading cards," (low-priority items) if any, and what you expect to get in return for giving up these items.
D. Decide in general what you expect to get in return for any concessions you make.
E. Set a bottom line for the contract as a whole.

**II. AN ASSESSMENT OF THE BALANCE OF POWER**

A. Evaluate what the other side stands to gain by this association, and what you stand to gain. Be sure to make a fair evaluation, in order to avoid a false sense of power.
   1. Evaluate what you can offer them in this deal, what they can offer you, and who needs whom the most.
B. Decide what you can say or do in the negotiations to impress on the other side your position of power (remembering all the time that you are walking a fine line between trying to attain your goals as completely as possible while still reaching a mutually satisfying agreement).

**III. DETERMINATION OF STRATEGY BASED ON I AND II**

A. Determine your opening stance, and make a summary of your opening statement.
   1. Is your position going to be flexible or hard-line?
   2. Do you have the power to enforce your position?

B. Decide whether to negotiate the high-priority items or the medium- and low-priority items first.

C. Decide whether to set any preconditions (always be careful on this point).

## Report Format

See the section on the format of reports in Appendix 2 on Business Writing (pp. 135–137). Organize your negotiations progress report within the following sections:

1. Pre-Negotiations Strategy
   a) Goals
   b) Assessment of the balance of power
   c) The tone to be established at the beginning of the negotiations
   d) The order of discussion of the items (commissions, exclusive contract, and so on)
2. The Negotiations
   a) What occurred during the negotiations?
   b) Did the negotiations follow your strategy and how successful was your strategy?
3. The Tentative Contract Agreement Reached between XYZ and Long-range
   a) Commission
   b) Exclusive contract
   c) Fixed price versus flexible price contract
   d) Coverage of advertising costs and authority over advertising campaigns
   e) Coverage of shipping expenses
4. Recommendation
   a) Should your management accept the contract?
   b) What impact will this contract have on your company's earnings in the coming years?

# WRITING: REPORT ON NEGOTIATION PROGRESS

In order to prepare a report on your group's progress in negotiations, first fill in your negotiations worksheet. Then, based on notes taken during the negotiation meeting, write a report to your respective board of directors using the guidelines above.

# VOCABULARY

**achieve,** *v.*   To reach your goals. (Example: "We hope to achieve our goals of. . . .")

**agreement,** *n.*   Reaching a mutually acceptable compromise to which both sides agree.

**balance of power,** *n.*   An analysis of the strengths and weaknesses of both sides to determine which side has the strongest bargaining position.

**bargaining,** *n.* (**to bargain,** *v.*)    Negotiating with the purpose of coming to an agreement.

**bargaining power,** *n.*    The power of one's position in the process of negotiating.

**bottom line,** *n.*    The lowest you are willing to go to reach an agreement. (Also: the line at the bottom of a financial report showing profit or loss.)

**CIF (cost, insurance, and freight),** *n.*    The manufacturer pays CIF to the port of delivery of the importer. This is naturally favorable for XYZ.

**concessions,** *n.*    Compromises made by one side in order to reach an agreement. Concessions from one side are expected to be matched by concessions from the other side.

**conditions,** *n.*    Terms of a contract or demands of the bargaining teams.

**confirm,** *v.*    To make certain. ("We confirmed the date of the meeting.")

**convince/persuade,** *v.*    To get the other side to agree that your point of view is correct.

**deadlocked,** *adj.*    When the negotiating process cannot proceed because both sides are unwilling to compromise.

**demands,** *n.*    Your opening position in a negotiation; what you hope to achieve.

**final offer,** *n.*    Your last offer before breaking off negotiations.

**flexible,** *adj.*    Willing to negotiate, not rigid in your demands.

**flexibility,** *n.*    The state of being flexible.

**FOB (free on board),** *n.*    A point to which the transportation costs are borne by the seller and at which the title passes to the buyer.

**to get in on the ground floor,** *v.*    To get into a business or market early on so as to take advantage of its growth potential from the beginning.

**hardball, softball,** *adj.*    Describing two approaches to negotiations. *Hardball* suggests inflexibility, or trying to force the opposition to accept your conditions, while *softball* suggests a more flexible approach in which you try to reach an acceptable compromise.

**to have connections,** *v.*    To have people who can help you. In this case, these connections would be people in business.

**inflexible,** *adj.*    Unwilling to negotiate.

**inflexibility,** *n.*    The state of being rigid or inflexible.

**negotiations,** *n.* (**to negotiate,** *v.*)    The process of bargaining in an attempt to reach a mutually satisfying agreement or contract.

**objectives,** *n.*    Your goals; in this case, what you hope to obtain.

**priority,** *n.*    How you rate something in terms of its importance (high, medium, or low).

**proposal,** *n.* (**to propose,** *v.*)    What you offer as a basis for contract negotiations; often followed by a **counterproposal**, *n.* which is the other side's proposal in response to yours.

**renegotiations,** *n.* (**to renegotiate,** *v.*)   Negotiations carried out when a contract is renewed.

**sanctions,** *n.*   Penalties that can be imposed on the other side if they fail to accept your position.

**to shy away,** *v.*   To avoid.

**strategy,** *n.*   The plan you have for achieving your goals.

**trading cards/tradables,** *n.*   Demands that you are willing to give up in trade for some of your other demands.

**traits,** *n.*   Characteristics.

**ultimatum,** *n.*   A final proposal or terms whose rejection will result in the breaking off of negotiations.

**unyielding,** *adj.*   Refusing to compromise.

# LABOR RELATIONS

## Midland Heating and Cooling vs. The Primary Sheet Metal Workers of America, AFL-CIO

## CULTURAL BACKGROUND: UNION-MANAGEMENT RELATIONS

See the discussion of characteristics of American negotiation in the case Long-range Golf Equipment Seeks a Distributor (Case 4). The negotiations in this case may be even harder as, traditionally, union-management negotiations are quite tough. Try to put yourself in the mind frame of the negotiators, imagining how they would think and react, and carry out the negotiations as they would be performed in the United States. Remember, the *paternalistic* system of some countries, in which workers are guaranteed a job for life and a number of fringe benefits and thus feel loyalty to the company, does not exist in the United States. Thus, negotiations are much harder. Workers often feel that they are fighting for their livelihood because they believe that jobs are being lost to developing third-world countries.

# CASE

This case involves negotiations between management and union representatives. In this case, the Primary Sheet Metal Workers Union will represent union shop workers in wage negotiations. The case allows you to practice English in a competitive negotiation situation. The negotiation has been simplified to allow you to solve the case within a reasonable time frame. In actuality, wage negotiations are more complex and are influenced by labor legislation, which varies from country to country. Still, an effort has been made to present a realistic case here, given the limitations of time. This case will be solved within an American framework because creating a case fitting all political systems would be impossible.

Negotiations require a certain amount of secrecy. The material given here is restricted to information that would be common knowledge to both sides. Position papers, which are secret, will be provided to both sides by the instructor. They will form the point of departure for your negotiation strategy. Do not allow them to be seen by members of the opposing group.

## Midland Heating and Cooling

Midland Heating and Cooling was founded in 1954 by William and Robert Carothers. Their primary product is industrial heating and cooling units, and their primary customers are companies with large factories. The company is located in Toledo, Ohio, and employs 850 workers, which is approximately one-half of the work force employed during the company's peak years in the middle 1970s. In 1986, Midland employed 1,250 workers, but downsizing and the recession have taken their toll on the work force. The streamlining undertaken in the 1980s allowed Midland to remain profitable, and the income statements from the last three years reflect this:

| Year | Sales | Net Profit after Taxes | Return on Sales (%) | Market Share (%) |
|------|-------|------------------------|---------------------|------------------|
| 2001 | $55,890,000 | $5,600,000 | 10.2 | 2.25 |
| 2000 | 63,976,000 | 6,100,000 | 9.6 | 2.34 |
| 1999 | 66,450,000 | 6,150,000 | 9.3 | 2.50 |

Despite falling sales, return on sales is improving. The union claims that the increased productivity of the workers, up 10 percent over the last three years, is the cause of the increased return on sales. Although encouraged by this trend, management is concerned about the falling market share that can only be reversed by keeping salary raises moderate. However, the union is quick to point out that wages over the past contract period of three years have kept up with neither inflation nor the industry's average, citing these figures:

| | |
|---|---|
| Inflation for the past three years: | 12 percent (4 percent per year) |
| Salary increases at Midland for the past three years: | 10 percent |
| Salary increases for the industry for the past three years: | 12 percent |

Management claims that their workers *are* getting higher salaries if one looks at the salaries and benefit package as a whole, because the cost of health insurance has gone up 34 percent over the past three years. Management has hinted that they may have to drop health insurance coverage for their workers if costs continue to rise. At present, it costs Midland $7,000 per year to insure each worker and his or her family. Furthermore, management estimates for the present year show a 10 percent decline in sales due to the recession, which means the company must cut costs in order to maintain its market share. Naturally, the workers will be expected to carry their share of the burden to allow Midland to remain competitive. There is no immediate threat of Midland going bankrupt since their equity level is a respectable 30 percent, but management is concerned about the effects of the recession and the company's declining market share.

## POINTS FOR DISCUSSION

Discuss how wages and working conditions are determined in your country, and compare this method with the union versus management approach described in this case. Do you have a union and management system? If not, what system is used to determine wages and working conditions? If so:

a. What are typical demands from workers? Are strikes used as sanctions?
b. Is the relationship between unions and management confrontational or cooperative?

## CASE ACTIVITIES

### Negotiating a Union-Management Agreement

You will be negotiating the package for the factory workers, with one group acting as management representatives, the other as union representatives. All the workers are represented by the Primary Sheet Metal Workers of America, AFL-CIO (the leading federation of unions in the United States). At present, the average salary for journeymen is $16.00 an hour based on seniority. There is only one shift, so there will be no question of shift differential. It has been standard practice in these negotiations to set an across-the-board percentage increase for each of the three years in a contract period. There is nothing that says that you cannot negotiate a one-year contract, but this has not been the practice in the past.

At present, the workers have the following benefits:

1. Health care insurance (major medical) for the worker and all family members living with him or her up to the age of 18.
2. A pension plan based on an equal sharing of the cost between management and the workers.
3. Paid holidays beginning with two weeks the first four years and three weeks after that.
4. Additional paid national holidays.
5. A clothing allowance for work clothes.
6. Time and a half for overtime over forty hours per week.

The workers have recently expressed concern over rumors that Midland intends to subcontract some of the work, and management knows this will be an issue. In addition, the union is against hiring part-time workers because that can lead to layoffs. Management cites the rising cost of health care as one reason for wanting to hire part-time workers, as these workers do not have to be covered by health care insurance. In these times of rising unemployment, the workers want a no-layoff guarantee and *job posting*. Job posting refers to the announcing of all jobs through the local union and internal promotion. COLAs (cost of living adjustments) are a standard union demand. COLAs mean that the workers will be compensated for inflation so that wage increases will represent real increases in buying power, thereby counteracting the trend in which the workers actually suffered a 2 percent decrease in buying power over the last three-year period. Naturally, management is against COLAs because they increase costs, making the estimation of future costs difficult; this, in turn, complicates the company's ability to bid successfully on contracts.

After each team has prepared its negotiation strategy (by filling out a negotiations worksheet like the one in Case 4, Long-range Golf Equipment Seeks a Distributor), they will meet at the negotiation table to try to work out a contract. The following questions will be considered:

1. Wages
2. Cost of living adjustments (COLAs)
3. A no-layoff guarantee
4. Part-time work
5. Subcontracting (buying certain parts or products from an outside producer instead of producing them, which would mean loss of jobs at Midland)
6. Job posting

After the teams have worked out a contract, they will present the result orally to the class. During the oral presentation, the team representatives will discuss their individual strategies and how successful they were in achieving their goals. They will explain why they agreed to the concessions they made and what they obtained in return for these concessions. There will be as many negotiations as there are teams (naturally, two teams per negotiation).

## LANGUAGE MASTERY EXERCISE

### Practicing Common Negotiation Phrases and Techniques

Negotiating involves the use of certain phrases to help master the process. Learn the following phrases, which you will use in your negotiations.

CHECKING THAT YOU HAVE UNDERSTOOD:

> Please correct me if I'm wrong, but . . .
> Could I ask a few questions to see whether I have understood your position?
> Could we go through that again?

SHOWING WILLINGNESS TO COOPERATE:

> We would like to settle this issue in a mutually satisfactory way.
> We'd be happy to settle this point in a mutually cooperative way.

PROPOSING A SOLUTION TO REACH A COMPROMISE:

> What if we were to . . . ?
> Supposing we tried . . . ?
> Wouldn't a fair solution be . . . ?

### SHOWING UNDERSTANDING:

We appreciate your problem, but  . . .

We can understand your difficulty, but  . . .

### FOCUSING ON DIFFICULTIES:

The main problem as we see it is  . . .

Where we have difficulty with your proposal is  . . .

### REJECTING AN OFFER:

I'm afraid we won't be able to accept that [*diplomatic*].

I'm afraid that you are going to have to meet our requests on this item if we are going to reach an agreement.

That is totally out of the question [*strong*].

### ACCEPTING AN OFFER:

I think we can accept that.

I think we can agree on that.

## VOCABULARY

**across-the-board increase,** *n.*    A wage increase given to all or nearly all employees at one time. This is in the form of a percentage or dollar-and-cents increase, such as 5 percent or $0.50 per hour.

**agreement,** *n.*    A contract or mutual understanding between a union and a company setting forth the terms and conditions of employment, such as salaries, benefits, and other working conditions.

**apprentice,** *n.*    One who is learning a trade or craft and who receives lower wages than a journeyman.

**arbitration** (American), *n.*    A situation in which parties unable to agree on a contract have submitted the final decision to a third party.

**attrition,** (British: **natural wastage**), *n.*    Reducing the work force through retirement, not layoffs.

**bargaining,** *n.*    Negotiating a contract (in this case, a contract to set forth the conditions of employment).

**bottom line,** *n.*    In this case, as far as you are willing to go to meet the other party to reach an agreement.

**COLAs (cost of living adjustments),** *n.*    Compensation for inflation so that wage increases represent real wage increases. This is a common union demand, but at present, COLAs are rarely awarded by management.

**collective bargaining,** *n.*    A process in which representatives from the union and management work out a contract specifying the conditions of employment.

**counter-proposal,** *n.* An offer made in response to an offer made by the other party in negotiations.

**deadlocked,** *adj.* When negotiations reach an **impasse**, meaning that no further progress can be made; this generally means that the decision must be turned over to an arbitrator.

**downsizing,** *n.* Reducing the size of a company's workforce.

**earnings,** *n.* The amount of money received by a worker, including salary, bonuses, commissions, overtime pay, and so on.

**to employ,** *v.* To hire.

**employee,** *n.* Anyone who works for an employer.

**employer,** *n.* A person, association, or company having workers in its employ.

**equity,** *n.* Real assets (all things owned by a business and having some money value).

**grievance,** *n.* Any complaint by an employee or by a union about any aspect of employment.

**health insurance,** *n.* As the United States does not have national health insurance, unions must negotiate to obtain health insurance coverage for their workers.

**journeyman,** *n.* A worker in a craft or trade who has served an apprenticeship and is qualified for employment at the journeyman's rate of pay.

**layoff,** *n.* Temporary or indefinite termination of employment, usually due to a lack of work. This is not the same as discharge (firing).

**lockout,** *n.* When unions refuse to accept an employer's conditions, the employer can close the factory to the present employees and even hire new employees. This is the employer's sanction, which corresponds to the union's sanction of a strike.

**market share,** *n.* The percentage of the total market that a product has.

**mediation,** *n.* A situation in which a neutral person, or **mediator**, works with labor and management to help them reach an agreement.

**musts,** *n.* Important demands that you must get if you are going to accept an agreement.

**negotiations,** *n.* Discussion with the intent of reaching an agreement.

**picketing,** *n.* The act of patrolling at or near the employer's place of business during a strike to inform the public that there is a labor dispute in progress or to prevent strike breakers from entering the place of employment. **Picket,** *n.* One who does the picketing.

**productivity,** *n.* An index to measure the efficiency of a plant in utilizing its work force and equipment.

**raise,** (British: **rise**), *n.* An increase in wages.

**ratification,** *n.* The acceptance by the members of a union of a contract worked out between the representatives of the union and management.

**real wages,** *n.*   The real worth of one's wages (present and future) in terms of buying power, which is affected by inflation.

**recession,** *n.*   A temporary decline in business activity.

**seniority,** *n.*   The length of time an employee has worked at a company. Seniority is frequently a factor in determining promotions and layoffs.

**shift,** *n.*   The set period of time one works, such as 8:00 A.M. to 4:00 P.M.

**shift differential,** *n.*   Different rates of pay for different shifts.

**shop steward,** *n.*   The representative of the union at the place of work.

**strike,** *n.*   A work stoppage on the part of the employees to force management to meet the union's demands.

**strikebreakers,** *n.*   Employees hired while the original work force is on strike so that the company can continue its operations; also called **scabs** (a derogatory expression).

**strike fund,** *n.*   The amount of money a union has to support its workers while they are on strike.

**to subcontract,** *v.*   To buy certain parts or items from another producer.

**trading cards,** *n.*   Demands that you are willing to trade away in order to get your most important demands — that is, your "musts."

**wage,** *n.*   The price paid by the employer for work or services rendered by an employee.

**wage cut,** *n.*   A reduction in wages.

**work day,** *n.*   The time spent by an employee at work during a normal day, usually eight hours.

# ENVIRONMENT AND BUSINESS LEADERS' SOCIAL RESPONSIBILITY

## Northern Electrical Services vs. the Environmentalists

## CULTURAL BACKGROUND: ENVIRONMENTAL GROUPS

Due to increased concern for the fate of our planet, environmental groups have become both more popular and stronger. There are a number of groups, such as the Sierra Club and Greenpeace, which, through demonstrations and lobbying (providing information to politicians in the hope of influencing the way they vote), have begun to have a strong impact both on people's awareness of the dangers of increased pollution and on political decisions. Organizations like these have local groups that monitor local conditions. Political activism at the local level is typical in the United States, as people's loyalties are strongly connected to their local environment. On the other hand, Americans tend to feel just as strongly that the individual should decide his or her own fate, and that feeling carries over to companies in a free-enterprise system, prompting a dislike of regulations. Because many environmental regulations in the United States are determined by the federal (national) government, it is not uncommon for local residents to react against them, especially if the loss of jobs is a result of the regulations. Thus, this case brings out the conflicts between local loyalties, dislike of federal regulation, and fear of loss of jobs. Americans would be very emotional in a meeting such as the one in this case and would express their feelings freely.

# CASE

This case deals with one of the basic questions that most business leaders will face eventually: environmental responsibility. Industrial waste, though not the only source of pollution, has been a focus of environmental groups, such as the Sierra Club and Greenpeace, with a special emphasis on waste dumping and air pollution. It has been claimed that business leaders have frequently avoided their environmental responsibilities by pretending not to know about their company's emissions or claiming that expenses associated with cleanups and factory modernization would be prohibitively expensive. When faced with demands from environmental groups and governmental agencies, business leaders sometimes threaten plant closures. The effect may be that the local population, fearing unemployment, turns on environmental groups. Politicians, fearing defeat in the next election, may decide not to pressure businesses to pollute less.

However, according to World Watch, an environmental organization, if we do not seriously reduce pollutants being released into the atmosphere within forty years, we will face an environmental catastrophe. One possible scenario is that global warming, due to the greenhouse effect, will lead to mass flooding of low-lying areas and a radical increase in the total desert area. Another problem is the thinning of the ozone layer due to CFC (chlorofluorocarbons) gases, which will lead to a dramatic rise in the number of skin cancer cases.

## POINTS FOR DISCUSSION

1. In your country, are industrial leaders fully aware of the amount of pollution their companies emit into the environment? If yes, what are they doing to reduce it? If not, why not? Is it because they don't want to accept the responsibility and costs associated with such pollution, or is it due to a lack of information?

2. Should industrial leaders be more responsive to the problem of pollution? What can be done, if necessary, to make them responsive?

3. What sanctions (such as fines, jail sentences, and so on) would be most effective in cases of repeated environmental offenses on the part of local industries?

## CASE ACTIVITIES

### A Public Hearing

Many companies' environmental records are being investigated. Such is the case with Northern Electrical Services. This company is located in a town of 12,000 people along the Connecticut River in Connecticut. It employs 800 people and is the town's largest employer in an area with over 10 percent unemployment. If the company were to close operations, it would be an economic disaster for the community. Not only would the unemployment figures double immediately, but the effect on local businesses would threaten the entire economic base of the community.

Northern Electrical Services services parts for electrical power plants. PCBs, a toxic material, were once used in producing many of the components the company services, and tests done by local environmentalists show that a ten-mile down-river stretch of the Connecticut River has high concentrations of PCBs in the river sediments. In addition, PCB concentrations in fish caught in the river are twice the FDA (Food and Drug Administration) standards of two ppm (parts per million) for levels of PCBs in fish. The number of cancer patients in the local area is 50 percent higher than the national average. In addition, the number of spontaneous abortions in the local area is 40 percent higher than the national average. Although there is no definite proof that the PCBs in the river sediments are the direct cause of these high rates of illness, it is difficult to find any other explanation. In any case, the possibility of a health risk has limited the use of the most important recreational area the townspeople have — the Connecticut River.

Another major problem allegedly caused by Northern Electrical Services is the emission of sulfur dioxide and nitrogen oxide from their heating unit, which burns fossil fuels (oil, gas, and coal). The company's plant, which was constructed in 1945, has inadequate cleansing equipment in its smoke stacks. The management has estimated that the installation of the most advanced filters would cost $2 million dollars, which is approximately half of the company's annual profits. It is estimated that this equipment would eliminate 99 percent of all sulfur dioxide and nitrogen oxide, which would greatly improve the air quality in the area. As it is now, poor air quality is blamed for nausea, headaches, and a high rate of respiratory diseases in the area. Forty percent of all school-age children suffer from asthma. Northern Electrical Services, on the other hand, claims that their sulfur dioxide and nitrogen oxide emissions are within the EPA (Environmental Protection Agency) limits of 1.2 pounds per million BTUs and 0.6 pounds per million BTUs respectively. Thus, they feel that they are adhering to the law and do not feel any responsibility to install new filters. An opinion poll taken in a local newspaper found that 62 percent of the population felt that Northern Electrical Services had a responsibility to install the new filters; 28 percent felt that emission controls were adequate, while 10 percent had no opinion.

In terms of responsibility, the local environmentalist organization's representative wrote a letter to the editor of the local newspaper stating that Northern Electrical Services should be held responsible for cleaning up the entire stretch of the Connecticut River polluted with PCBs — a process that would cost an estimated $25 million dollars. Naturally, the company's spokesperson responded that this demand was unrealistic, since it would force the closing of the plant. The plant is not highly profitable as it is, and even the cost of installing smokestack equipment could push the administration to consider closing the plant.

The local environmentalists further demand a study of health conditions of the workers at Northern Electrical Services paid for by the company. Its purpose would be both to help improve the possibility of limiting the number of deaths from cancer through early detection, and to determine if workers at the factory are more prone to develop cancer. If this was the case, the environmentalists would bring a *class-action suit* (a lawsuit representing the interests of a group of people) on behalf of the workers.

With the obvious conflicts of interest and strong emotions, tempers have been flying. In a few cases, the tension has led to violent confrontations between workers, who are afraid of losing their jobs, and environmentalists. Thus, the mayor of the town has called a hearing. She has invited representatives from the management of Northern Electrical Services, the environmentalists, the factory workers, and representatives of the State Department of Environmental Protection. In addition, all residents of the town are welcome to attend. Each group participating in the meeting will have to prepare its role separately, and then come to the meeting with carefully prepared positions and arguments.

### Management of Northern Electrical Services

You will try to present your company in the best light, talking about your civic concern and showing what you have done for the community and what your business means for the local economy. You will present a study that confirms that your emissions of sulfur dioxide and nitrogen oxide are within the EPA limits stated above. You will also emphasize that there is no proof that the PCBs stem from your factory. You will explain the financial situation of your company and the limitations that situation puts on meeting the demands raised by the environmentalists.

You must work out a position much like that needed for other negotiation cases in this book (see Cases 4 and 5). Determine how far you are willing to go to meet environmentalists' expected demands and where your bottom line is. What is your attitude going to be? Will you deny all responsibility and threaten to close the plant, or are you willing to make some concessions? You should keep in mind that if it is proven that you have exceeded EPA limits for sulfur dioxide and nitrogen oxide emissions, you may be charged fines levied by the Connecticut State Department of Environmental Protection, which has the final authority in this case. Your team will consist of representatives from management, plus your highly paid lawyers.

## The Workers

You have two conflicting concerns. Your major concern is the possible loss of your jobs, and thus you basically are aligned with management and against the environmentalists. However, you are also concerned about your health and the health of your family. Information about the high incidence of cancer and respiratory diseases in your community concerns you and will affect what you say in the meeting.

## The Environmentalists

Naturally, you are the most outspoken group. You will come to the meeting armed with statistics, charts, and a list of demands. Your statistics will present a different picture than that of the management of Northern Electrical Services. You will try to enlist the support of the local residents.

## Local Residents

You share similar concerns with the workers; that is, you are concerned with both the economic and the health aspects of the case. You are free to express individual opinions or formulate a unified position for your entire group.

## The Connecticut State Department of Environmental Protection

Your group consists of four to five members of the department. You will listen to arguments from all participants and formulate a judgment. If you find that Northern Electrical Services has broken the law, you can force them to take necessary steps to bring air pollution within EPA standards. You can even force them to clean up the down-river stretch of the Connecticut River if it is proven that they are the sole, or major, polluter. You can also levy fines. One of your members will chair the meeting. (See Meeting Terminology and Procedures in Case 3.)

Each group will prepare individually, and then come to the town meeting well prepared.

### The Meeting

The chairperson will call the meeting to order. The management from Northern Electrical Services will be allowed to present their case at the front of the room. After they are finished, the environmentalists will be allowed to present their case and their demands at the front of the room. Then the discussion will be opened to the floor, which means that anyone can speak, either as a representative of a group or as a person expressing an individual opinion. The representatives of the management and the environmentalists will remain in front of the class to answer any questions or respond to any comments.

After the chairperson feels that the positions have been adequately presented, he or she will adjourn the meeting and set a date for a follow-up meeting. In the follow-up meeting, the representatives of the State Department of Environmental Management will present their decision, beginning by announcing whether or not Northern Electrical Services has broken the law. If the Department representatives determine that Northern Electrical Services *has* broken the law, they must announce which specific points the company is responsible for, and what they must do to remedy the situation. Also, Department representatives must determine whether any fines are going to be levied, and if so, how much the company will be charged.

## LANGUAGE MASTERY EXERCISES

### Presenting an Opinion and Responding to Others' Opinions

In debating questions such as the one in this case, you will have to (1) present an opinion, and (2) agree and/or disagree with others' opinions. Below you will find expressions commonly used in this kind of situation, followed by an exercise in using these expressions.

#### PRESENTING AN OPINION

It seems to me . . . *or* It appears to me . . . [*weak*]
I feel that . . . *or* I think that . . . *or* It is my opinion that . . . [*neutral*]
I am convinced that . . . *or* I strongly/firmly believe that . . . [*strong*]
There is no question/doubt that . . . [*very strong*]

#### GETTING ANOTHER PERSON'S OPINION

Mr. Smith, I would like your opinion/input on this matter.
Mr. Smith, what do you think/feel about this matter?

#### RESPONDING

#### Agreeing

I generally agree . . . [*agreement, but with reservations*]
I agree . . . [*neutral*]
I fully/completely agree . . . [*strong*]

### Disagreeing

I'm afraid that I cannot agree . . . [*polite disagreement*]
I can see your point, but . . . [*polite disagreement*]
I cannot totally agree . . . [*partial disagreement*]
I cannot completely agree . . . [*partial disagreement*]
I strongly/totally disagree . . . [*strong*]

## Verbal Exercise

One student should express an opinion and then, using the above phrases, the other students should in turn express agreement or disagreement and state why. After three or four students have expressed their opinions about the original opinion or any of the other students' responses, have a new student express a new opinion and get other students' responses.

# WRITING: EXPRESSING YOUR OPINION

1. Write a letter to the local newspaper expressing your point of view on this case. (This exercise is for all groups except the Connecticut State Department of Environmental Protection group.)

2. The Connecticut State Department of Environmental Protection group will write a report summarizing (a) the information presented at the meeting, and (b) their decision in the case, supported by the facts presented in the course of the meeting.

# VOCABULARY

**abatement,** *n.*   Reducing the amount of, or eliminating, pollution.

**air pollutant,** *n.*   Any substance in the air which could, in high enough concentration, harm human beings, animals, vegetation, or other material.

**air pollution,** *n.*   The presence of air pollutants that have a harmful effect on human beings, animals, vegetation, or other material.

**to align,** *v.*   To be on the same side as someone else.

**biodegradable,** *adj.*   Able to break down or decompose rapidly under natural conditions and processes.

**carbon dioxide ($CO_2$),** *n.*   A colorless, odorless, nonpoisonous gas which results from burning fossil fuels. Carbon dioxide is a major contributor to the greenhouse effect.

**carcinogenic,** *adj.*   Cancer-producing.

**chlorofluorocarbons (CFC),** *n.*   Gases that deplete the ozone layer.

**class-action suit,** *n.*   A law suit brought on behalf of a group of people.

**cleanup,** *n.*   Actions taken to clean up a polluted area (in this case, dredging the river to remove sediments containing PCBs).

**desulfurization,** *n.*    The removal of sulfur from fossil fuels to reduce pollution. Desulfurization is a process that, along with filtering or scrubbing, can significantly reduce the amount of air pollution from factories like the one in this case.

**dredging,** *n.*    The removal of mud from the bottom of water bodies, using a machine. Dredging might be necessary to remove the PCBs in the sediments of the river in this case. But dredging can also produce negative side effects such as silting, which can kill life in the river.

**effluent,** *n.*    Waste water that flows into bodies of water.

**emission,** *n.*    Pollution discharged into the atmosphere from smokestacks and the like. The nitrogen oxide and sulfur dioxide emitted by the factory in this case are emissions.

**emission standard,** *n.*    The maximum amount of air-polluting discharge legally allowed from a single source.

**enforcement,** *n.*    The action of forcing companies to obey laws (in this case, environmental laws like the Clean Water and Clean Air Acts).

**to enlist,** *n.*    To seek the support of.

**EPA,** *n.*    The U.S. Environmental Protection Agency is the government agency charged with enforcing environmental legislation.

**to exceed,** *v.*    To emit more pollution than allowed by environmental legislation.

**greenhouse effect,** *n.*    The warming of the earth's atmosphere caused by a buildup of carbon dioxide or other gases. It is believed by many scientists that this buildup allows light from the sun's rays to heat the earth but prevents the escape of heat from the earth's atmosphere.

**to levy,** *v.*    To demand payment.

**to monitor,** *v.*    To check regularly.

**National Ambient Air Quality Standards (NAAQS),** *n.*    Air quality standards established by the EPA.

**National Emission Standards for Hazardous Air Pollutants (NESHAPs),** *n.*    Emission standards set by the EPA for air pollutants not covered by NAAQS.

**nitrogen oxide, (NOX),** *n.*    Gases produced in fossil fuel combustion.

**ozone ($O_3$),** *n.*    A gas found in two layers of the atmosphere, the stratosphere and the troposphere. In the stratosphere (the atmospheric layer beginning seven to ten miles above the earth's surface), ozone forms a protective shield protecting the earth from ultraviolet radiation which, in too large doses, causes skin cancer. This layer is rapidly being depleted by CFC gases.

**PCBs,** *n.*    A group of toxic chemicals used in transformers and capacitators for insulating purposes. Further sale or new use of PCBs was banned by law in 1979.

**pollutant,** *n.*    Any substance introduced into the environment that produces undesired environmental effects.

**pollution,** *n.*    The presence of matter or energy whose nature, location, or quantity produces undesired environmental effects.

**sediments,** *n.*    Soil, sand, and minerals washed from land into water. In this case, sediments could have carried PCBs into the riverbed, where fish feeding on the bottom would have ingested them.

**sulfur dioxide (SO$_2$),** *n.*    A heavy, pungent gas produced by industrial fossil fuel combustion.

# BUSINESS

# ORGANIZATION

# AND MANAGEMENT

## Commutair:
## Employee Motivation
## and Management Theory

## CULTURAL BACKGROUND: WORK FORCE MOTIVATION

This case reflects various aspects of British culture, where there is a democratic tradition in which employees are used to fighting for their rights and managers are aware of the importance of motivation in a service-sector company. In cultures like that in Great Britain, which tend to emphasize the individual, there is a tendency to try to motivate the work force to perform better. In cultures in which there is a strong loyalty to one's company, there is not the same emphasis on motivational theory, as motivation is built into the employees' attitude toward the company and the company's expectations of the employees. In these cultures, employees are expected to work hard because of their loyalty to the company, while in cultures that stress individualism, the employees must be motivated to work hard.

Thus, motivational strategies are considered an important part of the activities of the human resources (also called personnel) department within cultures that emphasize the individual.

# CASE

Commutair, a small commuter airline based in Newcastle in the United Kingdom, has flights between Newcastle, Aberdeen, and Edinburgh, as well as flights from these cities to London. The airline has recently applied for concessions for routes from the three northern cities to Oslo and Bergen (Norway), Gothenburg (Sweden), and Aarhus (Denmark). However, recent developments have begun to create uneasiness in the company. Judging from an increased number of customer complaints, there seems to be growing customer dissatisfaction. The complaints center around lost baggage, overbooking, delayed flights, inadequate information to passengers, and impoliteness. The president of the company, Tom Waters, fears that some of these problems can be tied to employee dissatisfaction. In addition, absenteeism is increasing, which supports management's fears of growing employee discontent. A brief survey of employee opinion has revealed dissatisfaction with pay (which is 10 percent under the industry average), the monotony of work (especially at the check-in counter), and frustration with managers who are not willing to listen to suggestions and complaints from "front-line" employees in response to customer demands and complaints.

Waters has followed up the survey with interviews, receiving the following responses. John Jacobs, a baggage handler, complained about eight-hour shifts with no coffee room in which to take a break, as well as problems with the electric baggage trucks which result in breakdowns and the need to reload the baggage onto new trucks. Margaret McKinney, a flight attendant, reported constant customer complaints (including a lack of snacks in tourist class and the absence of newspapers in business class) to her manager four months ago and has still received no reply. The check-in personnel are frustrated with reservation personnel for constant overbooking and have continually complained to their manager. One check-in employee, Jennifer Roberts, said that if the situation was not remedied soon, she would quit. She cannot stand the constant complaints she is getting, particularly since it does not appear as if anything will be done about the situation. Reservation personnel are also frustrated, as they receive constant complaints from the check-in personnel without being able to do anything about company policy concerning overbooking. (The reservations manager has insisted that overbooking is necessary to insure that flights are full, despite last-minute cancellations.)

Company President Waters is afraid that the application for new routes will be jeopardized if something is not done soon to reverse the rise in employee — and customer — dissatisfaction. He has asked the Director of Human Resources to set up a committee, consisting of members of her staff and other employees, to discuss the present situation and write a report suggesting necessary changes. As members of this committee, you must consider the major complaints of the employees, as well as possible changes the administration must make to meet these demands. Basically, you are being asked to consider what motivates front-line employees in an airline in general, and what must be done specifically in response to Commutair employees' complaints. How can the front-line employees be motivated to be more service-minded? Finally, what changes in management philosophy and organizational structure must be made to meet employee needs?

## POINTS FOR DISCUSSION

1. Compare the attitude of people within your culture toward work and the necessity for motivation with the situation in this case. Are your workers naturally motivated as a result of respect for, and loyalty to, the management and the company? If not, what are the typical means used by management to motivate workers?

2. How important is a knowledge of motivation theory for managers?

3. How much motivation theory have you learned in your studies or on the job?

4. Discuss what would best motivate employees in a company such as Commutair. Is money or job satisfaction the most important issue?

## CASE ACTIVITIES

### Management/Employee Discussions

Each group will function as a separate committee. Each committee will consist of (a) front-line employees with specific demands and (b) members of the Human Resources Department who possess a good knowledge of motivation and management theory. The employees on the committee should represent specific employee groups, such as check-in, baggage, cabin, and reservations personnel. You should begin by discussing what motivates personnel in front-line jobs such as yours. You can discuss this in general, using motivation theory, and then talk about what would motivate you in your specific job.

The next step will be to discuss managerial theories and approaches that management should adopt to meet the employees' demands. Here you will have to step out of your roles as employees and look at the problem from the point of view of consultants trying to consider the needs of both management and employees. You should discuss managerial theories relevant to a service company and devise a managerial policy statement for Commutair. This statement should include (1) a statement of management's attitude toward their employees, (2) a motivational package to meet the needs of the employees, and (3) changes in organizational structure to increase communication and give front-line employees more say in company policy. In addition, it should include a statement about the importance of a customer- and service-oriented attitude among the employees. The statement of policy should be illustrated with concrete examples of how this policy and attitude will be implemented in the future. (See the Vocabulary list on pages 66 – 67 for more ideas concerning motivation).

## The Meeting

This case will be carried out as a committee meeting and an open discussion of the points mentioned above. The results of the meeting will be reported to the class and also written up in the form of a report to be handed in. Your oral and written reports will cover the following areas:

1. A managerial policy statement concerning management's attitude toward the employees.

2. A motivational package offered to the employees to help meet their demands. This package might include pay raises, profit sharing, better shifts, job rotation, more influence on decision making, and so on.

3. Proposed changes in the organizational structure to meet employee demands (see the present organizational chart shown in Figure 7-1).

4. A statement of a customer- and service-oriented policy expected to be followed by all levels of employees.

## Tips in Solving This Case

In preparing this case, consider the following success stories in the airline industry.

1. **Donald Burr, People Express.** Although now defunct, People Express was extremely successful for a brief period of time, and Donald Burr was famous industry-wide as a motivational genius. Even though his company went bankrupt (due to overexpansion) and his ideas proved to be less successful near the end, they could be useful in formulating a motivational package. (See Harvard Business School Case 483-103, "People Express.")

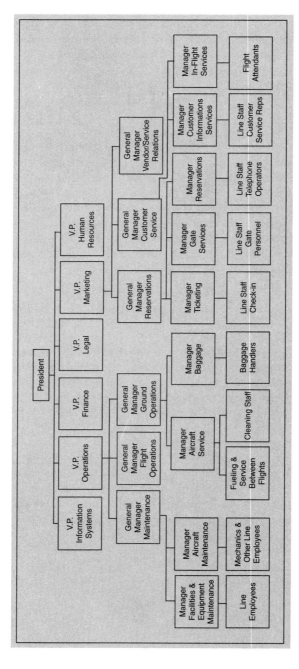

**Figure 7-1**    Organizational Chart: Commutair

2. **Jan Carlzon, SAS.** Carlzon has been very successful as head of SAS. Even more important for you, he has written and spoken extensively on the subject of employee motivation and managerial theory. (See Jan Carlzon, *Moments of Truth*, Cambridge, Mass.: Ballinger Publishing Co., 1987.)

3. **Alaska Airlines** is one of the few U.S. airlines enjoying economic success. Like Commutair, it is a small airline and bears watching. See recent articles.

4. **Harvard Business School Case 575-118,** "Southwest Airlines," analyzes another successful small airline.

Harvard Business School Case 9-482-017, "Note on Rewards Systems," gives a good overview of successful management/motivational strategies. Other sources of information are standard textbooks in Organization and Management. All Harvard Business School cases can be obtained from Harvard Business School Case Services, Harvard School of Business, Boston, MA 02163, USA.

## LANGUAGE MASTERY EXERCISE

### Word Choice and Attitudes

A positive attitude is important in business, and your choice of words is vital in creating the right attitude. Compare the statement "Our jobs are boring" with the statement "Our jobs could be more stimulating and our performance better if. . . ." The first statement is negative and reflects a passivity, whereas the second one is positive and reflects a desire to improve the situation.

Working in pairs, take the following sentences related to this case and create more positive statements either by using the hints as starters or by making your own entirely new sentences.

1. There is no communication between front-line employees and the decision makers.

   *Hint:* Better communication between front-line employees and decision makers would . . .

2. Management doesn't have a personnel policy that considers our needs.

   *Hint:* Work motivation would be improved if . . .

3. There are too many levels in our present organizational structure.

   *Hint:* We could respond better to customers' needs if . . .

4. We have no say in the running of our company.

   *Hint:* If we could have more say in the running of our company, . . .

5. The monotony in our jobs is unbearable.

   *Hint:* We would be . . . if . . .

6. Our salaries are far too low.

   *Hint:* We would be more . . . if . . .

7. Our company has no personnel policy.

*Hint:* Perhaps our job performance would . . . if . . .

# WRITING: MEETING REPORT

Each group should hand in the report described previously in "The Meeting" section.

# VOCABULARY

**absenteeism,** *n.*   The number of workers absent from work.

**to assess,** *v.*   To observe and evaluate someone's job performance.

**behavior modification,** *n.*   A technique that aims at changing an employee's behavior in a desired direction.

**compensation,** *n.*   A reward or payment for services.

**to evaluate,** *v.*   To rate a person's job performance.

**evaluation,** *n.*   The rating of a person's job performance. Synonym: **assessment,** *n.*

**fringe benefits,** *n.*   Any rewards given to an employee in addition to salary, such as a company car, an expense account, a free home phone, and so on. Synonym: **perk,** *n.* (considered slang by some people, but often used).

**gratification,** *n.*   Satisfaction of a need.

**incentive,** *n.*   Something that stimulates performance, such as a **bonus** (additional monetary compensation), **profit sharing** (sharing a percentage of the profits with the employees), or **stock options** (allowing employees to buy shares in the company at a favorable price).

**to implement,** *v.*   To put into practice.

**job design,** *n.*   The way job tasks are structured and carried out, including the following options:

> **job enrichment,** *n.*   Tailoring job tasks so that work is more satisfying for the employees.

> **flextime,** *n.*   Allowing employees to determine their work schedules within certain latitudes.

> **4/40,** *n.*   A work week made up of four 10-hour days.

> **quality control circles,** *n.*   A group of employees with similar tasks and responsibilities who meet regularly to discuss how they can improve job performance and products.

> **job rotation,** *n.*   A system that provides an employee a variety of tasks to reduce monotony and boredom.

**merit-based compensation plan,** *n.*   Salary based primarily on an employee's performance.

**motivation,** *n.*   Something that encourages or drives a person to act in a desired way.

**performance,** *n.*   The way an employee carries out his or her job.

**promotion,** *n.*   Raising an employee to a higher position in the company.

**to promote,** *v.*   To raise an employee to a higher position.

**raise,** *n.*   An increase in salary.

**recognition,** *n.*   Public acknowledgment of a good job performance.

**reinforcement,** *n.*   Something that causes certain behavior to be repeated or inhibited. **Positive reinforcement** encourages a desired behavior; **negative reinforcement** discourages undesired behavior.

**reward,** *n.*   A token given in recognition of good job performance.

**to reward,** *v.*   To provide a token in recognition of good job performance.

# BUSINESS

# ORGANIZATION

# AND MANAGEMENT

## Unhealthy Leaders: Sterling Forklift

## CULTURAL BACKGROUND: ANGLO/AMERICAN MANAGEMENT STYLES

This case, like Case 7 on Commutair, emphasizes the importance of creating an atmosphere in which employees are encouraged to perform at their best. In many cultures, bosses are so highly respected that their management style would not be questioned. However, in Anglo/American cultures, this is not the case. In this case, the employees of the British company, Sterling Forklift, consider the managerial style of their company's president so destructive of good working conditions that they feel obliged to confront him. The relatively open nature of British society allows for conflict between employees and their employer. The British have a long tradition of class conflict and confrontation between unions and management. Management has not always been responsive to workers' needs and, as in this case, must sometimes be forced to face these needs. Unlike managers in some other cultures, British managers are not so secure in their position that they cannot be confronted. Conflict is accepted as part of the relationship between workers and management, and British society allows for the conflict to be expressed.

# CASE

In a recent Norwegian book about management style, the author states that managers' leadership styles can actually lead to health problems and high absenteeism among the employees. One of these unhealthy styles is exhibited by Tom Masters, the founder and president of Sterling Forklift. Thus, this case deals not just with reorganization, but also with human personalities and conflicts. No matter where people work, they are going to run into conflicts of ideas, personalities, and management styles. The ability of employees and managers to resolve these conflicts satisfactorily will affect not only their working environment, but also the company's overall performance.

This case involves conflicts between the Engineering and Production Departments of Sterling Forklift — conflicts that are intensified by Masters's pressure on employees. Due to the pressure they are under, the two heads of the departments could easily turn to blaming each other as a way of avoiding Masters's anger. Naturally, this would have a negative effect on the working environment at

Sterling Forklift, as well as on the working relationship between engineering and production.

Sterling Forklift of Sterling, Scotland, makes battery-powered forklifts. It has been expanding rapidly, as it has managed to position itself in a new market created by government regulation requiring a reduction of pollution in the workplace. The company is headed by Tom Masters, the founder of the company. He is a hardheaded engineer with an eye for figures and a corresponding lack of psychological insight into employee motivation. The original forklift model produced by Sterling Forklift was Masters's "baby," and although he has hired engineers to further its development, he is constantly "dropping by" and more or less dictating to them how to carry out their jobs. The Production Manager, James Dickerson, an Englishman, and the Engineering Manager, William McRoberts, a Scot, feel that Masters is constantly pressuring their workers. They are professionals and do not want to be treated like assembly-line workers. However, Masters cannot seem to make this distinction. Masters's management style is particularly troubling to McRoberts, who has a degree in engineering and an MBA. Besides Masters's impolite manner, his management style includes monthly meetings with the managers, in which the managers must account for the past month's performance. These meetings in Masters's office take on the character of calling the employees on the carpet (criticizing them). Masters has even yelled at McRoberts during several of these meetings and stated point-blank that if McRoberts cannot perform up to expectations, he should consider finding employment elsewhere. The two criteria Masters uses to measure the Engineering and the Production Departments' performances are (a) cost efficiency and (b) quality control. McRoberts's department has recently experienced Masters's anger due to their slowness in working out problems in a new model that is now three months behind schedule. On several of his visits to the Engineering Department, Masters has embarrassed McRoberts by criticizing him in front of his staff.

Dickerson has also experienced Masters's abrasive management style. Masters is a stickler for cost efficiency and quality control, and Production is not living up to his expectations, especially in the area of cost efficiency. Dickerson feels that Masters's criticism is unfair, as Dickerson has been calling for a reorganization of the assembly system from bays to an assembly-line. Masters refuses to listen to Dickerson, saying that the conversion of the factory would be too expensive in terms of both the cost of the conversion and lost production time. The conversion is estimated by Masters to cost £1.7 million, plus another £300,000 in carrying the cost of overheads during the conversion, as well as the costs of overtime pay to train workers on the new assembly-line and to build up inventory. Dickerson counters that this conversion would increase productivity by 20 percent, which would compensate for the cost in approximately three years (the new assembly-line is expected to generate a £670,000 incremental cash flow). However, Dickerson's argument has been ignored (see point 2, Power barriers, on page 72, for a possible explanation).

In addition, both Dickerson and McRoberts are beginning to sense discontent among their staff, and there has been talk about some of the employees looking for new jobs. Employee morale is at an all-time low, which might explain the failings in quality control. Due to the somewhat isolated location of the plant, replacing these employees could be difficult. McRoberts is particularly afraid of losing Robert Smith, who is an old-timer with a number of practical solutions and experience in both Engineering and Production. Dickerson is afraid of losing his best employee, David McNulty, whom he brought over from the United States. Smith was recently criticized by Masters for initiating changes in their new model in an attempt to solve some of the problems in it. Smith had not cleared the changes with Masters, and although he had solved one of the basic problems with the model, all he got for his effort was criticism. Dickerson has been informed by Smith and other staff members that if he cannot "protect" them from Masters, they will consider quitting. Unfortunately, Masters considers the clearing of all decisions through him a must, which is typical of his "hub and spoke" concept of organizational structure (like a wheel, all communication must go through the center—the hub—making decision making centralized). This structure has, unfortunately, prevented interdepartmental cooperation, which has only made a bad situation worse. Masters's criticism about cost efficiency and quality control has created pressure on both Engineering and Production. McRoberts and Dickerson have started blaming each other. Production has claimed that the specifications have been unclear, and Engineering has claimed that Production does not know how to read the drawings. Pressure has mounted to the point where both McRoberts and Dickerson have decided to call a meeting to air and, they hope, to solve the problems. McRoberts and Dickerson see three main problems:

1. Problems created by Masters's management style, resulting in employee discontent.
2. Practical problems of the factory's outmoded production system.
3. Conflicts between the Engineering and Production Departments.

Both Dickerson and McRoberts know that they must confront Masters, and that they must work out a strategy for how to deal with him. Dickerson also knows that the costs of the conversion equal the sum of last year's profits, although this expense will be spread over a number of years. Thus, he knows he will meet resistance on this suggestion and has worked out estimates showing that an assembly-line will reduce production time per unit from ten to eight hours. This will result in savings that will pay for the £2 million in three years. Finally, Dickerson and McRoberts must work out their differences in front of Masters to show him that they are trying to solve problems. They hope that this will create some goodwill with Masters, prompting him to stay off their backs. Otherwise, growing tensions will result in insurmountable personnel problems. In preparing for the meeting with Masters, Dickerson and McRoberts will not only have to take into consideration Masters's personality, but also the following barriers to change:

1. **Value barriers.** The proposed changes conflict with certain individuals' perceptions (in this case, those of Masters) and philosophies of how the company should be run and how employees should be managed. In this latter

concern, Masters must be made aware of the importance of treating professionals as professionals.

2. **Power barriers.** Certain changes, especially reorganization, threaten certain individuals' positions and power in a company. In this case, Masters may perceive the meeting as a plot to undermine his power through greater employee freedom and decentralized decision making, which in turn would conflict with his perception of how a company should be run. He may fear that his "hub and spoke" approach may be undermined by interdepartmental cooperation. At the same time that he wants greater cost efficiency, he might be afraid of the interdepartmental cooperation that may be necessary to achieve it because he may lose control of the decision-making process.

3. **Psychological barriers.** These barriers often come from a general fear of change, resulting from personal insecurity and the resulting preference for maintaining the status quo. Does Masters's top-down approach stem from personal insecurity that will make him resistant to all change? If so, how can Dickerson and McRoberts approach him to overcome his fear?

## POINTS FOR DISCUSSION

1. Discuss bosses you have had, and give concrete examples of what made them good or bad bosses.
2. What are common mistakes that bosses make, and how, in a diplomatic way, can they be made to see these mistakes?

## CASE ACTIVITIES

### Productive Criticism of Management Styles

Dickerson and McRoberts have called a meeting with the following people (who will be played by you, the students):

Tom Masters, President
James Dickerson, Production Manager
David McNulty, Production Department Employee
William McRoberts, Engineering Manager
Robert Smith, Engineering Department Employee

The stated purpose of the meeting is to work out problems between Engineering and Production and to consider remodeling the factory's production facility. An unstated item on the agenda is Masters's management style. Masters suspects this and feels threatened. The first item (see the agenda in Figure 8-1) is basically designed to create goodwill with Masters, but concrete results must be achieved. Here you can draw from the experience of Smith and McNulty, who should contribute concrete suggestions on how to improve cooperation, such as including Production people in Engineering operations so that they can become

```
Jan. 17, 199_

12:00 P.M.

1. Cooperation between engineering and production
2. Assembly-line production and factory remodeling.
3. Any other business.
```

**Figure 8-1**   Agenda for Meeting

familiarized with the workings of Engineering and make suggestions, in terms of production problems, that might arise from certain design features. McNulty has worked in both Engineering and Production and would be the perfect partner to develop interdepartmental cooperation, as he understands both sides of the engineering/production process.

After reaching some concrete solutions, move on to item two on the agenda, where once again Engineering and Production exhibit a desire to cooperate to develop an assembly-line system. The second part of this item is to convince Masters to convert production to an assembly-line system. Masters is skeptical on three grounds: (1) cost; (2) the fact that the factory will have to be closed, and thus the problems of meeting delivery schedules and loss of sales and possible layoffs that such a closing will entail; and (3) a general skepticism about loss of control over the decision-making process (see the list of barriers to change on pages 71 – 72). The representatives from Engineering and Production will have to develop arguments and suggestions to convince Masters, such as employees working overtime to build up inventories to cover the period when the factory will be closed, cooperation between Engineering and Production in designing and building the assembly-line that will save money and keep the layoffs at a minimum, and so on. Smith has designed assembly-lines before and could provide the drawings.

The final item on the agenda, though not stated as such, will address Masters's management style, the problems it is causing, and the effects on the company and its personnel.

| Sales | Net Profit after Taxes | Return on Sales | Market Share in Great Britain |
|-------|------------------------|-----------------|-------------------------------|
| £40,000,000 | £2,000,000 | 5% | 4.5% |

**Figure 8-2**   Profit and Loss Figures for Sterling Forklift, Ltd. for 199 — (the previous year). These figures reflect a low net profit of 5 percent, which suggests a need for increased efficiency.

In preparation for this meeting, all those students playing Masters, Dickerson, McRoberts, Smith, and McNulty will meet to develop their roles and contributions. Let us say there are four students playing Masters. They will meet to define their attitudes toward the first two items on the agenda and their fears and attitudes toward the final, unstated item on the agenda. Those playing Dickerson will meet to discuss what they can contribute to a cooperative effort between Production and Engineering, in order to build a case that will convince Masters of the necessity of converting the factory to an assembly-line system. Those playing McRoberts will discuss what they can contribute to create better cooperation between Engineering and Production. Those playing Smith and those playing McNulty will discuss their roles and contributions to the meeting. Finally, students playing the four employees will also discuss how to confront Masters about his management style. After each participant has prepared his or her role, the Dickersons, McRobertses, McNulties and Smiths, who will be performing together in the meeting, will get together and discuss a common strategy. Those playing Masters will continue their discussion of their role. Thus, the two preparation phases will look like this (based on a class of 20 students):

### Phase 1

| Group 1 | Group 2 | Group 3 | Group 4 | Group 5 |
|---|---|---|---|---|
| 4 Masters | 4 McRoberts | 4 Dickersons | 4 McNulties | 4 Smiths |

### Phase 2

| Group 1 | Group 2 | Groups 3, 4, and 5 |
|---|---|---|
| 4 Masters | 1 McRoberts | Same composition as Group 2 |
|  | 1 Dickerson |  |
|  | 1 McNulty |  |
|  | 1 Smith |  |

## The Meeting

You will hold as many meetings as you have persons playing each character, with one Masters, Dickerson, McRoberts, Smith, and McNulty in each meeting. After each meeting is concluded, have a discussion in which all the groups discuss how they dealt with Masters and what conclusions were reached. The participants should make the following contributions:

### McRoberts:

Should chair the meeting and make a brief statement about how he and Dickerson have established a team consisting of employees from both Engineering and Production to work to create better communication between the two departments.

### Smith and McNulty:

Should provide details about how this team approach works in practice, including how employees develop drawings for products in order to avoid misunderstanding and to take into account ease of production when products are being designed. Smith and McNulty should also contribute to the second item on the agenda, the assembly-line, with drawings of an assembly-line and an explanation of how it will be more efficient.

### Dickerson:

Should introduce item two on the agenda and then turn the discussion over to McNulty and Smith, who will give details and present an argument in favor of the assembly-line approach. Dickerson will also diplomatically introduce the question of Masters's leadership style and make an appeal for greater decentralization of decision making and less pressure on employees, based on a concern for the employees and the overall success of the company.

### Masters:

Will act his role according to the personality described in the case.

## LANGUAGE MASTERY EXERCISE

### Diplomatic Language

Dealing with personal conflicts such as the ones in this case requires the use of diplomatic language. In the writing section on "Word Choice and Attitudes" in Case 7 (page 65), a series of diplomatic formulations is outlined. Working in pairs and using those formulations, the hints given below, or formulations which you choose yourself, revise the following sentences. Remember that you want to appeal to Masters's desire for cost efficiency and quality control, while not threatening him.

1. We want to install an assembly-line production system.

    *Hint:* We feel that . . .
    Competing factories with assembly-lines . . .

2. The present system of production is not efficient.

    *Hint:* If we installed assembly-line production, we could . . .

3. Your attitude toward us is destructive.

    *Hint:* We feel that we would perform better if . . .

4. Your leadership style prevents necessary cooperation between Engineering and Production.

    *Hint:* Cooperation would be easier if . . .

5. You are pressuring us too much.

    *Hint:* Pressuring us slightly less would . . .

6. We must have the opportunity to cooperate.

    *Hint:* Wouldn't it be better if . . .

7. It is obviously cheaper and more efficient to have assembly-line production.

   *Hint:* What would you say if we could show you that . . .

8. Our best people are going to quit if changes are not made around here.

   *Hint:* We are afraid that . . .

9. Why are you so stubborn and why can't you listen to us?

   *Hint:* Sometimes we feel . . .

10. We demand more decentralized authority.

    *Hint:* We would like to propose . . .

# WRITING: MEMOS

Masters should write a memo to the employees expressing his perception of the outcome of the meeting and proposing any planned changes in his managerial approach.

Dickerson and McNulty should write a memo to the Production staff stating how the decisions at the meeting will affect production routines, including cooperation with Engineering if any agreement on this item was reached.

McRoberts and Smith should write a memo similar to that written by Dickerson and McNulty, only directed to the Engineering staff.

# VOCABULARY

**accountability,** *n.*     Responsibility for the outcome. The person who is *accountable* enjoys the responsibility of making his or her own decisions, but is also responsible for the success or failure of the operation.

**to air a problem,** *v.*     To openly discuss a problem in hopes of solving it.

**authoritarian,** *adj.*     A personal or leadership style in which all power and decision making are vested in the leader or boss.

**bottom-up,** *adj.*     A managerial style in which employees have an influence on decision making. (See *top-down*).

**to breathe down someone's neck,** *v.*     To constantly put pressure on someone and check repeatedly on what they are doing.

**to call on the carpet,** *v.*     To criticize someone for bad on-the-job performance.

**to collaborate,** *v.*     To work together with others.

**collaboration,** *n.*     Working together, often on a specific project.

**company culture,** *n.*     The shared values, beliefs, and ways of doing things in a company.

**compromise,** *n.*     Settling differences by mutual concession.

**to compromise,** *v.*     To settle differences by mutual concession.

**conflict,** *n.*     The blocking of goals and expectations of one individual or group by another individual or group, usually leading to frustration.

**conflict resolution,** *n.* The solving of conflicts. (See Business Organization and Management textbooks for conflict resolution strategies.)

**to confront,** *v.* To face someone and express disagreement.

**confrontation,** *n.* An open dispute.

**to cooperate** *v.* To work together.

**cooperation,** *n.* Working together. *interdepartmental cooperation* refers to cooperation between departments like Production and Engineering.

**decentralized management,** *n.* A management style in which decision making is delegated to employees at lower levels in the organization.

**decision-making process,** *n.* The process by which decisions are made, which also involves deciding who is to make the decisions.

**to delegate,** *v.* To assign power and/or responsibilities.

**delegation,** *n.* The act of giving the power of decision making to employees at levels below that of the one in charge.

**eye for figures,** *adj.* To be good at, and interested in, anything dealing with numbers — in this case, accounting and profit and loss.

**to get wind of something,** *v.* To hear about something indirectly.

**hardheaded,** *adj.* Stubborn.

**horizontal communication,** *n.* Communication between departments at the same level in the organization (for example, between Engineering and Production).

**incremental cash flow,** *n.* The amount of additional cash receipts expected for a period of a time if a project is undertaken.

**to iron out/work out the bugs,** *v.* To improve a product so as to solve technical problems.

**job satisfaction,** *n.* Satisfaction stemming from working conditions and the atmosphere in an organization.

**managerial style,** *n.* See your Business Organization and Management textbook for a description of various managerial styles and their consequences.

**MBO,** *n.* Management by Objective.

**open channels,** *n.* A condition in which (a) employees are free to communicate their ideas to management, and (b) management takes these ideas seriously. In an open-channels system there is **vertical communication**.

**payback period,** *n.* The time it will take to earn back the total amount of money invested in a project.

**personality conflict,** *n.* A situation in which two or more people do not get along due to differences in personality.

**stickler,** *n.* One who insists on something; a *stickler for costs* would be someone who insisted on keeping costs low.

**top-down,** *n.* A management style in which all decisions are made at the top.

# BANKING

## Smith Brothers and Florida Central

## CULTURAL BACKGROUND: LOAN APPLICATIONS

Capital for small businesses is usually provided by banks. In the United States, when a bank loan officer interviews a small business owner who is applying for a loan, he or she may try to evaluate the personal characteristics of the loan applicant as well as get answers to financial questions. The personal aspect of the interview is to determine how serious the loan applicant is, as well as his or her qualities as a businessperson because the loan officer naturally wants to make sure the bank gets its money back. One aspect of the loan application process in the United States that may vary from many other cultures is the importance of the personal contact between the loan officer and applicant, and the loan officer's resulting evaluation of the applicant.

# CASE

Smith Brothers Building Materials Company, Inc. was founded by Wilbur Smith in 1942. Elmer and Zachary Smith, the two youngest sons of the founder, have been managing the company since 1985. All of the company stock is held by a family trust. The company operates six stores throughout the state of Florida. Two stores are located in Orlando, one in Miami, one in West Palm Beach, one in Sarasota, and one in St. Petersburg. Smith Brothers employs a total of 195 people.

Throughout the years, Smith Brothers has utilized the banking services provided by the First Federal Bank of Orlando. Unfortunately, however, Zachary Smith has become dissatisfied with his relationship with First Federal for a variety of reasons, including the high turnover among account officers. Zachary believes that the level and quality of service received from First Federal has declined because of this personnel problem. Florida Central, First Federal's biggest competitor, has tried unsuccessfully for years to solicit business, trust, and personal associations from the family and its business. In light of the current situation, Zachary Smith has been seriously considering developing a relationship with Florida Central. The company's long history of profitable operations and the excellent reputation of the current management make Smith Brothers a very attractive customer for any bank. Although Zachary may be persuaded to develop a relationship with Florida Central, he intends to maintain relationships with a number of different banks to insure that he always receives the level and quality of service that he desires.

A Smith Brothers loan application at Florida Central Bank, dated March 12, 2002, requests a $2.5 million line of credit with the following terms: an interest rate of the national prime rate plus .3 percent, unrestricted use of funds, and no personal guaranty (i.e., the Smith Brothers will not be personally responsible for repayment of the loan if the company is unable to pay it back). Zachary and Elmer Smith have enclosed a statement expressing the reasons for their request. In this document, they assert that the loan is needed to meet seasonal working capital needs related to the building materials industry. The brothers also indicate that they will increase the amount of their loan payments during their slow season, when they would have less money tied up in inventory. Financial statements prepared from the records of the company are also included in the application for examination by the loan officers.

Although Smith Brothers Building Materials appears to be an excellent company, the loan officers at Florida Central have requested that Zachary and Elmer Smith meet with them to discuss the particulars of the loan application. The two Florida Central loan officers, Alexandra Hamilton and Joshua Hall, have some reservations about the loan; they would like to gather more information about the current financial position of the organization and the company's reasons for switching banks before making any decisions about whether or not to grant the brothers' request for a loan. The loan officers must make a determination about the character of the borrowers, their creditworthiness, their capacity to repay the loan, and their ability to put up collateral to secure it. After reviewing the application together, Hamilton and Hall have prepared a number of questions for their interview with the Smith brothers. While the bank has been courting this family's business for many years, the loan officers must negotiate a deal that provides the best possible return for the bank. The loan officers must balance the benefits of securing the Smith family's business against the potential profits for the bank.

Hamilton and Hall have compiled the following list of questions and requests for the Smith brothers. They believe that this line of questioning, along with the additional data requested, will provide them with enough information to make a good decision concerning the creditworthiness of Smith Brothers Building Materials. Students playing the roles of the Smith brothers should prepare answers to these questions, which are based on Hamilton and Hall's analysis of the Smith Brothers' accounts. These students must study the accounts and prepare an explanation in response to these questions. Remember that Hall and Hamilton will also be evaluating the Smith brothers' character and business sense. Thus, those who play the roles of Zachary and Elmer Smith must appear serious and be able to answer these questions in a convincing manner.

1. Would it be possible for you to provide us with audited financial statements? In addition, we would like more detailed information about the subsidiaries.

2. Why have accounts receivable more than doubled in the past year? Have your internal controls changed? We would also like to examine a current accounts-receivable aging schedule if possible.

3. Why were assets shifted from cash to marketable equity securities in 1994? Has your cash management strategy changed?

4. Could you give us an idea of what you intend to do with the loan proceeds?

5. Why did inventory show a drastic increase in 2001?

6. Finally, we would like to discuss the loan terms that you requested in your application. First, failure to obtain a personal guarantee for a loan violates bank policy concerning the extension of credit. Second, the interest rate you requested of prime rate plus .3 percent would prevent the bank from recognizing any type of profit. This rate is far too low to be attractive to the bank. Also, would you object to providing some piece of property as collateral if the loan committee deems it necessary?

The Smith brothers have been informed of the issues to be addressed in their interview with the loan officers by a friend employed at the bank. This has enabled them to effectively prepare for their meeting with Hamilton and Hall.

## POINTS FOR DISCUSSION

1. Discuss what criteria a loan officer would use in evaluating an application such as the one in this case. Consult a banker to get his or her criteria.

2. As a loan officer, what might make you skeptical about granting this loan?

3. What questions might a loan officer ask in the interview with Zachary and Elmer Smith to determine the soundness of the business?

4. How reasonable are the terms requested by Smith Brothers?

## CASE ACTIVITIES

### Applying for a Loan

Half of the groups will prepare the roles of the Smith brothers and develop convincing arguments to support their loan application, preparing answers to the questions above, as well as working out a position in terms of the interest rate negotiations. The other half of the groups will prepare the roles of the loan officers by analyzing the balance sheet from Smith Brothers and reviewing the questions to be asked of Zachary and Elmer Smith. Try to understand the questions in light of the balance sheet (see Figure 9-1). For the meeting of the Smiths and the loan officers, the class will be divided into groups of four (the two Smiths and the two loan officers). There will be as many meetings as there are teams of Smiths and loan officers. In the meeting, the loan officers will ask the questions above and will negotiate the interest rate of the loan and any other conditions they feel are necessary. At the same time, the loan officers will formulate an opinion as to whether or not the loan should be granted, based on the conditions established, the creditworthiness of Smith Brothers, and the character of the two brothers.

## SMITH BROTHERS BUILDING MATERIALS
Balance Sheet
December 31, 2001

| Assets | 12/31/00 | 12/31/01 |
|---|---|---|
| *Current Assets* | | |
| Cash | $1,542,000 | $323,000 |
| Marketable Securities | 287,000 | 1,281,753 |
| Accounts Receivable — Gross | 368,000 | 991,491 |
| Reserve for Bad Debt | −42,000 | −84,000 |
| Accounts Receivable — Net | 326,000 | 907,491 |
| Inventory | 3,985,000 | 4,516,000 |
| **Total Current Assets** | **6,140,000** | **7,028,244** |
| | | |
| *Noncurrent Assets* | | |
| Prepaids | 52,000 | 78,000 |
| Due from Officers | 85,000 | 85,000 |
| Due from Subsidiaries | 1,315,000 | 1,523,000 |
| Total Fixed Assets | 1,217,000 | 978,000 |
| Accumulated Depreciation | −608,500 | −487,000 |
| Net Fixed Assets | 608,500 | 491,000 |
| **Total Noncurrent Assets** | **2,060,500** | **2,177,000** |
| | | |
| **Total Assets** | **8,200,500** | **$9,205,244** |
| Liabilities | | |
| | | |
| *Current Liabilities* | | |
| Accounts Payable | $1,349,000 | $1,457,000 |
| Accruals | 394,000 | 372,000 |
| Taxes Payable | 160,000 | 142,000 |
| **Total Current Liabilities** | **1,903,000** | **1,971,000** |

*continued*

**Figure 9-1**    Balance sheet

*continued*

**Noncurrent Liabilities**
Deferred Taxes

| | | |
|---|---|---|
| Deferred Taxes | 17,500 | 29,000 |
| **Total Liabilities** | **1,920,500** | **2,000,000** |

**Equity**

| | | |
|---|---|---|
| Common | 650,000 | 650,000 |
| Additional — PIC | 20,000 | 20,000 |
| Retained Earnings | 5,610,000 | 6,535,244 |
| **Total Equity** | **6,280,000** | **7,205,244** |
| **Total Equity and Liabilities** | **8,200,500** | **9,205,244** |

**Figure 9-1**   Balance sheet *(continued)*

## The Meeting

Hold the meeting between the loan officers and the Smith brothers. After all the groups have completed their meetings, hold a class discussion in which you address the results of the various meetings. What did the loan officers decide about granting the loan and on what terms? What were the main factors that led to their decision?

# LANGUAGE MASTERY EXERCISE

## Informal Meetings

This is a more informal meeting than in Case 3 ("Other People's Money"), and the vocabulary used reflects the situation. Learn these phrases for use in the meeting. Test your mastery of them by working in pairs and asking each other for sentences for opening, asking someone else's opinion, agreeing, and so on.

### OPENING

JOSHUA HALL (JH):   Thank you for coming. We would like to take a closer look at your application and ask some questions.

### QUESTIONS AND ANSWERS

JH: Perhaps we should first look at your sales figures for 199 __ .
They seem flat. Could you explain that?

ZACHARY SMITH (ZS): Yes, I think that I can explain that.
A simple explanation is . . .

JH: Second, why were assets shifted from cash to marketable equity in 199 __ ? Has your cash management strategy changed?

ZS: Yes, with falling interest rates and a rise in the stock market,
we felt that it was more advantageous to have some of our assets in securities.

### SOLICITING SOMEONE ELSE'S COMMENTS OR OPINION

JH: Alexandra, do you have any questions?

JH: Alexandra, what's your opinion?

### CONCLUDING A SUBJECT

ALEXANDRA HAMILTON (AH): Mr. Smith, do you have anything else you want to add?

### INTERRUPTING

AH: Excuse me, Mr. Smith, but I have a question.

### MOVING ON

JH: Could we go on to question four?

### CREATING A POSITIVE CLIMATE

ZS: I think you will agree that . . .

### STATING PREFERENCES

ZS: We'd rather . . .
We'd prefer to . . .

### PRESENTING THE OTHER SIDE

ZS: On the other hand, . . .
We must not forget . . .
However, we must take into consideration . . .

### AGREEING

JH: I agree with you [*neutral*].
I completely/totally agree with you [*strong*].

ZS: I disagree [*neutral*].
I completely/totally disagree [*strong*].
AH: I'm afraid that I can't quite agree [*more diplomatic*].
Have you considered the consequences of your position [*to raise questions and get the other side to reconsider its position*]?
ZS: I can see your point, but . . . [*creates a common understanding while also presenting disagreement*].

### EXPRESSING RESERVATIONS

JH: I cannot completely agree with your position.
I have some reservations about your proposal.

## WRITING: LOAN APPLICATION RESPONSE LETTER

Write a letter from the loan officer either approving or rejecting Smith Brothers' loan application. If you have decided to grant the loan, state its conditions (i.e., interest rate, the necessity to provide a guaranty, and so on). If you refuse the loan, do so in a polite manner.

## VOCABULARY

**accounts-payable aging,** *n.* A schedule that lists and analyzes the accounts payable in terms of the length of time outstanding.

**accounts-receivable aging,** *n.* A schedule that lists and analyzes the receivable accounts in terms of the length of their time past due.

**acid test ratio,** *n.* A measure of liquidity; the ratio is determined by dividing current assets, less inventories, by current liabilities.

**capacity,** *n.* The ability to repay the loan, usually determined by examining current and future financial positions.

**character,** *n.* Features or attributes that make up and distinguish the individual; when extending credit, an understanding of the applicant's character makes it possible to evaluate the risk involved in granting them a loan.

**collateral,** *n.* Property, such as securities, inventories, land, equipment, or accounts receivable, that is pledged by a borrower to protect the interests of the lender; the borrower would have to forfeit this asset if they became unable to make the required payments.

**compensating balance,** *n.* The average demand (checking account) a bank requires a regular borrower to maintain as part of the loan agreement. It is often 10–20 percent of the face amount of the loan.

**credit,** *n.* An amount or sum placed at a person's disposal by a bank.

**current ratio,** *n.* The ratio of current assets to current liabilities; a measure of an organization's liquidity.

**inventory turnover,** *n.*   A measure of how quickly the inventory is sold; computed by dividing the cost of goods sold by the average inventory.

**line of credit,** *n.*   A formal or informal understanding between a bank and a borrower that indicates how much credit the bank will extend to the borrower.

**liquidity,** *n.*   The ability to meet obligations as they become due. A firm that is liquid can, by definition, support its operational goals.

**marketable equities,** *n.*   Stocks, bonds, and other investments that are easily and quickly sold to obtain cash.

**operating profit,** *n.*   Gross profit less operating expenses.

**promissory note,** *n.*   A written document signed when a bank loan is approved. The note specifies the amount borrowed, the interest rate, the repayment schedule, any collateral put up as security for the loan, and any other terms and conditions to which the bank and borrower may have agreed.

**receivables,** *n.*   Money owed to a company due to goods or services delivered, but not yet paid for.

# INTRODUCTION TO OPEN-ENDED CASES

The remaining cases in this book are open-ended. This means that not all the information necessary to solve them is provided in the cases. Each group will have to research the topic and provide the material to solve the cases. The intention is to help develop information-finding skills to go along with the skills that have already been developed in the previous cases. Another feature of these cases is that they are closely related to local business conditions or are classic cases in the industry (such as Case 14, "Saturn: Can American Automobile Manufacturers Compete with the Japanese?"). Thus, they provide the opportunity to become familiar with actual business questions and problems. Once again, everyone will be expected to play an active role in solving the cases, and will have to seek out information.

Before solving the cases, the class should brainstorm (suggest ideas with no limits) as to where you can best find the necessary information to solve the cases. This activity is invaluable because it will help develop creative thinking, which is one of the most important skills in dealing successfully with the current business climate in an age of information technology. Even though gathering information may be an unfamiliar task, brainstorming will help you develop creative means of obtaining necessary information, a skill that will be very useful in the future.

# MARKETING

## Penetrating the Market with Long-range Golf Clubs and Bags

## CULTURAL BACKGROUND: INFORMATION GATHERING

Marketing techniques vary from country to country. If this case is set in a non-English-speaking country, use that country's approach. If the case is set in an English-speaking country, contact marketing students to get their input on how they would solve the case, and/or read marketing textbooks to get relevant information. Remember, the cases in this book are designed to encourage the development of information-gathering skills, so use the sources of information available to you. The case provides you with the basic information, but discussions with others can provide even more information that will be useful in solving the case.

# CASE

The purpose of this case is to develop a marketing strategy for Long-range products. The case will be based on conditions in the country where you are presently residing. Thus, you will have to do the necessary market analysis based on information to which you should have access. This case is realistic, in that you would have to do the same market analysis if you were going to introduce a new product. *Do not assume that the conclusions regarding your contract in "Long-range Golf Equipment Seeks a Distributor" (Case 4) are necessarily valid in this case. Your means of distribution will depend on other factors, such as your market analysis, segmentation, and market mix (the four P's: product, price, place, and promotion). Remember that all these factors are interdependent; thus, you cannot choose a means of distribution independent of the market analysis, segmentation, and the four P's.*

## POINTS FOR DISCUSSION

1. What are the four P's in marketing and what do decisions involving them consist of? Expand on the information provided in this case by either reading marketing textbooks or interviewing marketing students or experts.
2. What are the basic aspects of market research?

# CASE ACTIVITIES

## Developing a Marketing Strategy

Each group will develop a marketing strategy that will include the following information:

1. Market analysis
2. Market segmentation and selection of target group(s)
3. Positioning
4. The four P's (product, price, place, and promotion)

### Market Analysis

How much is currently being spent on golf clubs and bags in your target market? What percentage of that amount is being spent on clubs and bags in the price range of the equipment you produce? What is the predicted growth in sales in this market over the next five years? Answers to these questions will help you determine what clubs you will launch in the market. We assume that you produce a full range of golf clubs, and that only some of the lines will be appropriate for your target market (it is up to you to determine what range of golf clubs Long-range produces). Use established market forecasting tools to determine these figures, or obtain accurate figures from the national golf association in your country. Analyze the market in terms of (1) demographics — age, gender, and geographic concentration; (2) economics — salaries and professions; and (3) cultural factors — lifestyles, self-image, aspirations. Who are your major competitors and, realistically speaking, what percentage of the market share can you expect to capture in three years?

### Market Segmentation and Selection of Target Group(s)

Segmentation involves dividing the market into segments according to criteria such as age, gender, income, occupation, class, location, lifestyle, self-perception (the person's image of himself or herself), and usage level (the Sunday golfer versus the impassioned golfer who plays as often as possible). Once you have segmented the market, you must choose the target market for your market penetration. Choosing a target market involves finding the segment of the total market that you will strive to capture. This will form the basis for your positioning and market mix (the four P's).

### Positioning

In positioning you will try to choose the right product(s) and give them the right image to capture the chosen target market. For example, you may choose to emphasize the high-tech clubs in your range if your target market is avid golfers who view themselves as good golfers who could be even better with the right clubs. Or you might try to appeal to the Sunday golfer who needs a forgiving club (a club that produces a good shot even if the ball is not perfectly hit). In addition, you will consider product decisions. How do prospective customers decide what to buy — are they buying based on needs, wants, or perceived benefits? What criteria (such as quality, price, and so on) are used to evaluate the product? What information (such as data on score improvement, style and status, the pros who use the clubs, and so on) is necessary to convince customers to buy?

Based on your target market, what range of clubs (how many different lines), and what end of the market (up-market, popular, or someplace in between) do you wish to promote in the beginning? What about golf accessories like bags, shoes, gloves, and the like? How much do you intend to launch in the beginning; and if you intend to increase your line, how quickly do you want to do so?

## The Four P's: Product, Price, Place, and Promotion

The four P's must be in accordance with what you have outlined above. Marketing must be an extremely integrated process, because each individual element influences and is influenced by the other elements.

**PRODUCT:** Which of the products that you currently produce are you going to choose for your market penetration? Naturally, this will depend on your target group. If you are targeting the discerning golfer, you will choose the upper-market range of your line. This decision also involves the choice of products other than golf clubs. Are you going to concentrate on golf clubs alone, or are you also going to launch accessories (bags, clothes, and so on) as well? Are you going to launch everything all at once or phase different products in over time?

**PRICE:** Your choice of target market and products will, of course, influence the price range of the equipment you plan to launch.

**PLACE (CHANNEL OF DISTRIBUTION):** The two P's above will influence your choice of distribution network. If you are targeting the discerning golfer and positioning up-market clubs to capture this market, you will want to distribute them through pro shops (shops at golf courses run by a professional golfer) or other exclusive shops. On the other hand, the Sunday golfer who decides on the basis of price rather than quality may be best reached through department stores like Sears in the United States or Alders in England.

**PROMOTION:** First, you will have to determine your promotional goals. Then you will have to establish a promotion budget that will in turn affect your decisions about promotional mix. You should break down the total amount you intend to spend the first year for each item in your promotional mix, including:

1. *Public relations.* For example, you might hire a golf pro to do a series of golf clinics using Long-range clubs.
2. *Advertising.* Break down your advertising budget into (a) television, (b) radio, (c) newspapers, and (d) magazines.
3. *Sales promotion.* For example, you might hold contests for top salespersons and for buyers of Long-range clubs and bags.

4. *Personal selling.* This item would include commissions, salaries, and operating expenses for your distributor or sales force.

Once you have decided on your mix, you must decide how to effectively use each of the four P's. What is your public relations and sales promotion strategy? What media channels and approach are you going to use? In developing this strategy, you have to work closely with the market segmentation and target market people in your group. The characteristics (life-style, self-perception, attitudes, class, occupation, and so on) of your target market are important factors in designing an advertising strategy. After gaining a thorough knowledge of your target group(s), sketch out the type of television and radio spots you want to use (describe a typical spot in terms of what will be said and done), and lay out advertisements for newspapers and magazines. Explain how these spots and advertisements will convey the intended image of your product and convince the potential buyer (that is, describe the strategy behind your campaign). Based on your budget, provide information about frequency and channels (which television and radio stations and which newspapers and magazines) to be used.

After discussing these market strategy areas in your group, assign the tasks of presentation to each of your group members. One member should handle the market analysis and provide answers to the following questions:

1. How much is currently being spent in the golf club and bag sector?
2. What percentage is being spent on clubs and bags in the price range of the equipment you plan to launch?
3. What is the predicted growth in sales in golf clubs and bags in your market over the next five years?
4. Who are your major competitors, and what market share can you expect to capture in three years?

Use overheads and/or other graphic representations to present your findings.

One member should handle segmentation and selection of the target market. Use charts to depict and present your target group(s). State clearly the characteristics of your target market, such as (a) age, (b) gender, (c) occupation, (d) income, (e) class, (f) life-style and self-perception, and (g) user frequency. Explain why, given these characteristics, you have chosen this segment.

One to two members should present the four P's, working in close conjunction with the market segmentation/target market people in your group. These members should show how your four P's coincide with, and are geared toward, the target market.

In presenting your promotional campaign, make graphics or layouts of your intended ads, and explain them in terms of their impact on the target market you want to reach. For the television and radio spots, either tape existing spots and explain how similar spots could be used to sell *your* clubs and bags, or sketch a scenario orally, covering a thirty-second spot (that is, describe what television viewers or radio listeners will see or hear in your commercials). Discuss frequency and timing of your spots or advertisements, as well as channels (which television and radio stations and which newspapers and magazines). Present an overhead with your promotional budget. Discuss public relations and sales promotion ideas. Be creative!

One group member should present your channel(s) of distribution. Will you primarily use pro shops, general sporting goods shops or department stores, or a mix? What channels would best reach your target market and represent the image of your product that you are trying to promote?

The emphasis in this presentation should be on being professional and creative. To achieve this, do your homework so that you know what you are talking about and are prepared. Do a trial run so that your presentations flow smoothly and are tied together. Use your imagination and consult other sources of information, such as your national golf association and distributors of golf equipment.

## LANGUAGE MASTERY EXERCISE
### Professional Presentation

This case requires a group presentation, so here are some examples of the vocabulary needed to make a professional presentation.

#### GREETING

Good morning/afternoon/evening.

#### INTRODUCTION (OF THE GROUP AND THE TOPIC)

*Note:* Each group should choose an anchorperson who introduces the group and subject and provides a conclusion. This person can also make part of the presentation, depending on the number of members in the group.

We represent Marketing Research, Inc. and are going to present our recommendations for the launching of Long-range Golf Equipment.

Our group consists of Eva, who will present the segmentation of the market and target market selection; Thomas, who will discuss positioning; Roberta, who will cover product and price; and myself, Alice. I will discuss place and promotion.

As I have outlined, our presentation will analyze the market potential for Long-range clubs and bags including segmentation, target market, positioning, and the four P's. First, Eva will present the segmentation of the market and target market selection. Eva. (Eva should then step forward, say "Thank you, Alice," and begin her presentation.)

#### OPENING STATEMENTS

Let me begin by saying . . .
I would like to begin by . . .

**CHANGING THE SUBJECT**

Now that we have looked at the segmentation, let us look at the selection of the target market.

*Note:* To make smooth transitions, use sequencing words such as *first, second, third,* or *first, next, then.* In addition, use transition expressions such as the following:

## For addition

In addition

Equally important

Furthermore

## For comparison

Similarly

Likewise

## For contrast

On the other hand

However

Despite

Although

## To show cause and effect

Thus

Therefore

Consequently

As a result

**HIGHLIGHTS**

Most important, . . .

What you must remember, . . .

Interestingly enough, . . .

**CONCLUSION**

In conclusion, . . .

In summary, . . .

Practice structuring your presentation in advance of the in-class performance, using the above structuring devices.

# WRITING: MARKET REPORT

Write a report to the management of Long-range Sports Equipment in which you summarize your (1) market analysis, (2) market segmentation and the target market you have chosen, as well as why you chose this segment, (3) a strategy for positioning Long-range products, and (4) the four P's.

# VOCABULARY

**advertising,** *n.*   The promotion of an idea, goods, or services through the media.

**advertising agency,** *n.*   An agency whose function it is to develop an advertising campaign.

**brand,** *n.*   A name associated with a specific product (for example, *Coca-Cola, Ford, General Electric*). A *trademark* is a brand that has been given legal protection.

**break-even analysis,** *n.*   A technique to discover what volume of sales is necessary to reach a break-even point (where the seller covers his or her costs).

**cannibalization,** *n.*   A situation in which one product reaches a market share at the expense of other products in the same market produced by the same producer.

**disposable income,** *n.*   The personal income left after deductions for social security, insurance, and taxes.

**F.O.B. (free on board),** *n.*   Any point to which the transportation costs are born by the seller and at which the title passes to the buyer.

**implementation,** *n.*   The putting into practice of a marketing strategy.

**margin,** *n.*   The difference between the cost of production of an item and its selling price.

**market penetration,** *n.*   Entering a new market with a product.

**market share,** *n.*   The percentage of a total market that a product has.

**marketing mix,** *n.*   The combination of factors to be considered in marketing: price, promotion (advertising and personal sales), place (channels of distribution), and product. This is traditionally known as the four P's.

**marketing research,** *n.*   Research done to determine the conditions and potentials of a market.

**positioning,** *n.*   Meeting the needs of a market by either developing a new product, altering an existing product, or changing the image of an existing product through advertising.

**pricing,** *n.*   Setting a price on a product or service.

**prime time,** *n.*   The viewing time on television when most people are watching (usually considered to be between 7 and 11 P.M.).

**product differentiation,** *n.*    Any difference (real or imaginary) intended to set a product apart from its competitors and, it is hoped, make it more attractive to the consumer.

**pro shops,** *n.*    Golf equipment shops run by a professional golfer (the *pro*). The pro may give advice on selecting the proper equipment and give golf lessons. These shops tend to be up-market.

**segmentation,** *n.*    The dividing of a market into segments on the basis of geographical areas, demographics (income, age, gender, ethnic groups, and the like), lifestyles, and attitudes.

**target market,** *n.*    After segmentation, the segment of the market at which a company chooses to aim their product.

**telemarketing,** *n.*    Using the telephone to sell a product.

# MARKETING

## Costa de los Años de Oro

# CULTURAL BACKGROUND: INFORMATION GATHERING

Please refer to the section on "Cultural Background: Information Gathering" in Case 10 (page 89) in preparation for this case.

# CASE

On a recent vacation, you overheard a conversation between two older people (for the purposes of this case, if you live in Europe or Africa, your vacation was in the Canary Islands; if you live in Latin America, it was in the Caribbean; if you live in the Far East, it was in Bali, in which case you will have to change the name of the resort). The people you overheard were complaining about their vacations, and you found their complaints interesting. First, they complained about the lack of availability of extended-stay vacations — say six weeks to three months — for people in their age group. Second, they complained about being jammed in with the disco crowd, and the resulting noise, and so on. Third, they complained about the lack of activities for senior citizens. A couple of days later, you met a local contractor who had access to plots of land to build a resort. You asked for his business card and mentioned that you might be interested in a business deal.

## POINTS FOR DISCUSSION

1. How important are people over 65 as a market, and what products could be successfully promoted in this market? (Try to think of products that are not currently being promoted in this market.)
2. Why is this an increasingly important market, or why is it not?
3. How important are travel and recreation for older people in your culture? Are these people's ideas about travel changing?

## CASE ACTIVITIES

### Market Research: Vacations for Senior Citizens

Upon returning to your country, you start investigating the possibility of a vacation community for senior citizens. You begin by carrying out the following market research to determine (a) if in fact there is a market for a senior citizens' resort and (b) what facilities and activities such a resort should contain. At the same time, you investigate the possibility of opening a travel bureau exclusively for senior citizens to serve that market.

Your market research should include the following:

## Market Segmentation

Do a demographic study of the people in your market area to find out the numbers of senior citizens. Include a gender, income, and occupational status breakdown. (Also find out what percentage of this group is still working full- or part-time, and what percentage is available for long-term vacations.) Is there an imbalance between men and women? Obtain some general information about lifestyle and self-perception (the image they have of themselves, including user frequency, or the frequency of travel; vacation destination; average length of stay; and future travel plans). Also consider benefit segmentation (what people in this market area expect to get in exchange for the money invested, such as companionship, knowledge, excitement, and so on).

## Target Market

Do a profile of your target group, including gender breakdown by percentage, marital status (are there a large number of singles?), preference in terms of the class of hotel facilities (rating from tourist to luxury or using the star system used by tour operators), and expectations in terms of what is offered by a resort. Investigate whether this market is being adequately served. If you find that it is not, move to the next step.

## Positioning

Develop a concept to meet the needs of the market. Begin with your philosophy. What is your concept of vacationing and your attitude toward your target market? How do you view the needs, both personal and recreational, of this group? Include a design of the facilities you intend to build, showing how they will meet the needs of the target market. This design should be graphically represented by pictures of the total facility, with reference to specific facilities and services that your market survey has indicated that senior citizens want. It should also include room plans for rooms that are geared to the needs of people in this group. You should also provide activity schedules based on your market research.

In carrying out this survey, do both primary (if possible) and secondary research. The primary research can be done in the form of a questionnaire to be filled out by senior citizens, while the secondary research can be done through professional journals and by contacting travel agents or tour operators.

Considering your chosen positioning, briefly draw implications for the three remaining P's (you have already adequately described the product above): *price* and comfort level, *packages* in terms of length of stay and what the price includes, and *promotion* (what media will you use to promote the product?).

Here are a few tips for gathering the information necessary for this case.

Tour operators and travel bureaus should have a good deal of information about the market and brochures that you can use for your graphics. In addition, senior citizens' organizations might have some information. You might want to go to a social meeting of a group of senior citizens to have them fill out a market survey questionnaire. Don't forget your grandparents or parents. They may possess a wealth of information if they belong to your target market.

The presentation will consist of your group's presentation of the findings of your market survey, grouped in the categories outlined above: (1) segmentation, (2) target market, and (3) positioning (including a graphic presentation of the resort you are planning to develop to meet the demands of the market). You should assign each segment of the presentation to one or two group members so that every group member participates. Assign a group member the role of anchorperson; this person will give a general introduction and conclusion. Although all groups should come prepared to present, the teacher may choose two groups to present so that the presentation phase will not be too repetitive.

# LANGUAGE MASTERY EXERCISES

## Presentation

Refer to the "Professional Presentation" section of Case 10, "Penetrating the Market with Long-range Golf Clubs and Bags" (pages 93 – 94) for language suggestions.

## Social Dialogues

Much business takes place in a social setting. Study the social English presented below and practice the dialogues in pairs until you feel comfortable with them. (The responses should come naturally without your having to think about them.)

### INTRODUCTIONS

DAVID SANCHEZ (DS): Good morning, my name is David Sanchez [or, I am David Sanchez], and I represent the resort Costa de los Años de Oro.

ROBERTA JOHNSON (RJ): How do you do. Roberta Johnson, Tour Product Development Manager for Mansfield Tours. Pleased to meet you.

DS: Nice to meet you, Roberta/Ms. Johnson.

*Note:* Different cultures have different degrees of formality. In some cultures it is acceptable to start using first names from the beginning. However, if in doubt, use titles and last names.

### INTRODUCTION OF OTHERS

DS: Ms. Johnson, I would like to introduce you to our Marketing Manager, Alberto Gomez (AG). Alberto, this is Roberta Johnson.

RJ: Pleased to meet you, Mr. Gomez.
AG: Nice meeting you, Ms. Johnson.

> *Note:* Mr. Gomez could also say simply, "Nice meeting you."

### SEEING PEOPLE AGAIN

DS: Nice to see you again, Ms. Johnson. How have you been?
RJ: Fine, and you? How has business been?

> *Note:* Do not say, "Nice to *meet* you again." The verb *to meet* is only used for the first meeting.

### INVITING AND ACCEPTING

RJ: Can I take you out to lunch?
DG: Thank you very much.
RJ: My pleasure. We can look at the contract over lunch.
DG: Sounds like a good idea.

### REJECTING AN INVITATION

DAVID SMITH (DS): Bill, would you like to come over for dinner on Friday?
BILL JONES (BJ): I'd love to, but I'm afraid I am busy/have a commitment/will be out of town.

### THANKING

DS: Thanks for helping me out with that contract. I never would have finished it without your help.
BJ: Think nothing of it. I was glad I could help you.
*or* You're quite welcome.
*or* Don't mention it.

# WRITING: MARKETING REPORT

Write a report in which you summarize (1) your market segmentation and the target market you have chosen, as well as your reasons for choosing this segment; (2) a strategy for positioning the resort; and (3) the four P's.

# VOCABULARY

For important terms in this case, see the Vocabulary list for Case 10: Penetrating the Market with Long-range Golf Clubs and Bags on pages 95–96.

# ENVIRONMENT

## Industrial Pollution: Charting Pollution and Proposing Solutions

## CULTURAL BACKGROUND: RELATIONS BETWEEN BUSINESS AND ENVIRONMENTALISTS

Environmental issues can be very sensitive, especially from the point of view of business and industry. Thus, an investigator may not receive full cooperation in the attempt to uncover material. Most countries do have environmental organizations that can provide useful information. However, due to the sensitivity of the situation described in this case, be careful not to antagonize local businesses, while at the same time try to obtain the information necessary to solve the case.

# CASE

This is an extension of the case Northern Electrical Services vs. the Environmentalists (Case 6), and the knowledge you gained in solving that case can be applied here. In this case, you are to play the role of an environmentalist group investigating industrial pollution in your area. Begin by targeting one of the major industrial polluters in your area to find out the extent and type of air and water pollution emitted from their company. Local environmental groups can often be helpful in providing this information. Check on whether this company is exceeding nationally set limits (if your country has national standards) or emitting significant amounts of pollutants (in the event that your country does not have national standards), and find out if its management has been warned about their infractions. If they have been warned, find out why they have resisted making the required improvements. If the company does exceed nationally set limits (or emits large amounts of air and/or water pollution), make an estimate of the impact on the health of the local residents. This may be difficult to determine accurately, as it is difficult to isolate the effects of one company's emissions from the total amount of pollution. However, once you have determined the type of pollutants emitted by the targeted factory, you can make an educated guess as to the effects on the health of the local population by seeing if disorders associated with those pollutants are prevalent in your area. Once again, local environmentalist groups can provide valuable information. Often, health studies have already been conducted.

## POINTS FOR DISCUSSION

1. Which companies are the major polluters in your area?
2. Have they made any progress in reducing their pollution recently? If so, how have they done so? If not, why not?
3. What can be done to make these companies more environmentally responsible?

## CASE ACTIVITIES

### Preparing and Presenting Environmental Issues

The environmentalist group should use graphs to present the national standards (or accepted international standards, if your country has no national standards) compared with the company's emissions. These graphs should show incidences of illness (such as cancer, spontaneous abortions, and asthma) which could be associated with the pollutants emitted by the company that you have targeted and compare the number of these incidences with the national average. If there is a significant difference between the national and local averages, be prepared to present and explain this discrepancy.

At the same time that the environmentalist group is preparing a presentation of the amount and effects of the pollution emitted by the targeted company, a second group should prepare the role of management of the same company. They should prepare a defense of their present emission practices. They should also try to guess what improvements the environmentalist group is going to recommend and estimate the costs of these improvements, based on information provided by environmental groups, state environmental agencies, producers of environmental clean-up equipment, or the company's management itself. They should prepare a negotiation position that will include:

1. A statement of their feelings of civic responsibility toward the local community and what they are doing to fulfill their pledge of civic responsibility.
2. An estimation of the costs of installing equipment to meet the emission standards expected to be proposed by the environmentalists.
3. The future of the company if they are forced to cover the costs of reducing the amount of pollution emitted from their facilities. You can describe several possible scenarios, based on the costs per percentage of clean-up and the impact on your company's finances. For example,
   a) To remove 90 percent of the sulfur dioxide from our emissions will require equipment at a cost of $X and will have the following impact on our company's finances. . . .
   b) To remove 95 percent of the sulfur dioxide from our emissions will require. . . .

## Presentation

The case will involve the presentation of the environmentalist group's findings to the management group. The environmentalist group will graphically represent the following findings:

1. The amount and type of water and air pollution emitted by the company in question (an educated guess).
2. A comparison with accepted standards (either national or recognized international standards).
3. An estimation of the impact of these emissions on the health of the local population (including a commentary linking local incidence of illness to these pollutants, if the incidence of these illnesses significantly exceeds the national average).
4. Recommendations to the company as to what they should do to reduce the amount of pollution emanating from their company and, if possible, the costs of these procedures.

After the environmentalist group presents its findings, the management group can respond on the basis of the three points mentioned on page 104 (a statement of their sense of civic responsibility, an estimate of the costs of reducing pollution, and the impact on the finances of the company). They can choose a hard-line response, suggesting that they are already doing enough and that any increased expenses may force them to consider closing the factory. Or they may make a more flexible response, trying to meet the environmentalist group halfway. Management's response should lead to a discussion between the two groups. It is impossible to know where that discussion will lead, but if the environmentalist group is not satisfied with the result, they may suggest sanctions (such as fines and the like) that could be levied against the company to force them to comply with accepted standards.

Two groups will be chosen to present, one representing management and one representing the environmentalists. These two groups will be chosen at the last minute, so all groups must be prepared to present. The remaining groups' members can ask questions of those presenting after the initial presentations have been made.

# LANGUAGE MASTERY EXERCISE

## Tone: Confrontation versus Mutuality

The tone of the meeting between the environmentalists and the business management could be either one of *confrontation*, in which the environmentalists demand and management makes counterthreats, or one of *mutuality*, in which the two sides attempt to arrive at a solution. The sentences below will help you develop the vocabulary to deal with either situation. Practice them in pairs until you feel confident in their use. One student should read the first response (that of the environmentalists) and test whether the second student makes an appropriate response.

### Confrontation

1. ENVIRONMENTALISTS (E):  We demand an immediate cleanup.
      MANAGEMENT (M):  You realize that such expenses will cause our factory to become unprofitable, thus forcing its closing.

2. E:  You realize that your company is the major polluter in this area.
   M:  Can you show us conclusive proof that *we*, rather than another company, are the major polluter?

3. E:  If you do not install cleaning systems in your smokestacks, we will block the entrance to your factory.
   M:  Have you considered the impact of your actions on the local economy and the possible reaction among the workers at the factory?

4. E:  You are using loss of jobs to create fear among the local population and avoid your responsibility to the community.
   M:  We are showing responsibility to the local community by providing many well-paid jobs.

5. E:  You are the greatest health threat to our community.
   M:  Studies we have undertaken show that we are not exceeding accepted limits on emissions.

### Mutuality

Responses to environmentalists' claims can also be met with a sense of having a mutual interest in cleaning up the environment, as expressed by the following responses.

In this pair work exercise, the student representing the environmentalists should make a claim or demand and the student representing management should respond in a manner geared toward reaching a compromise solution. After the student playing the role of management has made his or her offer, the student playing the role of the environmentalists should respond to it. Use some of the following expressions or develop your own responses.

> We are prepared to . . .
> We are willing to . . .
> Would the following be acceptable . . . ?
> We have no objection provided that . . .
> We can meet you halfway and are willing to offer . . .
> We feel that a solution that would be mutually beneficial is . . .

## WRITING: NEWSPAPER ARTICLE

The material presented in your oral presentation will be written up in the form of a newspaper article to the local newspaper. This article should include the following:

1. A brief statement of management's position.
2. A brief statement of the environmentalists' position and demands.
3. A summary of the results of the meeting (Was a compromise reached, or does it look like the factory will be closed down and so on).

## VOCABULARY

See the Vocabulary list in Case 6: Northern Electrical Services vs. the Environmentalists on pages 57 – 59.

# INTERNATIONAL TRADE

## Competing Internationally

# CULTURAL BACKGROUND: BRITISH COMPETITIVENESS IN BUSINESS

Because this case involves four to six countries, most of which will be chosen by you, the students, it is not possible to provide a complete cultural background. In fact, an analysis of the cultural background and how it affects the competitiveness of the chosen company is part of the task of this case. However, to give an idea of what this analysis involves, several factors that may impact on companies in Great Britain can be noted. There is a strong sense of class and noticeable class divisions in Great Britain, which may result in conflicts between management and workers or may result in strikes that will reduce productivity. This class division may also influence management's attitude toward its workers and its managerial philosophy and style. Management may be less democratic, and decision making may be more centralized at the top, leading to a top-down (more authoritarian) managerial style. This may be met by a more confrontational attitude on the part of the workers and resistance to changes brought about by managerial decisions based on changing market conditions. British workers have traditionally been less productive than their European counterparts, although Britain has made progress in this area during recent years.

Another cultural factor of importance is the English educational system (note that the Scottish system is different). Two-thirds of English pupils leave school at the age of sixteen; the English system does not emphasize technical education and has a poorly developed apprentice system. This may lead to a poorly educated resource pool. In addition, the school system reflects the class division mentioned above. Many of the top leaders in English politics and business have attended exclusive private schools and then gone on to elite universities, such as Oxford and Cambridge, where they have not studied business subjects. As a result, they have often had little contact with the people they will manage and have not developed an understanding of them nor the interpersonal skills needed to deal with them. In addition, these leaders often develop a very conservative and risk-avoiding view of life and business, which can greatly limit their entrepreneurial spirit.

These are just a few examples of how culture affects business conditions and thus a country's competitiveness. In addition, one finds individual variations in *company* culture from company to company. It is important to analyze company culture as well, as it has a strong impact on competitiveness. Some important aspects of company culture are:

1. *The company's stated philosophy, how it is conveyed to the employees, and to what degree it is followed in the company's daily activities.* The philosophy should include information about managerial philosophy and decision-making practices (democratic or authoritarian, decentralized or centralized).

2. *How the company's management views its workers and what it does to increase job satisfaction.* This is often reflected in how decentralized the decision-making process is and the efforts the company makes to educate and upgrade the skills of its workers.

3. *The degree of information sharing between management and workers.* This is needed so that company goals are shared and so that workers can participate in shaping these goals.

4. *The company's equipment and interior design, which reflect management's attitude toward their products and those who produce them.* Are production facilities modern enough to efficiently produce *state of the art* products (the most advance products possible)? Are the facilities pleasant and healthy, reflecting management's concern for the job satisfaction and health of its workers?

# CASE

Recent decades of steadily declining market shares have shown British manufacturers that British industrial dominance is a thing of the past. British manufacturers assumed that their position as market leaders, established before World War II, would go unchallenged, but they have seen that position erode steadily. Faced with the consequences of European unification, such as the *four freedoms* (the free flow of capital, goods, services, and work force), the British economy is likely to become even more vulnerable to the threats posed by the French, Germans, Italians, and Spanish. Thus, the National Economic Development Council has called a seminar to look at the future of British manufacturing. The purpose is to analyze the present state of one industry sector of British manufacturing, whether it be automobiles, steel, electronics, or whatever. The sector to be analyzed and the British company to be used in this case should be chosen by the class.

## POINTS FOR DISCUSSION

Discuss some or all of the following factors, stating how and to what degree they impact on a company's ability to compete internationally:

1. Production costs
2. Human resource pool

3. Product quality

4. Research and development

5. Governmental policy (tax, regulation, support, and import restrictions, and so on)

6. Capital costs and the access to capital

7. Impact of exchange rates

8. Use of information technology and computer-assisted design to more rapidly adapt to changing world markets

9. Use of logistical strategies, such as just-in-time delivery, to cut costs

10. Use of joint ventures and coalitions to develop a synergy effect

11. Use of international marketing strategies

12. Organizational structure and its impact on competitiveness

## CASE ACTIVITIES

### Researching International Trade

This is an open-ended case in which you must research the subject in order to solve the case. After choosing one representative British company in one industry, choose the major competitors in each of three to five other EU (European Union) countries. Make a comparative study of the British company in regard to some or all of the factors mentioned in the Points for Discussion above. Based on this comparison, make a prognosis for the possible future success of the British company and a list of changes that will need to be made in order for this company to succeed in the EU.

This case should be presented in several sessions. First, the British company should be presented by a group whose presentation will include some or all of the areas just described. In the next session, the other groups will present their companies and compare them with the British company in these areas. In the final session, the group presenting the British company will present the future strategy for competition, taking into account what they have learned about the competitors. Naturally, they will have to propose changes in the company and the means of carrying out these changes. There must be enough time between each session to allow the groups adequate time to prepare.

## LANGUAGE MASTERY EXERCISES

### Terms for Comparison: Comparatives and Superlatives

In this case you will be comparing companies. You will use the *comparative* form of adjectives when comparing two companies, and the *superlative* form when comparing more than two companies:

## Comparatives

Comparatives are used to compare two subjects.

| Adjective | Comparative Form | Example |
|-----------|------------------|---------|
| good | better | Our products are better than theirs. |
| bad | worse | Their profits were worse than expected. |

Use *-er* endings to make regular one- or two-syllable adjectives into comparative adjectives. For example, the comparative form of *smart* is *smarter:*

Barbara is *smarter* than Joe.

Use *less* or *more*, plus the adjective, to make comparative adjectives from regular adjectives with three or more syllables. For example, the comparative form of *complicated* is *more* (or *less*) *complicated:*

Their system is *more complicated* than ours.
Our system is *less complicated* than theirs.

*Note:* Use *as . . . as* when making equal comparisons.

Our products are *as* good *as* theirs.

## Exercise: Using Comparatives

Using the following nouns and adjectives, make sentences comparing two companies.

*Examples:*

| Noun | Adjective |
|------|-----------|
| 1. costs | high |

Our costs were higher than theirs.

| Noun | Adjective |
|------|-----------|
| company | profitable (*equal*) |

Our company is as profitable as Company X.

| Noun | Adjective |
|------|-----------|
| 1. profits | high |
| 2. costs | low |
| 3. workers | productive (*equal*) |
| 4. designers | creative (*equal*) |
| 5. employees | highly educated |
| 6. technology | highly developed |
| 7. production costs | expensive |
| 8. financial position | solid |
| 9. design | advanced (Use the word *less* in the sentence.) |
| 10. prices | competitive (Use the word *less* in the sentence.) |

### Superlatives

Superlatives are used to compare three or more subjects.

| Adjective | Superlative Form | Example |
|---|---|---|
| good | best | Our company is the best of the three. |
| bad | worst | Their products are the worst of the five displayed. |

Use *-st* endings to make regular one- or two-syllable adjectives into comparative adjectives. For example, the superlative form of *fast* is *fastest:*

This is the *fastest* machinery on the market.

Use *least* or *most*, plus the adjective, to make superlative adjectives from regular adjectives with three or more syllables. For example, the superlative form of *impressive* is *most* (or *least*) *impressive:*

The *least impressive* product was made by Company X.
The *most impressive* product was made by Company Y.

*Note:* In making equal comparisons of three or more subjects, use the same form as used in comparing two subjects.

Our products are *as* good *as* all of our competitors' products.

### Exercise: Using Superlatives

Using the adjectives and nouns in the Exercise on page 112, make sentences in the superlative.

## WRITING: REPORT ON COMPETITIVE POSITION

Each group will write a separate report stating the competitive position of their company and suggesting necessary changes to improve that competitive position. This report should be complete with a vocabulary list of terms relevant to this case and their definitions.

## VOCABULARY

**brand,** *n.*   The name associated with a specific product, such as Coca-Cola, Ford, Phillips.

**business climate,** *n.*   The general conditions for doing business and producing goods in a country, including such factors as government regulations and support, interest rates, and union-management relations.

**coalitions,** *n.*   Formal, long-term alliances between firms that link aspects of their business without actually entering into a merger.

**consumer confidence,** *n.* The confidence consumers have in a company's products, which is often reflected in consumer loyalty (the degree to which a consumer will purchase the same brand when making new purchases).

**economies of scale,** *n.* The advantages gained by large-scale production, which reduces per unit cost of products.

**EU,** *n.* The European Union.

**job security,** *n.* The likelihood that a worker will not be laid off (that is, have his or her employment terminated, due to a lack of work).

**joint venture,** *n.* A partnership formed by two or more companies to cooperate on some special business activity.

**just-in-time logistics,** *n.* Delivering goods to customers directly, based on computerized models, to save warehousing costs.

**loyalty,** *n.* A relationship of trust and concern, developed between employers and employees, that causes workers to feel secure in their jobs and to make a maximum effort.

**market mix,** *n.* The combination of the four P's (product, price, promotion, and place) that best meets the needs of the consumer.

**market research,** *n.* Research done to determine the conditions and the potentials of a market.

**market shares,** *n.* The percentage of the total market that a product achieves in a given market.

**positioning,** *n.* Meeting the needs of a market by (a) developing a new product, (b) altering an existing one, or (c) changing the image of an existing product through advertising.

**product differentiation,** *n.* Any difference, real or imaginary, that sets a product apart from competitors' products and, it is hoped, makes it more attractive to the consumer.

**production costs,** *n.* The costs of producing goods, including fixed costs (such as factories), direct costs (such as labor), material costs, and capital costs (such as interest on loans).

**production time,** *n.* The length of time it takes to produce a product.

**productivity,** *n.* The average amount of goods produced by a worker in a given amount of time. The higher the productivity, the lower the cost per unit.

**prognosis,** *n.* A prediction about future business conditions and potential markets and sales.

**quality,** *n.* How good or bad a product is. Ways of evaluating quality include *customer satisfaction studies* (which indicate how satisfied customers are with the product) and *recall* (the number of products that have been recalled due to mistakes in production, which must be corrected).

**recall,** *n.* Having to call in products to correct mistakes in production. A high recall percentage raises questions about the quality of a product.

**R & D** (Research and Development), *n.* Studies involving the discovery of new potential products and the development of the actual product.

**recognition factor,** *n.*   The degree of familiarity among consumers of a company's brands.

**synergy,** *n.*   The effect gained by merging the strengths of two or more companies.

**target market,** *n.*   After segmentation, the segment (a part of the total market) at which a company chooses to aim their product.

# REFERENCES

The following two works should provide you with the information and vocabulary to solve this case. If these textbooks are not available in your library, look for other textbooks on competitive analysis.

Oster, Sharon M. *Modern Competitive Analysis*. Oxford: Oxford University Press, 1990.

Porter, Michael. *Competition in Global Industries*. Boston: Harvard Business School Press, 1986.

# BUSINESS

# ORGANIZATION

# AND MANAGEMENT

## Saturn: Can American Automobile Manufacturers Compete with the Japanese?

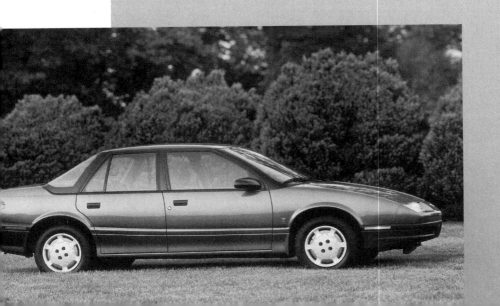

## CULTURAL BACKGROUND: AMERICAN AND JAPANESE BUSINESS CULTURES

This case provides the opportunity to analyze two business cultures and discover their strengths and weaknesses. Solving it will give you insight into differences in human resource policies, including the relation between management and workers, attitudes toward research and development, and the ability to react quickly to changing markets and production techniques and their impact on productivity. It is a classic case providing a look into the business cultures of two leading industrial nations — useful information for future businesspersons like yourselves.

# CASE

In your studies, you have undoubtedly encountered the problem American manufacturers have had competing with the Japanese. Here is a chance to use your theoretical knowledge. When General Motors (GM) decided to produce the Saturn model, they took the radical step of starting a whole new company and factory outside of the parent company. This could be seen as an admission of defeat, in that GM seemed to be saying that they simply could not produce a competitive car within the present company framework, due to its bureaucratic rigidity and all that it entailed in terms of impeding changes in engineering, production, and human resource policy. In addition, this decision could have been an admission, explicit or implicit, of the many failings of American automobile manufacturing, not only at GM but across the board. Comparative figures from the time when the idea of Saturn was developed (1983) show the competitive advantages that the Japanese enjoyed.* In 1979, the market share captured by Japanese automobiles was 17 percent; three years later, in 1982, it had grown to 30 percent.

Cost differentials between Japanese and American automobiles show a competitive advantage in favor of the Japanese in 1983, the year this case takes place:

---

*Figures source: William J. Abernathy et al. *Industrial Renaissance: Producing a Competitive Future for America.* New York: Basic Books, 1983.

|                                                 | Japan   | USA     |
|-------------------------------------------------|---------|---------|
| Hourly wage rate (average) + benefits           | $11.91  | $23.31  |
| Total production costs per vehicle (average)     | $4,211  | $6,520  |
| Capacity utilization level                       | 95%     | 85%     |
| Capacity adjusted costs                          | $4,363  | $7,285  |

The cost of American cars averaged $2,922 more than Japanese cars for comparative models.

In terms of customer satisfaction, Japanese automobiles enjoyed this advantage: Approximately 75 percent of American car owners, versus 93 percent of Japanese car owners, said that they would purchase the same make of car again.

Management's attitudes towards their work force can be reflected in layoff figures, in that these figures represent human resource policy and consideration for the workers' welfare. In 1983, the Japanese no-layoff policy resulted in virtually no layoffs, while in the years between 1980 and 1984, Ford and Chrysler laid off 40 percent of their workers, and GM laid off 17 percent of its workers. One can hypothesize that workers who feel secure in their jobs will feel greater loyalty to the company, and that loyalty will be reflected in their job performance.

The figures listed here illustrate some of the problems American automobile producers faced in 1983. Such problems required a change in their approach to producing automobiles. Following are some of the problems that the Saturn project attempted to solve (and with which this case will deal).

## Engineering

Can American engineers produce a quality, gas-efficient car that can be assembled in a competitive number of working hours? Can engineering be responsive to consumers' needs, or do they expect the consumer to adapt to the engineers' product?

Take for example the complaint of American automobile makers that the Japanese market is restrictive, thus making market penetration difficult. While this is true, it is also true that the American cars exported to Japan have had the steering wheel on the left, as in American cars. However, the Japanese drive on the left side of the road and need the steering wheel on the right. Granted, American car manufacturers are finally producing cars with the steering wheels on the right for export. But how many years did it take them to adapt?

Another case of poor adaptation to consumers' demands is the slow response of the American automobile industry to the oil crisis in the 1970s. American companies kept on producing gas guzzlers long after it became apparent that the market was calling for more fuel-efficient cars. This left the door open for the Japanese penetration into the U.S. car market.

Then there is the question of quality. Japanese cars generally led the list of cars eliciting the least complaints from customers, whereas American cars more often fell nearer the bottom of the list. American cars have made some progress in this area in recent years. But this progress has been slow, and American-made cars have developed a bad reputation that their manufacturers are now struggling to overcome. When you discuss engineering, you are going to have to come up with ways for American automobile companies to be more consumer- and quality-oriented.

### Production

According to a recent television report, it takes GM an average of 44 working hours to assemble a car, while Ford and Japanese automobile makers take less than half that time. In designing your production facility, you will have to take this into account and, based on approaches from either Saturn or other successful car manufacturing plants, suggest ways of cutting production time.

### Human Resources

There are glaring gaps between the job security and family loyalty approach of Japanese employers and the periodic layoffs and plant-closing approach of American automobile employers. Does GM care about their employees? If not, will they be able to produce quality cars until they *do* start caring about the people that design and build them? You will have to design a human resource policy that is more responsive to the needs of employees, in hopes of increasing employees' motivation, which will in turn lead to greater output and quality.

### Organizational Structure

GM has been criticized for its deep and hierarchical structure, which makes the company too bureaucratic and, in turn, leads to a slowness in responding to market trends. Recent critics have wondered why it has taken GM so long to respond to obvious changes. Some analysts believe the nation's large firms might have avoided recent traumatic cost cutting if they had been more responsive to the fundamental competitive challenges of the last two decades. Perhaps creating separate, smaller companies with flatter organizational structures (i.e., fewer levels) like that of the Saturn project is the way of the future. In any case, you will have to set up a flatter, more responsive organizational structure for the Saturn project that can respond to changes in the market more rapidly than the present deep structure at GM.

## POINTS FOR DISCUSSION

1. Discuss in detail recent developments in the competition and cooperation between American and Japanese automobile manufacturers. Do recent improvements in American competitiveness reflect improvements in engineering, production, organizational structure, and human resource policy or are these improvements simply a result of the strength of Japanese currency, which makes Japanese cars too expensive?

2. Discuss whether the American automobile producers will be able to recapture

some of the market shares they have lost to the Japanese and what they will have to do to recapture these shares.

# CASE ACTIVITIES

## Corporate Organization

The purpose of this case is to give you insight into problems faced by large corporations and the opportunity to work on solutions to these problems in English. In this case, you will form task forces to discuss the areas mentioned above and outline a strategy for the establishing of the company to produce Saturns. Your meeting will consist of two representatives from each of the four departments suggested above: Engineering, Production, Human Resources, and Management. There will be as many task forces as the size of your class allows. After each task force has reached conclusions concerning the four areas mentioned above, compare notes in a classroom discussion, with each task force presenting and defending its conclusions and answering questions from the other task forces. In advance of the meeting, all members of each section should meet separately and discuss aspects of their area's problem. Thus, they will prepare in advance of the meeting. Diagrammed, the process will look like this:

### PHASE 1: PREPARATION

| Engineering | Human Resources | Management | Production |
|---|---|---|---|
| Student A | Student E | Student I | Student M |
| Student B | Student F | Student J | Student N |
| Student C | Student G | Student K | Student O |
| Student D | Student H | Student L | Student P |

### PHASE 2: TASK FORCE MEETINGS

Meeting 1: Students A, B, E, F, I, J, M, N

Meeting 2: Students C, D, G, H, K, L, O, P

This structure assumes that you have 16 students. If you have more students, you can have three or more task forces.

This is an open-ended case, which means that all the information necessary to solve the case is *not* provided here. Thus, you will have to research the case. Fortunately, the Saturn project drew much media attention, so you should find plenty of material in newspapers, magazines, and so on.

This case provides an opportunity for creative information-gathering techniques and case solutions. The engineers in the case should address the questions of design and quality that are available in Saturn brochures. The Production people should discuss ways of rationalizing assembly and present drawings of production facilities. Human Resources should outline a policy that is in line with employees' needs. Management should propose an organizational structure that is more responsive to employee suggestions (including open channels of communication and a flatter structure, for example). In addition, this group should discuss a more decentralized decision-making system and an organization that is more responsive to changes in the market.

The task forces should discuss solutions in the four areas mentioned above and prepare a presentation. *Although you will be referring to articles and other materials about the development of the actual Saturn project, you should discuss this case as if it were 1983 and* you *were developing the project.* Thus, you can make reference to the failings of GM and propose your solutions as a remedy for GM's problems.

When the task forces have come to a conclusion and have a strategy for the establishing of Saturn, their conclusions should be presented to the class, along with diagrams of (a) car designs, (b) more efficient assembly plants, and (c) a flatter, more responsive organizational structure. The task forces should also present statements concerning management and personnel policy and ways of insuring quality and production efficiency. Each task force should present and defend their conclusions. The other class members can ask questions and criticize the presenting task force's conclusions, which should lead to lively discussion.

## LANGUAGE MASTERY EXERCISES

See the exercises on pages 111 – 113.

## WRITING: GROUP PROJECT/REPORT

The information from the oral presentation should be written up in the form of a report. As this case is fairly advanced, the report can be considered a group project term paper, which will receive a grade.

## VOCABULARY

See the Vocabulary list in Case 13 ("Competing Internationally") on pages 113 – 115.

## REFERENCES

Also refer to articles in *Business Week*, the *Wall Street Journal*, and *Fortune*.

Daft, Richard L. *Organizational Theory and Design*. St. Paul, Minn: West Publishing, 1992.

Oster, Sharon M. *Modern Competitive Analysis*. Oxford: Oxford University Press, 1990.

Porter, Michael. *Competition in Global Industries*. Boston: Harvard Business School Press, 1986.

# Appendix 1
# TELEPHONE
# ENGLISH

The majority of your communication in English will be over the telephone. In fact, in international trade it is possible to have business relationships for years without ever seeing the people with whom you are dealing. It is through the telephone that you project an impression of yourself and the company you represent. Thus, it is extremely important that you master the skills necessary to communicate well over the telephone, which is the purpose of this Appendix.

The activities in this Appendix will make you aware of the subtle differences in communication that make a big difference in the impression you create. Not being aware of these differences can result in your seeming rude or arrogant, unsophisticated or not service-minded. It can take no more than saying "I want" instead of "I would like to" to create a bad impression. In addition, there is the cultural element that must also be understood in order to communicate effectively with native English speakers. First, you must be made aware of a standard form that English telephone conversations often have. Second, you should be aware of two extremely important cultural values that must be expressed: politeness and service-mindedness. So let us take a look at these elements and then practice them until they become second nature.

## ANSWERING A BUSINESS TELEPHONE CALL

### Seven Steps

Following is a list of seven steps you may use to answer the telephone in a business setting.

#### 1. GREETING

> Hello.
> Good morning.
> Good afternoon.

The greeting is optional and would mainly be used by switchboard operators (for example, *Good morning, General Foods*). However, it is appropriate if you are sure the call is coming from outside the company.

**2. IDENTIFICATION**

Accounting, David Warner speaking.

**3. OFFER OF HELP**

May I help you?
How may I help you?

This is also optional but recommended when dealing with customers. Thus, if you work in customer service, customer relations, or sales, offering help would be appropriate.

**4. EXCHANGE OF INFORMATION**

This is the core of the telephone conversation, in which information is exchanged, requests are made, meetings are arranged, and so on. It is here that you can show your sophistication by being informative, polite, and service-minded.

**5. CONFIRMATION OF MESSAGE**

If the caller has made a request, if a meeting date has been set, or if something has been decided, repeat it to be sure that both parties have understood the same thing or that the request is clear. This will help avoid misunderstandings. Confirmation of the message is expected as part of a conversation by English-speaking people, and it makes your telephone manners seem more sophisticated.

**6. CONFIRMATION OF ACTION**

You confirm that you will do what is requested or what has been decided. If time permits, you should follow this up by confirming your intended action in writing.

**7. CLOSING**

"Goodbye" is the standard closing, but you can make a good final impression in this call by adding something polite or service-minded, such as "If you have any other questions, don't hesitate to call," or "Thank you for calling. I'm looking forward to our meeting."

Now let's walk through a standard telephone call using the seven steps.

BJ: Good morning. Macintosh Customer Service, Bill Jenkins speaking. How may I help you? [Steps 1–3]

DJ: My name is Dick Johnson. I just bought a Macintosh LC II with Systems 7, but I didn't get the operations manual.

BJ: Oh, that's strange. It should have been included in the package. It's called Macintosh Reference 7. However, that's easy to solve. I'll send you a copy by UPS (United Parcel Service). You should get it in a couple of days. What's your address, Mr. Johnson? [Note that an American employee might refer to this customer as "Dick." The use of first names is very common in the United States, but much less common in Great Britain.]

DJ: It's 515 Wilson Avenue, Kingston, Rhode Island 02881. [Step 4]

BJ: Let me repeat that, Mr. Johnson. That was 515 Wilson Avenue, Kingston, Rhode Island 02881. [Step 5]

BJ: I'll put a copy of Macintosh Reference 7 in the mail and you should get it by Friday. [Steps 5 and 6] Is there anything else I can do for you? [A sign of service-mindedness.]

DJ: No. That should do it.

BJ: All right, but if you have any other questions, don't hesitate to call. [Once again, service-mindedness.] Goodbye.

DJ: Goodbye.

## Telephone Etiquette

As you can see, it takes so little to make a good impression, but it makes all the difference in the world. So let's look at some standard phrases that will help.

### Be Polite

Adding "please" always creates a polite tone, especially along with the conditional "could" and "would." Compare "Would you please repeat that" with "What?", or "I would like to speak to. . ." with "I want to speak to . . . ," or "I would appreciate your sending me" with "Send me. . . ." In each case, the first form is polite and the second is blunt. Also, do not forget "thank you" and "please." These phrases add another polite dimension. "Convenient" is another word that adds politeness and consideration to your conversation. For example, when planning a meeting, you might say, "What is a convenient time for you?" Or if you propose a time, you might phrase it, "Is that convenient for you?" The key is remembering how you would want to be treated on the telephone and using your own expectations as your guidelines.

### Be Service-minded

This is another attitude that will create a good impression. One tip is that if a caller has a problem, feel that it is your goal to solve it. For example, a positive response might be, "Yes, I understand the problem. Let me investigate a couple of possibilities, and I'll get back to you." Compare such a response with "I really do not know what we can do about that." If you do not have an immediate answer, do not just give up. Make an investigation, and see if you can find an answer. Finally, always stress that you will get back to the caller soon. And do it!

### Be Informative

Don't force people to ask questions. Be forthcoming. When you do get a question, give a complete answer. Try to imagine what information the caller would want if he or she knew it were available. For example, let's say that a customer calls to ask about material on an information system, and there is a new system just out on the market. You should say, "Are you aware that we just put System 7 on the market?" and then go into a brief description of its advantages. You can close by saying, "I'll send you brochures on both systems so that you can choose which is best for you." Or let's say someone calls for your office mate, who is in a meeting. You can answer, "Mr. Johnson is in a meeting" or "Mr. Johnson is in a meeting. I expect him back at two o'clock. Would you like to leave a message?" Obviously the latter response is much more professional.

## Practice

In the following conversations, practice the seven steps and the telephone etiquette suggested above.

### Taking a Message

You receive a call for your office mate who is not in the office. In a polite fashion, take a message. After you have done this once, reverse the roles and do it again.

#### KEY PHRASES

> Mr. Johnson's telephone, Peter Smith speaking.
>
> Mr. Johnson (1) is away from his desk, (2) just stepped out for a moment, (3) is in a meeting, (4) is not in today, (5) is on a business trip. Would you like to leave a message? [Another possibility is "Can I help you?"]
>
> Mr. Johnson is on another line. Would you like to hold or would you like to leave a message? Would you like him to call you back?

Remember to repeat the message to confirm it and then confirm that you will do what the caller requests. For example, "Thank you, Mr. Williams. I'll have Mr. Johnson call you at 790-8978 as soon as he comes in." If you want the caller to repeat a name, say "Excuse me, could you repeat that?" or "Could you spell that, please?" In confirming the caller's number, you could say, "That was 790-8978."

### Arranging a Meeting

Call and arrange a meeting.

#### KEY PHRASES

> Let's set up a meeting.
>
> When is it convenient for you?
>
> Wednesday is most convenient for me.
>
> Let me check my schedule/calendar.
>
> How about two o'clock? *Or* Is two o'clock all right/convenient?

Using the key phrases above, call to arrange a meeting. After you have done this once, reverse roles and do it again.

### Booking an Airline Ticket

Call and book an airline ticket. The airline agent will need information such as time and day of departure, class, smoking or non-smoking section, and time and day of return. The traveler will want to know price, seating (window or aisle seat), and whether it is a direct or nonstop flight.

#### KEY WORDS AND PHRASES

Departing

Arriving

Flight number

Tourist, business, or first class

Direct or nonstop

Check-in time

Using these words or phrases, book a ticket with an airline agent. After you have done this once, reverse roles and do it again. When you play the agent, be sure to confirm all details about the ticket.

### Dealing with a Complaint

Invent two situations in which a customer has a complaint. Play out the telephone conversations so that both of you play each role (customer and customer service representative) once. Dealing with complaints requires the utmost in language sophistication to avoid losing a customer. In this situation, you must calm the customer down, solve the problem, and reestablish good will.

#### KEY PHRASES

I'm sorry that this has inconvenienced you.

I'll get over there right away. *Or* I'll send a serviceperson immediately.

That almost never happens, but we will have someone there within an hour.

I'm sorry our delivery was late. We had a mix-up. But I'll see that it never happens again.

I'll see what I can do and get back to you immediately.

I'm afraid that there is nothing we can do at the moment. But I'll get back to you as soon as I can, say in a day or two.

You can invent as many situations as you feel are useful until you feel comfortable on the phone. Possible situations include reserving a table at a restaurant, selling a product over the telephone, or informing a customer that his or her account is in arrears (i.e., payment is overdue).

Following are more key words and phrases for using the telephone:

to dial

to transfer

to connect you
to be put on hold
to call back
to page (*v.*)
radio pager (*n.*)
switchboard
operator (*n.*)
information (*n.*) (British: *directory inquiries*)
local call (*n.*)
long-distance call (*n.*) (British: *trunk call*)
telephone number (*n.*)
extension (*n.*)
I'm sorry, you have the wrong number.

Use the above words to fill in the blanks in the following telephone conversations:

OPERATOR: This is ＿＿＿＿＿＿ . What city please?

MS. JONES: Boston. The telephone ＿＿＿＿＿＿
for A. J. Smiths.

OPERATOR: Their ＿＿＿＿＿＿ is 678-8897.

MS. JONES: Is that a ＿＿＿＿＿＿ or ＿＿＿＿＿＿
call from a 665 exchange?

OPERATOR: It's in the same area, so it's a ＿＿＿＿＿＿
call.

MS. JONES: Thank you, Operator.

SWITCHBOARD OPERATOR AT A. J. SMITHS: A. J. Smiths. Good morning.

MS. JONES: Mr. Johnson at ＿＿＿＿＿＿ 255, please.

SWITCHBOARD OPERATOR: Just a moment. I'll ＿＿＿＿＿＿ you.

MR. WILLIAMS: Accounting, Mr. Williams.

MS. JONES: Excuse me. Is this ＿＿＿＿＿＿ 255?

MR. WILLIAMS: No, I'm sorry. This is 253.

MS. JONES: Oh, the ＿＿＿＿＿＿ connected me
with the ＿＿＿＿＿＿ .

MR. WILLIAMS: No problem. I'll ＿＿＿＿＿＿ your call
to 255.

MS. DICKSON: Mr. Johnson's telephone.

MS. JONES: Is Mr. Johnson in?

MS. DICKSON: No he isn't, but I can _____ him.
He has a _____ . Oh, excuse me.
Mr. Johnson is in the next office. I can hear
his voice, but he's on another line. Do you
want me to put you _____ or do
you want to _____ later?

MS. JONES: You can put me _____ .

## The Alphabet

In taking or giving messages, it is essential to know the English alphabet because
many names and addresses must be spelled. So here is an alphabet review to help
master the sounds of each letter:

| [ei] | [i:] | [e] | [ai] | [u:] | [owe] |
|------|------|-----|------|------|-------|
| a (bay) | b (be) | f (left) | i (I) | q (cue) | o (go) |
| h (a + ch) | c (sea) | l (electric) | y (why) | u (you) | |
| j (jay) | d (deed) | m (them) | | w (double you) | |
| k (Kay) | e (me) | n (men) | | | |
| | g (gee) | x (exit) | | | |
| | p (pea) | z (zee) (British: zed) | | | |
| | t (tea) | | | | |
| | v (vee) | | | | |

| | |
|---|---|
| r (bar) | s (mess) |

After you have practiced the sounds as a class, break into pairs. One person
should spell personal and company names and addresses aloud while the other
writes them down. Reverse roles until you both can quickly recognize the words
being spelled and write them down.

# Appendix 2

# BUSINESS

# WRITING

The purpose of this Appendix is to provide you with important tips and a general introduction to the basic components of business writing: format, style, and tone. The material presented here will provide information and models to complete the written exercises in this book that deal with business writing.

## BASIC TIPS

1. Ask to see business correspondence in English at the place where you work. This will give you (a) the relevant vocabulary in your profession, and (b) a sense of the format used by your employer.

2. Purchase a handbook for business correspondence. Make sure that the book has examples of different kinds of correspondence, including memos, letters, and reports. The book should also have sample letters for different purposes, such as request for payment, request for information, acknowledgment, cover letter, and so on. The vocabulary for each type of letter is fairly standard; thus, in writing a letter, you can find the type of letter you are writing in your handbook and use that letter's vocabulary as a guide.

3. If at all possible, have someone who is a native English speaker correct the draft of your letter before you write a final draft. This could save you much embarrassment. Also, keep copies of your original draft and the final copy and review them periodically. This will help you see and eliminate the mistakes you made before. You will soon discover that business letters follow a formula consisting of phrases like the following:

   In response to your letter of . . .

   We regret that we cannot . . .

   We look forward to . . .

   You will soon learn these phrases by studying a handbook for business correspondence and by having your original drafts proofread and corrected by a native English speaker.

# FORMAT

## Letters

There are three basic letter formats: (1) *block style*, in which all the lines begin at the left-hand margin; (2) *modified block style*, in which the dateline, the complimentary close, and the sender's name and title at the end begin in the center of the page; and (3) *indented* (also called *modified block with paragraph indentations*), in which each first line of a new paragraph is indented five spaces and the sender's address and date are placed on the upper right-hand side of the page. Figures A-1 through A-3 give you examples of all three styles.

## Letterheads

Most business letters are typed on stationery with a printed address known as the *letterhead*. Thus, the placement of the sender's address will be predetermined.

## Dateline

There is a slight difference between the formats of American and British datelines:

American: May 22, 200–
British: 22 May 200–

## Inside Address

This is to be typed anywhere from three to twelve lines below the date, depending on the length of your letter. The shorter the letter, the more space there should be between the date and the inside address. Be sure to check the spelling of the name of the person receiving the letter, as well as his or her title and address.

## Salutations

The standard salutation for a man is *Dear Mr.* For women, the preferred salutation is *Dear Ms.* In the event that the name of the receiver is unknown, use *Dear Sir* or *Dear Madam*, or *Dear Sir or Madam* if the sex of the receiver is unknown.

## Subject

Many business letters begin with *SUBJECT:* or *Re:*, which states the subject of the letter. This aids the reader in knowing what the letter is about without having to read the entire letter.

Video Distributors
231 Allen Road
Wakefield, RI 02879


May 22, 200_

David Wilson
Wilson Video
451 Broad Street
Providence, RI 02905

Dear Mr. Wilson:

SUBJECT: Video Distributors' Catalogue for 199_

Thank you very much for your letter of April 22 requesting our 199_
catalogue. Please excuse the delay in sending you the enclosed
catalogue, which resulted from unforeseen problems at the printer.
I am sure you will agree that the catalogue was worth the wait. We
have doubled our holdings from last year by securing an exclusive
contract with Global Video Production. In addition, we have added
new lines of educational and business training videos.

As a means of promoting our new lines of educational and business
training videos, we have a special offer for the remainder of 199_.
Order five educational and/or business videos, and the sixth one is
free. We have designed promotional materials for each category of
video, which we will provide free of charge. We have also compiled a
list of potential customers in your area for each category of video.
Naturally, when you succeed, we succeed, and we are doing our utmost
to insure our mutual success.

We have streamlined our order processing service, which means three-
day delivery upon the receipt of your order. We are looking forward
to a continued profitable business relationship. If you have any
questions, please do not hesitate to call me.

Sincerely yours,



David House
Customer Service Representative

Enclosure

**Figure A-1**  Block style letter

Video Distributors
231 Allen Road
Wakefield, RI 02879


                              May 22, 200_

David Wilson
Wilson Video
451 Broad Street
Providence, RI 02905

Dear Mr. Wilson:

SUBJECT: Video Distributors' Catalogue for 199_

Thank you very much for your letter of April 22 requesting our 199_
catalogue. Please excuse the delay in sending you the enclosed
catalogue, which resulted from unforeseen problems at the printer.
I am sure you will agree that the catalogue was worth the wait. We
have doubled our holdings from last year by securing an exclusive
contract with Global Video Production. In addition, we have added
new lines of educational and business training videos.

As a means of promoting our new lines of educational and business
training videos, we have a special offer for the remainder of 199_.
Order five educational and/or business videos, and the sixth one is
free. We have designed promotional materials for each category of
video, which we will provide free of charge. We have also compiled a
list of potential customers in your area for each category of video.
Naturally, when you succeed, we succeed, and we are doing our utmost
to insure our mutual success.

We have streamlined our order processing service, which means three-
day delivery upon the receipt of your order. We are looking forward
to a continued profitable business relationship. If you have any
questions, please do not hesitate to call me.

                              Sincerely yours,



                              David House
                              Customer Service Representative

Enclosure


**Figure A-2**  Modified block style letter

Video Distributors
231 Allen Road
Wakefield, RI 02879

May 22, 200_

David Wilson
Wilson Video
451 Broad Street
Providence, RI 02905

Dear Mr. Wilson:

SUBJECT: Video Distributors' Catalogue for 199_

Thank you very much for your letter of April 22 requesting our 199_ catalogue. Please excuse the delay in sending you the enclosed catalogue, which resulted from unforeseen problems at the printer. I am sure you will agree that the catalogue was worth the wait. We have doubled our holdings from last year by securing an exclusive contract with Global Video Production. In addition, we have added new lines of educational and business training videos.

As a means of promoting our new lines of educational and business training videos, we have a special offer for the remainder of 199_. Order five educational and/or business videos, and the sixth one is free. We have designed promotional materials for each category of video, which we will provide free of charge. We have also compiled a list of potential customers in your area for each category of video. Naturally, when you succeed, we succeed, and we are doing our utmost to insure our mutual success.

We have streamlined our order processing service, which means three-day delivery upon the receipt of your order. We are looking forward to a continued profitable business relationship. If you have any questions, please do not hesitate to call me.

Sincerely yours,

David House
Customer Service Representative

Enclosure

**Figure A-3**    Indented style letter

## Complimentary Closings

These closings can be characterized by their degree of formality:

1. *Less formal:* Sincerely, Sincerely yours, Yours sincerely.
   These are the standard closings for an American business letter. Note that only the first word in the complimentary closing is capitalized.
2. *More formal:* Respectfully yours, Yours respectfully, Yours truly.
   The British tend to be more formal and thus use these complimentary closings more often than Americans do. These are also standard closings for letters beginning with *Dear Sir, Dear Madam*, or *Dear Sir or Madam*.

## Office Memorandums

Generally referred to as a *memo*, the office memorandum is the basic form of written communication between company employees and is less formal than a letter. It is used (a) for messages that are complicated, (b) to avoid making unnecessary telephone calls on subjects that are not urgent, and (c) when a record of the communication is necessary. Usually they are brief. Figure A-4 contains the basic elements of an office memo.

## Reports

Because there are so many different types of reports, it is not possible to deal fully with the subject of reports in this section. Instead, this section will provide you with a model as a guideline for writing reports.

### Title Page

A sample title page is shown in Figure A-5.

```
        TO: William Smith, Chief Shipping Clerk
      FROM: David House, Customer Service Representative
      DATE: June 10, 1994
   SUBJECT: Shipment of Order #3452 to Wilson Video

   Order #3452 to Wilson Video was supposed to be sent on June 5, 199_,
   in compliance with our three-day delivery policy. Per today's date,
   Wilson Video has not received the shipment. Please check the status
   of this shipment, and inform me.
```

**Figure A-4**   Interoffice Memo

A REPORT
OF THE NEGOTIATIONS BETWEEN
XYZ DISTRIBUTORS
AND
LONG-RANGE GOLF EQUIPMENT, INC.


Compiled by the XYZ Negotiations Team

David Williams, Marketing Manager

Joyce Daniels, Sales Manager

Connie Smith, Chief Legal Adviser


July 22, 200_

**Figure A-5**    Title page

### Executive Summary

The executive summary is a brief description of the contents of the report, which allows a reader to know if the report is relevant to his or her purposes without having to read the entire thing. It should be typed on a separate page. An example from the report named in the title page (see Figure A-5) is shown in Figure A-6.

### Table of Contents

The table of contents is placed before the summary. Prepared after the report is completed, it lists in order the numbers and titles of the sections or chapters in the report and the pages on which they begin. In numbering, you have a choice between the American system of calling the sections *chapters* (for example, *Chapter 1*) or the British system illustrated in Figure A-7. The table of contents should appear on its own page. The American form, using Roman numerals, capital letters, and cardinal numbers, is shown in Figure A-8.

### The Body

The body of the report follows the structure given in the table of contents. Each section's title is placed in a heading with the number and capitalized heading (for example, 4.0 The Negotiation). Each subsection is placed in a subheading with the first letter of each word capitalized (for example, 4.1 The Resulting Contract). So a page might begin as shown in Figure A-9.

## STYLE AND TONE

The discussion of style cannot be as concrete as that of format because the question of style is determined by company policy as well as personal writing style. To familiarize yourself with a given company's style, review business documents

---

```
                          EXECUTIVE SUMMARY


        On July 15, 200_, formal negotiations with Long-range were held
   to discuss terms of an eventual contract to distribute Long-range
   golf equipment. This report presents the pre-negotiations segment
   and XYZ's goals and strategies, as well as an assessment of the
   financial benefits of distributing Long-range golf equipment and an
   account of the negotiation process and resulting contact. Also
   included are our assessment of the contract and our recommendation
   on whether to accept the contract.
```

**Figure A-6**  Executive Summary

```
                    TABLE OF CONTENTS


TITLE PAGE                                          (i)

TABLE OF CONTENTS                                   (ii)

1.0  EXECUTIVE SUMMARY                               1

2.0  INTRODUCTION                                    2

3.0  PRE-NEGOTIATION                                 4
     3.1  Our Goals                                  4
          3.1.1  Musts
          3.1.2  Trading Cards
          3.1.3  The Bottom Line
     3.2  An Assessment of the Balance of Power      5
          3.2.1  How Much Do We Need Them?
          3.2.2  How Much Do They Need Us?

4.0  THE NEGOTIATIONS                                7
     4.1  The Resulting Contract                     8

5.0  AN ASSESSMENT OF THE CONTRACT                  12
     5.1  Our Goals Compared with the Results Achieved  12

6.0  RECOMMENDATION                                 15
```

**Figure A-7**  Table of Contents, British-style

written in English and talk to the persons responsible for typing the company's correspondence in English. These people have a wealth of information just waiting to be tapped.

However, certain generalizations *can* be made about English style, and these

```
III.  Pre-Negotiation
      A.  Our Goals
          1.  Musts
          2.  Trading Cards
          3.  The Bottom Line
```

**Figure A-8**  Table of contents, American-style

```
4.0  NEGOTIATIONS
     4.1 The Resulting Contract
     The contract reached contains the following terms . . .
```

**Figure A-9**   Body of a report

can serve as guidelines. First, English business style is concise. This means your writing should be brief and concrete. For example, the French expression *Je vous prie de bien vouloir* is translated as *please* in English. Certain cultures have a tendency to be more ornate, even metaphorical, in their writing style. But there is little room for poetic devices in English business style. Stick to the facts and keep it brief. Note the following examples of wordiness and accompanying suggestions for how to be more concise:

| **Wordy** | **Concise** |
|---|---|
| the question as to whether | whether (the question whether) |
| there is no doubt but that | no doubt (doubtless) |
| he is a man who | he |
| in a hasty manner | hastily |
| this is a subject that | this subject |
| owing to the fact that | since [Avoid using *the fact that*.] |

Politeness and service-mindedness are key elements in English business style. Thus, the use of polite phrases such as *We would appreciate it if, At your convenience, Please consider*, and *Thank you for your consideration* is considered good style. Note the service-mindedness reflected in the letter from Video Distributors (pages 132–133), in which David House emphasizes his interest in the success of Wilson Video.

Business writing style also strives for a fine balance between respect and equality between the persons who are communicating. The following examples will help you understand the proper balance.

1. Use *could, would,* or *might* to make what you write less blunt:

    That is impossible. [*blunt*]

    That would create unnecessary difficulties. [*more diplomatic*]

2. Do not present your ideas as an ultimatum.

    There is no possibility of meeting that deadline. [*ultimatum*]

    We find it difficult to meet the deadline. [*more diplomatic*]

3. Present your ideas more as opinion than as fact.

> Your figures are wrong. [*blunt*]
> We feel that your figures warrant revision. [*more diplomatic*]

4. Avoid using negative words.

> Your attitude is destructive. [*abrasive*]
> We would appreciate greater cooperation. [*more diplomatic*]

5. Present rejections as a result over which you had no control.

> I will not meet your salary demands. [*blunt*]
> I am afraid that our salary schedule does not allow us to meet your salary demands. [*more diplomatic*]

> *Note:* In rejecting demands, always preface your statement with a phrase like *I am (we are) sorry that* or *I am (we are) afraid that.*

6. Use the continuous form with words such as *think, hope, wonder*, and *plan*.

> I think you should accept our salary offer. [*blunt*]
> I was wondering whether you might accept our salary offer. [*more diplomatic*]

7. Do not adopt a subservient tone.

> We beg your forgiveness for our failure to meet the deadline. [*subservient*]
> Please excuse the delay in our delivery.

8. Try to elicit agreement.

> I think that you will agree that . . .

9. Use a question to make a proposal or express an opinion.

> Wouldn't it be better if . . .
> Don't you think this would be more appropriate?

10. Use qualifiers.

> We must express slight disagreement . . .
> We have some reservations . . .

11. In stating preference, use phrases like *We would rather* or *We prefer to.*

## Exercises

### Using Polite Phrases

Using the above or other polite phrases, rewrite the following sentences:

1. We cannot do that.
2. I don't want to meet you that early.
3. I want this by Thursday.

4. I cannot accept your proposal.

5. We expect you to accept an 8 percent commission.

6. That would create a problem.

7. Your analysis of the situation is incorrect.

8. Your claim for compensation has been rejected.

9. This year's sales results were bad.

10. We think it would be better if you changed your strategy.

### Responding to a Complaint

Analyze the accompanying letter, explaining how the writer has managed to respond politely and diplomatically to a complaint concerning construction noise at a resort hotel.

### Practicing Polite Responses

Write a letter using polite and diplomatic formulations in response to one of the following letters.

1. A letter of complaint due to delayed delivery of 100 Walkmans to an electronics store for which you are the major supplier.

2. A disagreement with the producer of tennis rackets for which you are the major distributor in your country. They have offered you a 7 percent commission on all sales, but you have requested 10 percent.

3. A letter from a dissatisfied tourist at one of your hotels complaining about construction noise. (Do not use the exact same wording as in the letter on page 142.)

4. Invent and describe a situation and then respond to it in the form of a letter.

## Achieving an Active Style

Create an active style by focusing on verbs rather than nouns and by using the active voice.

### Verb-Centered Writing

Note the emphasis on nouns that weakens the impact of this sentence:

> The committee made a *recommendation* that there was a *need* for an *improvement* in the company's billing routines.

This verb-centered approach is both more active and more concise:

> The committee *recommended* that the company *improve* its billing routines.

### Active Versus Passive Voice

In the active voice, the reader sees immediately who did the action and what he/she did because the actor is in the subject's place in the sentence. In the passive voice, the reader must wait until the end of the sentence to see who did the

Dear Mr. Wyatt:

I was sorry to hear from your letter of 10 January that you were dissatisfied with your stay on Tenerife in December of last year.

I have just been in contact with our local represenative in Alcudia concerning the problems with the construction noise at the Hotel Playa del Sol. He confirmed that the hotel found it necessary to carry out the construction work during this period and that the decision had been made on very short notice.

Unfortunately, Mansfield Tours was not informed of the decision before your arrival at the hotel, which made it impossible for us to alter your accommodation arrangement before your departure from London. Those guests who contacted our representative at the hotel were offered the opportunity to stay at one of our five-star hotels in the neighboring town at no additional expense.

You have requested a 50 percent discount for the inconvenience caused by the construction work. Because the incident was brought to our attention after your arrival, and because other accommodations were in fact available to you, we are unfortunately not able to give such a substantial refund.

However, our company policy states that our customers should always be 100 percent satisfied with their holiday, and I would therefore like to offer you and your spouse a weekend trip to Amsterdam, including accommodations at the Plaza Hotel, at our expense.

On behalf of Mansfield Tours, I regret the inconvenience you experienced during your holiday, and I sincerely hope this offer is acceptable to you. The tickets will be issued to you as soon as you contact our office.

Should you have any questions, please do not hesitate to write or call us. We hope that we can be of service in connection with any of your future travel plans.

Yours sincerely,


David Smith
Customer Service Manager

action, and sometimes the actor is not mentioned at all. In general, the active voice is stronger.

*Active voice:* The CEO made the decision.

*Passive voice:* The decision was made by the CEO.

However, the passive voice can be used when you wish to say what was done without pointing the finger at anyone. The passive voice allows you to be more diplomatic by allowing you to make your point without embarrassing anyone.

*Example:* An excellent opportunity to penetrate the Canadian market was lost.

## AN AUDIENCE-CENTERED APPROACH TO WRITING

Remember that you are communicating your ideas to an audience. In order to be effective, you *must* consider your audience's situation and priorities. When communicating, think of carrying on a dialogue with your audience. After you have written a couple of sentences, ask yourself what your audience would say to you after reading those sentences. Their interpretation of these preliminary sentences will influence how they interpret the remainder of your communication. Their response will be *cumulative* — that is, each sentence they read will influence how they interpret the rest of the communication.

The goal of much of your communication will be to get your audience to act in a specific way. To achieve this goal, you must formulate your communication in a way that is attractive to your audience. Thus, you must balance your goal of persuading the audience to act in a certain way with a consideration of their priorities and needs. Thus, you should provide them with the information they need and show how acting in the desired fashion *will benefit them.* For example, say your boss is under pressure to cut production costs and has asked you to evaluate production routines. You have researched the subject and developed routines that will cut costs in the long run, but will result in high initial costs. In order to persuade your boss, you must think of her situation:

1. She is under pressure due to the high costs of production.

2. She is of the old school of labor-intensive assembly.

3. She is very concerned with quality control.

4. Her boss is a "number cruncher" (a person who is concerned about costs).

Thus, your report cannot simply provide a conclusion to convert to robot-centered production. You must appeal to your boss's quality-control priority in order to overcome her reluctance to convert from a labor-intensive approach to a robot-centered approach. You can show that factory X, your competitor which uses the same robot-centered production system, has a record of only 2 percent of finished products that do not meet quality standards. Furthermore, you must also provide her with figures that will (a) convince her number-crunching boss that the initial investment will be profitable and (b) predict when this new system will pay back the initial investment. You must provide your boss with enough "ammunition" to look good when confronting her own boss. If she looks good, you look good, and your idea will be accepted. You might even be promoted to manage the conversion.

*The main thing is not to assume that your audience automatically thinks as you do. Analyze their situation and priorities and appeal to them. Remember that communication is a dialogue, not a monologue.*

# Appendix 3
# ELECTRONIC
# COMMUNICATION
# DEVICES

In our age of electronic communication, a few words must be said about such communication devices.

## E-MAIL

Electronic mail, or E-Mail, is second only to FAX messages in speed of transmission. Whereas a letter to Europe from the United States may take seven to nine days, an E-Mail letter takes less than thirty minutes. Your letter is electronically transmitted via your computer, which must be connected either to a modem or directly to a mainframe computer. It allows you to transmit messages to anyone who has a similar set-up and an E-Mail address. This address consists of a user identification code (ID) + @ + the computer network address, also known as the *node name*. The fee for a user code is nominal, and the cost of transmission usually depends on your position. Most university faculty can send E-Mail free, for example, while most students are on a pay-as-you-go basis.

When using E-Mail in a business setting, remember that initial contacts should be established by formal business letters. Once a working relationship is established, however, E-Mail can be an efficient means of communication.

## ELECTRONIC BULLETIN BOARDS

Electronic bulletin boards are open forums accessed through your computer. Let us say that you are an Apple user and want to access other Apple users to share experience and ask questions. You can access a bulletin board called AppleLink directly or through *Internet* (a worldwide network of interconnected computers to exchange information) by typing in the access code for AppleLink. Either way you must have an account number, which you get by paying a nominal fee to either Internet or AppleLink. Once you are into the bulletin board, you can type your message or question, which will show up on your screen and that of any other screen logged on to this AppleLink. Other users can then respond to your message or question, and their responses will appear on all screens logged on to AppleLink. There are many such bulletin boards which provide access to a great deal of expertise. You should become aware of electronic bulletin boards in your field of interest.

# INDEX

*Acknowledgment*

The financial statements in "Larry the Liquidator vs. New England Wire and Cable," the organizational charts in "Commutair," and the case "Smith Brothers and Florida Central" are reprinted by permission of Grace Murphy.

*Photo credits*

*p. 3:* Frank Siteman/Stock, Boston
*p. 12:* Peter Menzel/Stock, Boston
*p. 22:* Spencer Grant/The Picture Cube
*p. 33:* Spencer Grant/Monkmeyer
*p. 43:* Mitch Wojnarowicz/The Image Works
*p. 51:* Rob Crandal/The Image Works
*p. 60:* Mike Kagan/Monkmeyer
*p. 68:* Nancy Bates/The Picture Cube
*p. 78:* Bob Kramer/The Picture Cube
*p. 88:* Richard Pasley/Stock, Boston
*p. 97:* Mimi Forsyth/Monkmeyer
*p. 102:* Stephen Agricola/Stock, Boston
*p. 108:* Cameramann/The Image Works
*p. 116:* Courtesy of Saturn Corporation

## About the Author

DREW RODGERS teaches business communication and English at the School of Business, Oslo University College School of Management. His thirty years of teaching experience at colleges and universities in the United States, Switzerland, and Norway include courses in business communication, British and American studies, writing, and literature.